CHARLIE PALMER

WITH **JUDITH CHOATE**

DESIGN BY **JOEL AVIROM** AND **JASON SNYDER**

PHOTOGRAPHS BY **GOZEN KOSHIDA**

TEN SPEED PRESS
Berkeley ▪ Toronto

THE ART OF AUREOLE

INTRODUCTION My style of cooking is a very personal interpretation of the traditions of the classical French kitchen. The long-practiced techniques and base recipes of this culinary heritage have enabled me to stretch my imagination using fine-quality ingredients, intense flavors, unpredictable combinations and challenging resources to take my craft to its logical end as a statement of art on the table. It is in the Aureole kitchen that other cooks can find the same stimulation and experience their own expression of the creative process.

Like other creators, cooks practice their magic only with the desire that it awaken the diner's sense of taste. At the table, this means not only the stimulation of the palate but the arousal of all of the other senses as well. Aromas, colors and textures are only a few of the elements used to entice the diner. So, while the craft of the kitchen— technique, culture and practice—is a primary component in the development of the art, it is the refinement of the craft that carries the ordinary meal to the sublime. This refinement occurs not only in the kitchen but in the environment as well. For what good is the perfectly prepared meal if it is not served with pleasure in a serene and gracious setting? So, although The Art of Aureole

4

focuses on portraits of food from a conceptual view-point, the restaurants from which these recipes are taken very much emphasize the total dining experience. It is the skill of the waitstaff and other front of the house personnel that ensures that the art of the kitchen finds the proper frame.

It is important to clarify creative expression as it relates to culinary adventure. Just as in the other arts, creative license is only successfully taken when there is complete comprehension of the fundamental rules at the root of the experience. Innovation occurs when a cook takes what is known and introduces new elements into it backed by a full under-standing of the flavors and textures necessary to complement the taste upon which the mod-ification has been derived. Sometimes this occurs almost by divine inspiration, sometimes through trial and error and sometimes simply through the availability of unfamiliar ingredi-ents. However it occurs, it is this innovation that makes art out of the ordinary.

To the uninitiated, it might seem a bit presumptuous to think of food as art. But to those who celebrate the table, contemporary cooking has been elevated to the highest form of creativity. What was once simply a well-honed craft is now accepted as a definition of innovation, talent and accomplishment. Unfortunately, artistry on the plate, when appreciated, disappears with every bite. With *The Art of Aureole* it has been my intention to preserve the art of the moment with a creative expression of a recipe through its components rather than on a plated dish.

THE ART OF AUREOLE

APPETIZERS & SOUPS

Whole Roasted Foie Gras
with Peppered Peach Tatin

SERVES 6   1 cup sugar ▪ 2 tablespoons white wine vinegar ▪ 3 tablespoons butter ▪ 2 teaspoons butcher ground or cracked black pepper ▪ 3 ripe peaches, peeled, pit removed and cut in half, lengthwise ▪ 1 frozen puff pastry sheet ▪ 1 Grade A foie gras lobe ▪ Coarse salt to taste ▪ 6 stems basil, well washed and dried ▪ ¼ cup Basil Oil (see page 235) ▪ ¼ cup Natural Sauce (see page 234) ▪ Fleur de sel ▪ 1½ cup baby opal basil, well washed and dried ▪ 12 sprigs basil

1   Preheat the oven to 350°F and place a rack in the lower third of the oven.

2   Place the sugar in a heavy-duty saucepan over medium-low heat. Cook, stirring constantly with a wooden spoon and occasionally brushing down the sides of the pan with a wet pastry brush to prevent crystallization, for about 15 minutes or until the sugar is nicely caramelized (about 350°F on an instant-read thermometer). Immediately whisk in the vinegar and then the butter, whisking constantly until the butter is well incorporated.

3   Pour an equal portion of the caramel into each of six 4-ounce nonstick metal molds. Generously sprinkle the pepper over the caramel in each mold. Place a peach half into each mold, cut side down, nestling it into the caramel. The peaches may have to be trimmed a bit around the edges to correctly fit. Set aside.

4   Using a biscuit cutter or a small, sharp knife, cut 6 frozen puff pastry rounds to fit the top of each mold. Prick the top of each round with a fork and then fit a puff pastry round on top of each peach. Place on the lower rack in the preheated oven and bake for 5 minutes. Reduce the oven temperature to 325°F and bake for about 20 minutes or until the pastry is golden brown and crisp and the peach juice is bubbling around the edges. Remove from the oven and set aside on a wire rack. Raise the oven temperature to 400°F.

5   Using the tip of a sharp chef's knife, cut a crosshatch design about 1/8 inch deep across the top of the foie gras. Season both sides with salt. Place in a very hot heavy-duty, ovenproof sauté pan over high heat and sear, turning frequently, for about 4 minutes or until all sides are a deep mahogany color. Transfer to the preheated oven and roast, frequently turning and basting the lobe with its fat for about 5 minutes or until just about cooked through.

6   Immediately return to the stovetop over high heat and place the basil stems on top of the foie gras, basting the liver with its rendered fat for about 2 minutes or until it is just tender and spongy throughout. Transfer the foie gras to a wire rack to rest and to drain off excess fat. (At this point, you can present the whole lobe to your guests, continuing to baste with the basil-scented rendered fat.)

7   Invert a warm peach tatin onto each of 6 heated dinner plates, drizzling the caramel around each tatin. Slice the foie gras, on the bias, into 6 equal pieces and drape 1 slice over the peach tatin on each place. Season with the fleur de sel. Drizzle Basil Oil and Natural Sauce around the edge of each plate and randomly sprinkle baby opal basil over all. Place 2 basil sprigs into each tatin and serve immediately.

Port-Glazed
Foie Gras
and Tuna Terrine

SERVES 6 4 cups port ■ 1 Grade A foie gras lobe ■ ¼ cup white port ■ Coarse salt and freshly ground pepper ■ Approximately ½ teaspoon sel rose ■ 1 block yellowfin tuna, 6 inches long by 4 inches high by 4 inches wide ■ Red Wine Vinaigrette (see page 236) ■ 2 cups spicy baby or micro-greens

1 Place the port in a medium heavy-bottomed saucepan over medium-low heat. Bring to a simmer; then, immediately lower the heat and cook at a bare simmer for about 45 minutes or until reduced to a syrup consistency. Take care that the port does not simmer hard or boil or it will reduce too quickly and become bitter. Remove from the heat and set aside to cool. (Reduction may be made up to 1 week in advance of use and stored, covered and refrigerated.)

2 Place the foie gras on a plate and let stand at room temperature until soft enough to easily manipulate.

3 Separate the softened lobes by cutting the connecting tendon with a very sharp knife. Working from the back to the front, carefully push the liver away from the vein structure (two levels of veins are one on top of the other), taking care that the front layer of the liver is not broken or damaged. Remove and discard the veins. When all of the veins have been removed, fold the liver back together, incorporating any pieces that have loosened during the deveining process. When reassembled and viewed from the front, the foie gras should look intact.

4 Place the foie gras on a flat surface. Sprinkle with some of the white port and season liberally with salt and pepper. Dust lightly with sel rose. Turn and sprinkle the other side with white port and season as for the first side. Tightly cover with plastic wrap and refrigerate for 12 hours to cure.

5 Remove the foie gras from the refrigerator, unwrap and place on a sheet of parchment paper. Allow to rest until soft enough to manipulate.

14

6 Bring a medium saucepan of water to boil over high heat. Reduce the heat to a low simmer.

7 Make an ice-water bath in a medium mixing bowl.

8 Using your thumb, make an indentation down the center of the foie gras. Pour a small amount of the reduced port into the indentation, reserving the remaining for plate garnish. Roll the liver into a 2-inch round log-like shape. Tightly enclose with plastic wrap and place in the simmering water. Poach for 3 minutes; then, immediately lift the poached foie gras to the ice-water bath and let sit until well chilled.

9 Cut the tuna into three 2-inch-long blocks. Using a 2-inch round ring cutter, punch a hole out of the center of each tuna block the exact diameter of the foie gras log, reserving the holes for another use.

10 Remove the plastic wrap from the foie gras and cut the log into three 2-inch-thick pieces. Insert 1 piece into the hole in each tuna block. Season all of the outer sides of the tuna with salt and pepper.

11 Heat the oil in a large, nonstick sauté pan over medium-high heat. Add the tuna, searing only the 4 outer edges until just lightly cooked. The foie gras-filled sides must not touch the pan or the foie gras will begin to melt. Using a slotted spatula, carefully remove the tuna from the pan and place on a cutting board. Using a serrated knife, carefully cut each block into 2 equal pieces.

12 Place a piece of the tuna on each of 6 plates. Drizzle the reserved reduced port and some Red Wine Vinaigrette over the tuna and around the plate. Garnish with spicy, peppery baby or micro-greens.

Sautéed Foie Gras
Armagnac Apples

with Apple Purée,
and Cornbread Muffins

■ 1 cup honey ■ 2 tablespoons Armagnac ■ 1 Grade A foie gras lobe ■ Armagnac Apples ■ Cornbread Muffins ■ Apple Purée ■ Coarse salt and freshly ground pepper ■ 1 bunch mâche, well washed and dried ■ Fleur de sel

1 Place the honey in a small, deep, heavy-bottomed saucepan over low heat. Cook, stirring frequently with a wooden spoon, for about 15 minutes or until the honey is a deep golden color and nicely caramelized. Stirring constantly, very carefully, pour in the Armagnac. Remove from the heat and set aside to cool slightly.

2 When cool enough to handle safely, pour the honey into a plastic squeeze bottle and set aside.

3 Separate the foie gras lobes by cutting the connecting tendon with a very sharp knife. Working from the back to the front, carefully push the liver away from the vein structure (two levels of veins are one on top of the other), taking care that only require the front layer of the liver is not broken or damaged. (Six servings mousse.) Pat the liver dry with a clean kitchen towel. Place the lobe for a pâté or a cool, clean surface and, using a sharp knife dipped into very hot water, cut, at a slight angle, to make a ⅝- to ¾-inch-thick slice of foie gras weighing about 3 ounces. Continue cutting until you have 6 pieces of equal size, dipping the knife into very hot water each time you slice. Lay the foie gras pieces on a platter and, with the tip of the knife, cut a crosshatch design about ⅛ inch deep across the top of each piece. Cover and refrigerate.

4 If necessary, preheat the oven to 275°F to warm the Armagnac Apples and Cornbread Muffins.

5 Reheat the Apple Purée as directed in the recipe.

6 Place a medium, nonstick sauté pan over high heat. Remove the foie gras from the refrigerator and season both sides with salt and pepper. When the pan is very hot but not smoking, add the foie gras, scored side down. Using your fingertips, gently push the slices into the pan so that the foie gras immediately begins to render its fat. Cook for about 2 minutes or until the bottom begins to caramelize and quite a bit of fat has been exuded. Turn and brown the other side for 2 minutes or until nicely crisped. Using a slotted spatula, transfer the foie gras to a warm plate. Tent lightly with foil to keep warm.

7 Place equal portions of warm Apple Purée in the center of each of 6 warm dinner plates. Stack 2 Armagnac Apple rounds on top of one another in the center of the purée. Place a piece of foie gras on top of the apples. Place 2 muffins on each plate nestled into the purée. Drizzle the caramelized honey around each plate. Garnish each plate with a small bundle of mâche. Season the foie gras with fleur de sel and serve.

APPLE PURÉE

■ 2 Granny Smith apples, peeled, cored and chopped ■ 1 cup cold water ■ ½ cup dry white wine ■ ½ cup sugar

1 Combine the apples with the water and wine in a medium saucepan over medium heat. Add the sugar, stirring until the sugar has dissolved. Cover and bring to a simmer. Lower the heat and simmer for about 12 minutes or until the apples are very soft.

2 Remove from the heat and strain through a fine-mesh strainer, separately reserving the cooking liquid.

3 Transfer the apples to a blender and begin processing, adding the reserved liquid as needed to make a smooth purée. Scrape the purée into a small bowl and set aside until ready to use.

4 When ready to use, return to a small, nonstick pan and reheat over very low heat.

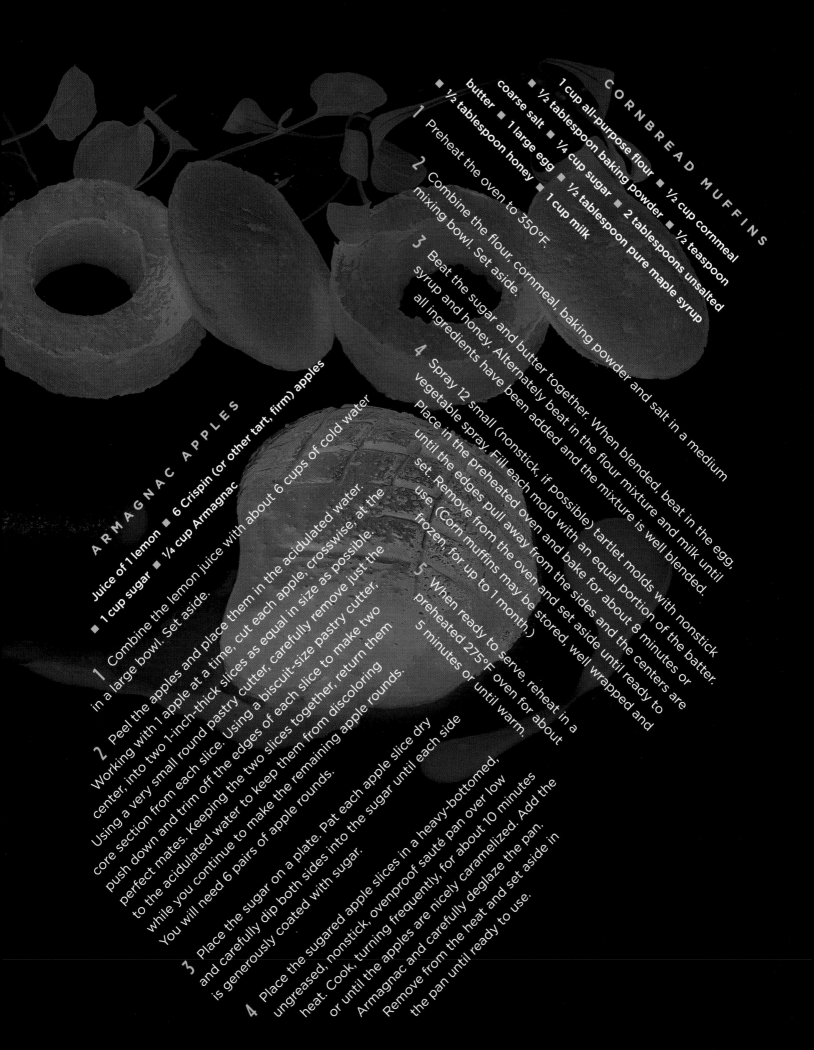

CORNBREAD MUFFINS

- **1 cup all-purpose flour** ■ **½ cup cornmeal**
- **½ tablespoon baking powder** ■ **½ teaspoon coarse salt** ■ **¼ cup sugar** ■ **2 tablespoons unsalted butter** ■ **1 large egg** ■ **½ tablespoon pure maple syrup**
- **½ tablespoon honey** ■ **1 cup milk**

1 Preheat the oven to 350°F.

2 Combine the flour, cornmeal, baking powder and salt in a medium mixing bowl. Set aside.

3 Beat the sugar and butter together. When blended, beat in the egg, syrup and honey. Alternately beat in the flour mixture and milk until all ingredients have been added and the mixture is well blended.

4 Spray 12 small (nonstick, if possible) tartlet molds with nonstick vegetable spray. Fill each mold with an equal portion of the batter. Place in the preheated oven and bake for about 8 minutes or until the edges pull away from the sides and set aside and the centers are set. Remove from the oven and set aside until ready to use. (Corn muffins may be stored, well wrapped and frozen, for up to 1 month.)

5 When ready to serve, reheat in a preheated 275°F oven for about 5 minutes or until warm.

ARMAGNAC APPLES

- **Juice of 1 lemon** ■ **6 Crispin (or other tart, firm) apples**
- **1 cup sugar** ■ **¼ cup Armagnac**

1 Combine the lemon juice with about 6 cups of cold water in a large bowl. Set aside.

2 Peel the apples and place them in the acidulated water. Working with 1 apple at a time, cut each apple, crosswise, at the center, into two 1-inch-thick slices as equal in size as possible. Using a very small round pastry cutter, carefully remove just the core section from each slice. Using a biscuit-size pastry cutter, push down and trim off the edges of each slice to make two perfect mates. Keeping the two slices together, return them to the acidulated water to keep them from discoloring while you continue to make the remaining apple rounds. You will need 6 pairs of apple rounds.

3 Place the sugar on a plate. Pat each apple slice dry and carefully dip both sides into the sugar until each side is generously coated with sugar.

4 Place the sugared apple slices in a heavy-bottomed, ungreased, nonstick, ovenproof sauté pan over low heat. Cook, turning frequently, for about 10 minutes or until the apples are nicely caramelized. Add the Armagnac and carefully deglaze the pan. Remove from the heat and set aside in the pan until ready to use.

Carpaccio of Beef and Porcini Foam with a Salad of Cress, Celery Leaves, Red Radishes and Onion

SERVES 6 12 ounces beef tenderloin, well trimmed of all fat and silverskin ■ 1 small red onion, peeled and julienned ■ 2 cups peppercress, well washed and dried ■ ½ cup tiny yellow celery leaves, well washed and dried ■ ¼ cup red radish slivers ■ Coarse salt and freshly ground pepper ■ 1 tablespoon porcini powder ■ 2 batches Phyllo Crisps ■ Porcini Vinaigrette ■ Fleur de sel ■ Porcini Foam

1 Tightly enclose the tenderloin in plastic wrap. Place in the freezer for 8 hours.

2 When ready to serve, combine the onion, peppercress, celery leaves, and radishes in a medium bowl and place in the refrigerator.

3 Remove the tenderloin from the freezer. Unwrap the meat and liberally season with salt and pepper. Place the porcini powder in a small sieve and gently shake the sieve over the tenderloin to evenly coat all sides with the powder. Using an electric meat slicer, cut the tenderloin, crosswise, into paper-thin slices. Place an equal number of slices in a circular pattern on each of 6 chilled dinner plates. Place a Phyllo Crisp in the center of each plate; then, top with another Phyllo Crisp.

4 Remove the salad from the refrigerator and add just enough Porcini Vinaigrette to lightly coat. Toss to blend and spoon dollops mound an equal portion of the salad on top of the Phyllo Crisps on each plate.

5 Lightly sprinkle fleur de sel over the carpaccio and spoon dollops of Porcini Foam around the edge of each plate. Serve immediately.

PHYLLO CRISPS

3 sheets phyllo dough, thawed ■ **¾ cup clarified butter** ■ **2 teaspoons porcini powder**

1 Preheat the oven to 350°F.

2 Line a baking sheet with parchment paper. Set aside.

3 Working quickly, cut each phyllo sheet in half, crosswise. Stack the phyllo and place on a clean, flat surface and cover with a damp kitchen towel.

4 Working with one sheet at a time, lay a phyllo sheet on a clean, flat surface and, using a pastry brush generously coat it with clarified butter. Place the porcini powder in a small sieve and gently shake it over the buttered phyllo to dust lightly. Place another sheet of phyllo on top and brush it with clarified butter and dust with porcini powder. Continue layering, brushing and dusting until all of the phyllo, butter and porcini powder has been used.

5 Using a 3-inch round biscuit cutter, cut out 6 stacked phyllo circles. Place the circles on a nonstick baking sheet. Place another baking sheet on top of the first sheet to hold the phyllo circles flat. Place in the preheated oven and bake for about 15 minutes or until the phyllo is crisp and golden brown.

6 Line a baking sheet with a triple layer of paper towel. Remove the phyllo rounds from the oven and place on the towel-lined baking sheet just until well drained and slightly cool. (If the towel absorbs too much butter, the crisps will start to reabsorb the oil and get soggy.) Transfer the crisps to wire racks until ready to use.

NOTE: Parmesan Phyllo Crisps are made following the above recipe, replacing the porcini powder with ½ cup freshly grated Parmesan cheese.

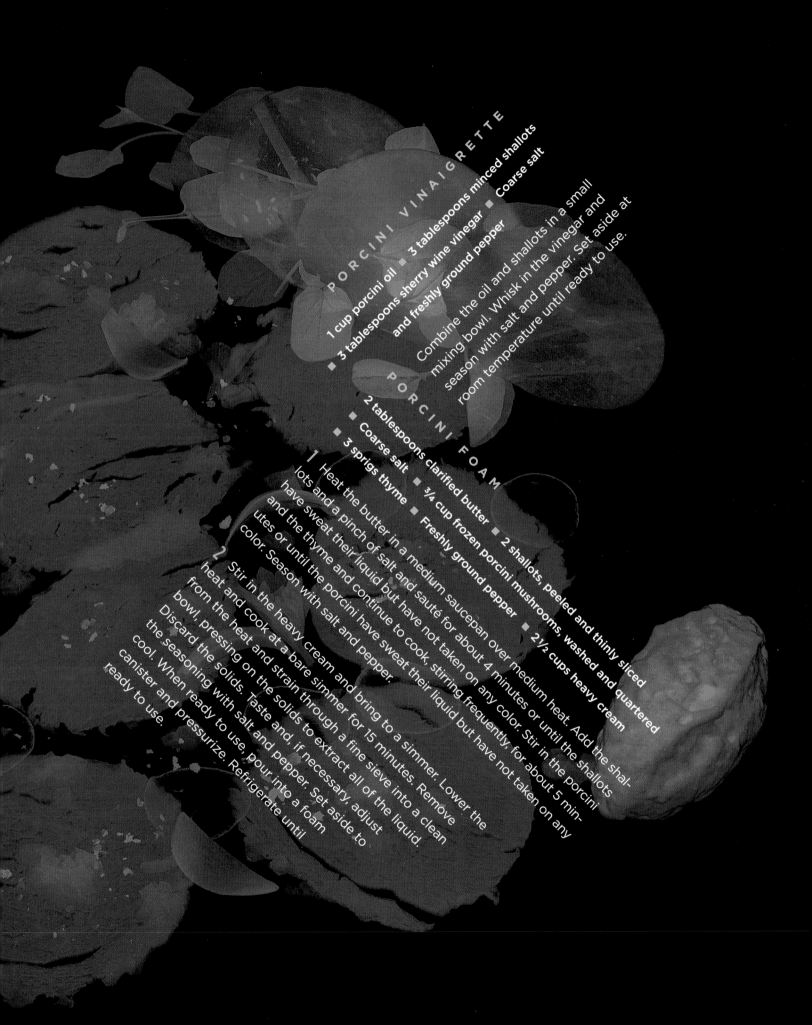

PORCINI VINAIGRETTE

- **1 cup porcini oil**
- **3 tablespoons sherry wine vinegar**
- **3 tablespoons minced shallots**
- **Coarse salt and freshly ground pepper**

Combine the oil and shallots in a small mixing bowl. Whisk in the vinegar and season with salt and pepper. Set aside at room temperature until ready to use.

PORCINI FOAM

- **2 tablespoons clarified butter**
- **Coarse salt**
- **3 sprigs thyme**
- **¾ cup frozen porcini mushrooms**
- **2 shallots, peeled and thinly sliced**
- **Freshly ground pepper**
- **2½ cups heavy cream**

1 Heat the butter in a medium saucepan over medium heat. Add the shallots and a pinch of salt and saute for about 4 minutes or until the shallots have sweat their liquid but have not taken on any color. Stir in the porcini and the thyme and continue to cook, stirring frequently, for about 5 minutes or until the porcini have sweat their liquid but have not taken on any color. Season with salt and pepper.

2 Stir in the heavy cream and bring to a simmer. Lower the heat and cook at a bare simmer for 15 minutes. Remove from the heat and strain through a fine sieve into a clean bowl, pressing on the solids to extract all of the liquid. Discard the solids. Taste and, if necessary, adjust the seasoning with salt and pepper. Set aside to cool. When ready to use, pour into a foam canister and pressurize. Refrigerate until ready to use.

Prosciutto
with Ricotta Flan
and a Sunny-Side-Up
Quail Egg

SERVES 6   ¼ cup aged balsamic vinegar   ■   18 thinly sliced pieces prosciutto   ■   18 spears very thin asparagus, trimmed and blanched   ■   2 tablespoons lemon oil   ■   Coarse salt and freshly ground pepper   ■   1 head frisée, well washed, trimmed and dried   ■   1½ cups baby arugula   ■   Parmesan Phyllo Crisps (see page 22)   ■   1 tablespoon clarified butter   ■   6 quail eggs   ■   Ricotta Flan   ■   Red Wine Vinaigrette (see page 236)   ■   Fleur de sel   ■   18 spears wild asparagus, trimmed and blanched   ■   Approximately ¼ cup extra virgin olive oil

1   Place the balsamic in a plastic squeeze bottle and set aside.

2   Leaving a 1-inch border, place 3 slices of the prosciutto in slightly overlapping slices around the edge of each of 6 dinner plates. Set aside.

3   Using a sharp knife, cut each asparagus spear, on the bias, into thirds. Place in a small bowl and toss with the lemon oil and salt and pepper. Set aside.

4   Combine the frisée and arugula in a small bowl. Set aside.

5   Place the Parmesan Phyllo Crisps on a clean flat surface.

6   Generously grease a nonstick griddle with the clarified butter. Place over medium heat and then set six 2-inch ring molds onto the griddle. When the griddle is hot, break a quail egg into each ring mold. Fry for about 2 minutes or just until the egg whites are set. Remove the griddle from the heat and gently remove the ring molds.

7   Place a Ricotta Flan on top of each Phyllo Crisp; then, place a fried quail egg on top of each flan. Set aside.

8   Place a small mound of the dressed asparagus pieces in the center of each prosciutto-ringed plate. Dress the frisée and arugula with just enough Red Wine Vinaigrette to lightly season. Toss to coat and place on top of the asparagus on each plate. Carefully place a Ricotta Flan on top of the salad. Season with fleur de sel and freshly ground pepper. Place 3 spears of wild asparagus on each plate in a decorative pattern. Make small dots of the balsamic around the edge of each plate and drizzle olive oil over all. Serve immediately.

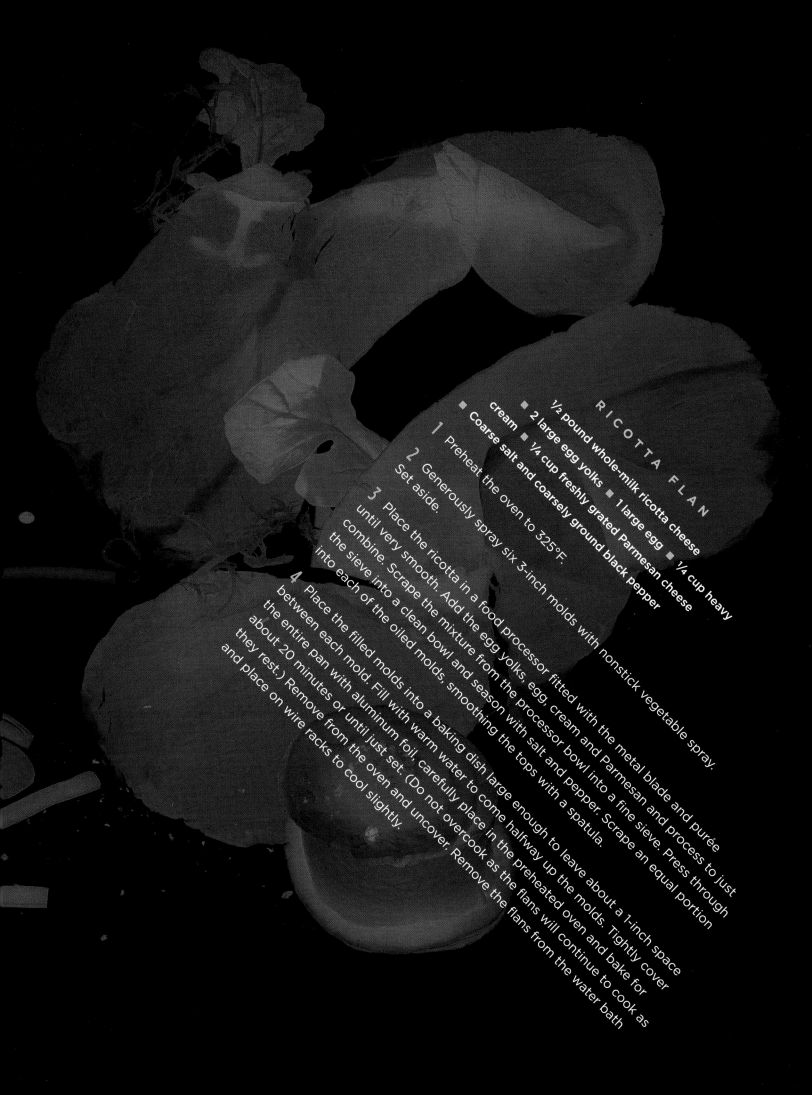

RICOTTA FLAN

- ½ pound whole-milk ricotta cheese
- 2 large egg yolks ◼ 1 large egg ◼ ¼ cup heavy cream
- ¼ cup freshly grated Parmesan cheese
- Coarse salt and coarsely ground black pepper

1 Preheat the oven to 325°F. Generously spray six 3-inch molds with nonstick vegetable spray. Set aside.

2 Place the ricotta in a food processor fitted with the metal blade and purée to just combine. Scrape the mixture from the processor bowl into a fine sieve. Press through the sieve into a clean bowl and season with salt and pepper. Scrape an equal portion into each of the oiled molds, smoothing the tops with a spatula.

3 Place the ricotta in a food processor fitted with the metal blade and purée to just combine. Add the egg yolks, egg, cream and Parmesan and process until very smooth. Scrape the mixture from the processor bowl into a fine sieve. Press through the sieve into a clean bowl and season with salt and pepper. Scrape an equal portion into each of the oiled molds, smoothing the tops with a spatula.

4 Place the filled molds into a baking dish large enough to leave about a 1-inch space between each mold. Fill with warm water to come halfway up the molds. Tightly cover the entire pan with aluminum foil, carefully place in the preheated oven and bake for about 20 minutes or until just set. (Do not overcook as the flans will continue to cook as they rest.) Remove from the oven and uncover. Remove the flans from the water bath and place on wire racks to cool slightly.

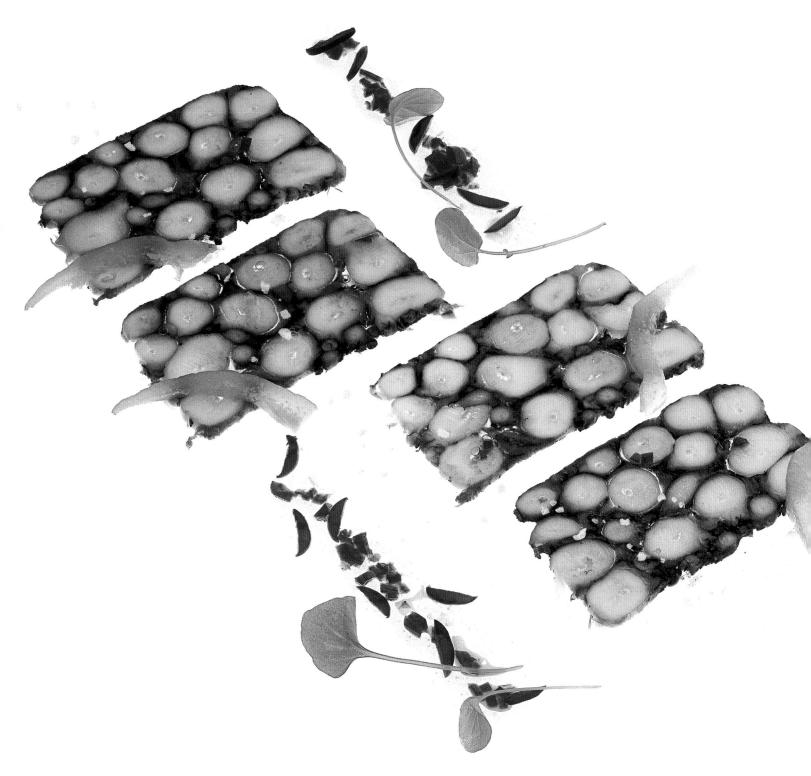

Terrine
with Pickled Lemon Rind
and Verjus Vinaigrette

1 Place the octopus in a large, heavy-bottomed saucepan. Add enough chicken stock to cover by 2 inches. Add the saffron and sea salt and place over medium-high heat. Bring to a boil; then, lower the heat to a bare simmer. Simmer slowly for about 2 hours or until the octopus is very tender. (If the octopus has been frozen, the cooking time may be substantially less.) Remove from the heat and allow to cool.

2 Line a 12 ½ inch by 4 inch by 4-inch terrine with plastic wrap, leaving about a 3-inch overhang all around.

3 When the octopus is cool enough to handle, remove the arms from the body, discarding the head, and cut them into 1-inch-wide strips. Place the arms in even layers in the terrine.

4 Strain the octopus cooking liquid through a fine sieve. Pour enough of the strained liquid into the terrine to cover all of the meat and form a top layer of liquid. Pull the plastic wrap up and over the octopus to tightly cover. Place a brick, another terrine of equal size or a couple of filled cans on top of the terrine to press it down firmly and refrigerate for 12 hours.

5 When ready to serve, unmold and unwrap the terrine. For the most perfect, even slices, cut the terrine on an electric slicer into ⅛-inch-thick pieces. Alternately, use a very sharp serrated knife.

6 Place 3 slices on each of 6 plates. Garnish with Pickled Lemon Rind and drizzle some of the Verjus Vinaigrette over the terrine and around the plate. Combine the potatoes, greens and olives and toss with a bit of the vinaigrette. Season with salt and pepper and place a small mound of the salad on each plate.

MAKES ONE 12½-INCH TERRINE

One 5-pound octopus, cleaned

■ **Approximately 10 cups chicken stock** ■ **Large pinch saffron threads**

■ **Sea salt** ■ **Pickled Lemon Rind**

■ **Verjus Vinaigrette** ■ **Fingerling potato disks, blanched** ■ **Baby greens**

■ **3 tablespoons Niçoise olive slivers**

■ **Coarsely ground salt and pepper**

PICKLED LEMON RIND

■ **3 whole lemons** ■ **4 allspice berries** ■ **2 bay leaves**
1 cinnamon stick ■ **1 tablespoon coarse salt** ■ **1 tablespoon**
coriander seeds ■ **1 tablespoon white peppercorns** ■ **2 cups water** ■ **1 tablespoon freshly**
grated turmeric ■ **1 teaspoon red chile flakes**

1 Using a small sharp knife, carefully remove the rind from each lemon in long, wide strips. Cut each strip into ¼-inch-wide strips and set aside.

2 Combine the allspice, bay leaves, cinnamon stick, salt, coriander, peppercorns, turmeric and chile flakes in a double piece of cheesecloth or muslin large enough to make a bag. Pull up the edges and tie closed with kitchen twine.

3 Place the water in a small saucepan. Add the sachet and place over high heat. Bring to a boil; then, lower the heat and simmer until the rind is tender. Remove from the heat and allow to cool. When cool, pour 15 minutes or until the lemon rind and simmer for 10 minutes. Add the lemon rind and simmer for about into a clean container; cover and refrigerate for up to 1 month or until ready to use.

4 Before serving, lift the lemon rind from the pickling liquid and drain on a double layer of paper towels.

VERJUS VINAIGRETTE

■ **1 cup verjus** ■ **1 cup port wine** ■ **2 tablespoons minced shallots**
■ **1 cup grapeseed oil** ■ **Coarse salt and freshly ground white pepper**

1 Combine the verjus, port and shallots in a small nonreactive saucepan over medium heat. Bring to a boil; then, lower the heat and simmer for about 30 minutes or until reduced by half. Remove from the heat and allow to cool.

2 Pour the verjus reduction into a clean bowl. Whisking constantly, add the oil. Season with salt and pepper. Store, covered and refrigerated, until ready to use.

Tuna Tartare
with Chile-Spiced Ponzu

SERVES 6   1 ½ pounds sashimi-grade, center-cut bluefin tuna, cut into ¼-inch dice ■ 1 cup olive oil ■ 1 teaspoon cayenne pepper ■ Coarse salt ■ Sesame Crisps ■ Chile-Spiced Ponzu ■ ½ cup pickled ginger ■ 1 cup baby red mustard greens

1 Place the tuna in a well-chilled bowl. Add the olive oil, cayenne and salt and lightly toss to combine. Firmly pack equal amounts of the tartare into each of six 2-inch ring molds. Place the molds on a platter, cover lightly with plastic wrap and refrigerate until ready to use.

2 When ready to serve, place one mold in the center of each of 6 luncheon plates. If necessary, run a knife around the edge of the mold to invert the tartare onto the plate. Place 2 Sesame Crisps at an angle into the tartare. Drizzle Chile-Spiced Ponzu around the edge of the plates and garnish with pickled ginger and baby red mustard greens. Serve immediately.

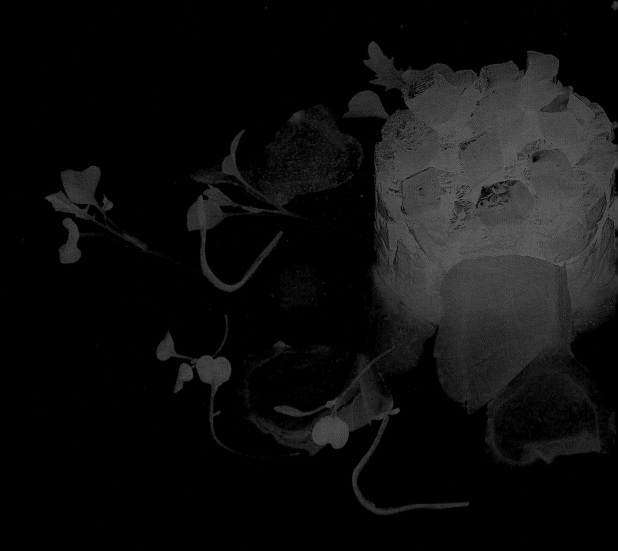

34

SESAME CRISPS

- 3/4 cup warm water ■ 2 tablespoons olive oil ■ 2 tablespoons sesame oil ■ 2 teaspoons sugar ■ 1 tablespoon dry yeast ■ 2 cups all-purpose flour ■ 2 teaspoons salt ■ 1 teaspoon sesame seeds ■ 3/4 teaspoon ground ginger ■ Pinch freshly ground white pepper ■ 1 large egg ■ 1 tablespoon cold water ■ Approximately 1/4 cup black sesame seeds

1 Combine the warm water, olive and sesame oils and sugar in a small warm bowl. Stir in the yeast and set aside to rest for a few minutes to allow the yeast to activate.

2 Place the flour, salt, sesame seeds, ginger and white pepper in a large bowl. Add the yeast mixture and stir just long enough to incorporate the liquid and have the dough come together. Form the dough into a ball and tightly wrap in plastic wrap. Refrigerate for at least 8 hours or up to 24 hours.

3 When ready to bake, preheat the oven to 275°F.

4 Line at least two baking sheets with parchment paper. Set aside.

5 Place the egg in a small bowl and whisk together with the 1 tablespoon cold water. Set aside.

6 Using a pasta machine, roll the dough out into 1/8-inch-thick sheets. Cut each sheet into whatever shape is desired (triangles and half-moons are particularly attractive).

7 Place the shapes on the prepared baking sheets. Using a pastry brush, lightly coat each piece with the egg wash and sprinkle with the sesame seeds. Place in the preheated oven and bake for about 12 minutes or until golden brown. Remove from the oven and cool on wire racks. Store, tightly covered, at room temperature.

CHILE-SPICED PONZU

- 1 1/2 cups freshly squeezed lemon juice ■ 1 1/2 cups soy sauce ■ 1 1/2 cups chicken stock ■ 1/4 cup sesame oil ■ 1/4 cup freshly grated ginger ■ 3 tablespoons red chile flakes ■ 3/4 cup peanut oil ■ 3 tablespoons ground cumin ■ 2 tablespoons coarsely ground black pepper

Combine the lemon juice, soy sauce and chicken stock in a medium nonreactive saucepan over medium heat. Stir in the peanut and sesame oils. Add the ginger, pepper, cumin and chile flakes and bring to a simmer. Remove from the heat and allow to cool. Strain through a fine sieve into a clean container. Store, covered, at room temperature until ready to use.

Grilled Sardines
with Caponata-Stuffed
Piquillo Peppers and
Crisp Red Onion Rings

1 Preheat the oven to 300°F.

2 Line a baking sheet with parchment paper. Place the Caponata-Stuffed Piquillo Peppers on the prepared baking sheet. Using a pastry brush, lightly coat each pepper with some of the olive oil. Place in the preheated oven and bake for about 5 minutes or just until very hot.

3 Preheat and oil a grill (either outdoor or stovetop). Using a pastry brush and the remaining olive oil, lightly coat the sardine fillets. Season with salt and white pepper. Place the sardines on the grill, skin side down, and grill for a few seconds to quickly impress grill marks on the skin. If further cooking is desired, place, skin side up, on a baking sheet in the oven with the peppers and bake for about 2 minutes or until just cooked through.

5 Place a pool of Yellow Tomato Coulis in the center of each of 6 luncheon plates. Place 2 peppers in the coulis on each plate. Arrange 3 fillets over the peppers on each plate. Garnish with Crisp Red Onion Rings and mixed herbs. Drizzle Basil Oil around the edge of the plate and serve.

SERVES 6 Caponata-Stuffed Piquillo Peppers ■ 3 tablespoons olive oil ■ 9 fresh sardines, cleaned and filleted ■ Coarse salt and freshly ground white pepper ■ Yellow Tomato Coulis ■ Crisp Red Onion Rings ■ ¼ cup chopped mixed herbs ■ Basil Oil (see page 235)

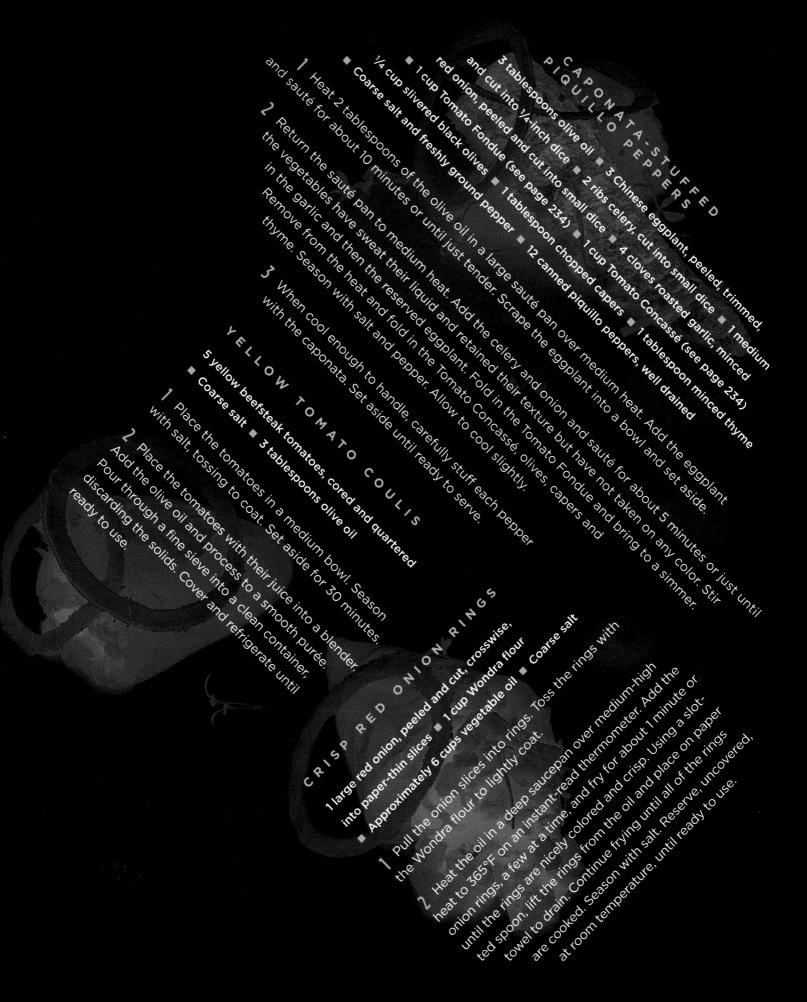

CAPONATA-STUFFED PIQUILLO PEPPERS

- **3 tablespoons olive oil**
- **1 medium red onion, peeled and cut into ¼-inch dice**
- **3 Chinese eggplant, peeled, trimmed, and cut into ¼-inch dice**
- **2 ribs celery, cut into small dice**
- **1 cup Tomato Fondue (see page 234)**
- **4 cloves roasted garlic, minced**
- **1 tablespoon minced thyme**
- **1 tablespoon chopped capers**
- **¼ cup slivered black olives**
- **12 canned piquillo peppers, well drained**
- **1 cup Tomato Concassé (see page 234)**
- **Coarse salt and freshly ground pepper**

1. Heat 2 tablespoons of the olive oil in a large sauté pan over medium heat. Add the eggplant and sauté for about 10 minutes or until just tender. Scrape the eggplant into a bowl and set aside.

2. Return the sauté pan to medium heat. Add the celery and onion and sauté for about 5 minutes or just until the vegetables have sweat their liquid and retained their texture but have not taken on any color. Stir in the garlic and then the reserved eggplant. Fold in the Tomato Fondue and bring to a simmer. Remove from the heat and fold in the Tomato Concassé, olives, capers and thyme. Season with salt and pepper. Allow to cool slightly.

3. When cool enough to handle, carefully stuff each pepper with the caponata. Set aside until ready to serve.

YELLOW TOMATO COULIS

- **5 yellow beefsteak tomatoes, cored and quartered**
- **Coarse salt**
- **3 tablespoons olive oil**

1. Place the tomatoes in a medium bowl. Season with salt, tossing to coat. Set aside for 30 minutes.

2. Place the tomatoes with their juice into a blender. Add the olive oil and process to a smooth purée. Pour through a fine sieve into a clean container, discarding the solids. Cover and refrigerate until ready to use.

CRISPED RED ONION RINGS

- **1 large red onion, peeled and cut, crosswise, into paper-thin slices**
- **1 cup Wondra flour**
- **Coarse salt**
- **Approximately 6 cups vegetable oil**

1. Pull the onion slices into rings. Toss the rings with the Wondra flour to lightly coat.

2. Heat the oil in a deep saucepan over medium-high heat to 365°F on an instant-read thermometer. Add the onion rings, a few at a time, and fry for about 1 minute or until the rings are nicely colored and crisp. Using a slot- ted spoon, lift the rings from the oil and place on paper towel to drain. Continue frying until all of the rings are cooked. Season with salt. Reserve, uncovered, at room temperature, until ready to use.

Nantucket Bay
with Sea Urchin

Scallops
and Mirin Emulsion

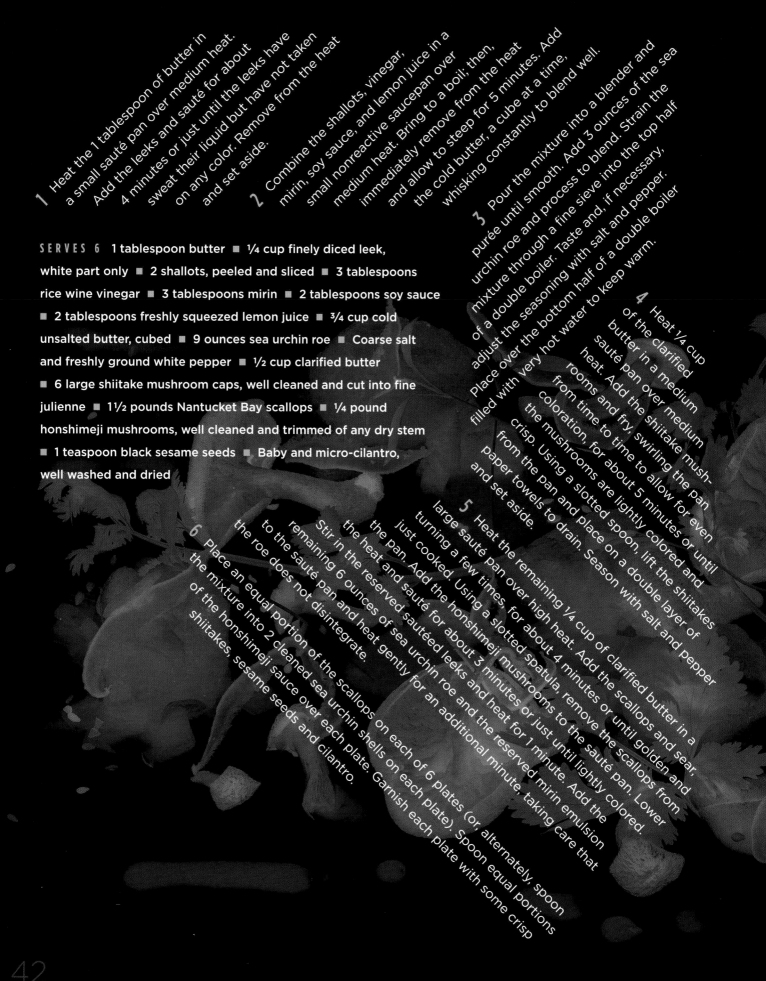

1 Heat the 1 tablespoon of butter in a small sauté pan over medium heat. Add the leeks and sauté for about 4 minutes or just until the leeks have sweat their liquid but have not taken on any color. Remove from the heat and set aside.

2 Combine the shallots, vinegar, mirin, soy sauce, and lemon juice in a small nonreactive saucepan over medium heat. Bring to a boil; then, immediately remove from the heat and allow to steep for 5 minutes. Add the cold butter, a cube at a time, whisking constantly to blend well.

3 Pour the mixture into a blender and purée until smooth. Add 3 ounces of the sea urchin roe and process to blend. Strain the mixture through a fine sieve into the top half of a double boiler. Taste and, if necessary, adjust the seasoning with salt and pepper. Place over the bottom half of a double boiler filled with very hot water to keep warm.

SERVES 6   1 tablespoon butter ■ ¼ cup finely diced leek, white part only ■ 2 shallots, peeled and sliced ■ 3 tablespoons rice wine vinegar ■ 3 tablespoons mirin ■ 2 tablespoons soy sauce ■ 2 tablespoons freshly squeezed lemon juice ■ ¾ cup cold unsalted butter, cubed ■ 9 ounces sea urchin roe ■ Coarse salt and freshly ground white pepper ■ ½ cup clarified butter ■ 6 large shiitake mushroom caps, well cleaned and cut into fine julienne ■ 1½ pounds Nantucket Bay scallops ■ ¼ pound honshimeji mushrooms, well cleaned and trimmed of any dry stem ■ 1 teaspoon black sesame seeds ■ Baby and micro-cilantro, well washed and dried

4 Heat ¼ cup of the clarified butter in a medium sauté pan over medium heat. Add the shiitake mushrooms and fry, swirling the pan from time to time to allow for even coloration, for about 5 minutes or until the mushrooms are lightly colored and crisp. Using a slotted spoon, lift the shiitakes from the pan and place on a double layer of paper towels to drain. Season with salt and pepper and set aside.

5 Heat the remaining ¼ cup of clarified butter in a large sauté pan over high heat. Add the scallops and sear, turning a few times, for about 4 minutes or until the scallops from just cooked. Using a slotted spatula, remove the scallops to the sauté pan. Lower the heat and sauté the honshimeji mushrooms to the sauté pan. Add the reserved sautéed leeks and the reserved mirin emulsion to the sauté pan and heat gently for 1 minute, taking care that the roe does not disintegrate.

6 Place an equal portion of the scallops on each of 6 plates (or, alternately, spoon an equal portion of the mixture into 2 cleaned sea urchin shells on each plate). Spoon equal portions of the honshimeji sauce over each plate. Garnish each plate with some crisp shiitakes, sesame seeds and cilantro.

Oysters

with Cucumber-Apple

Sorbet and

Green Apple

Mignonette

Line 6 oyster plates or other shallow dishes with shaved ice. Open the oysters and place 6 on each plate, nestling them into a bed of ice. Arrange some seaweed around the oysters. Spoon about ½ teaspoon of the Green Apple Mignonette over each oyster and then drizzle in a tiny bit of the olive oil. Place a small scoop of sorbet on each oyster and top with a dollop of wasabi tobiko. Serve immediately, garnished with seaweed strands, small sticks of apple and baby amaranth.

SERVES 6 **36 oysters** ■ **½ pound seaweed, blanched** ■ **Green Apple Mignonette** ■ **3 tablespoons fine quality, fruity extra virgin olive oil** ■ **Cucumber-Green Apple Sorbet** ■ **3 tablespoons wasabi tobiko** ■ **Large handful seaweed strands, well washed and dried** ■ **1 Granny Smith apple, peeled and cut into small sticks** ■ **1 cup baby amaranth, well washed and dried**

GREEN APPLE MIGNONETTE

4 large green apples, well washed and quartered ■ **2 tablespoons mirin** ■ **1 teaspoon rice wine vinegar** ■ **1 cup very finely diced green apple** ■ **1 tablespoon ascorbic acid**

1 Using an electric juicer, juice the quartered apples along with the ascorbic acid. Strain into a clean container and then measure out 1 cup. Stir in the finely diced apple and set aside at room temperature until ready to serve.

CUCUMBER-GREEN APPLE SORBET

4 large green apples, well washed and quartered ■ **1 teaspoon ascorbic acid** ■ **5 cups fresh cucumber juice, strained** ■ **2 cups mirin** ■ **½ cup rice wine vinegar**

1 Using an electric juicer, juice the apples along with the ascorbic acid. Strain into a clean container and then measure out 1 cup. Combine the apple juice with the cucumber juice, mirin, and vinegar. Place in an ice cream freezer and freeze according to manufacturer's directions for sorbet.

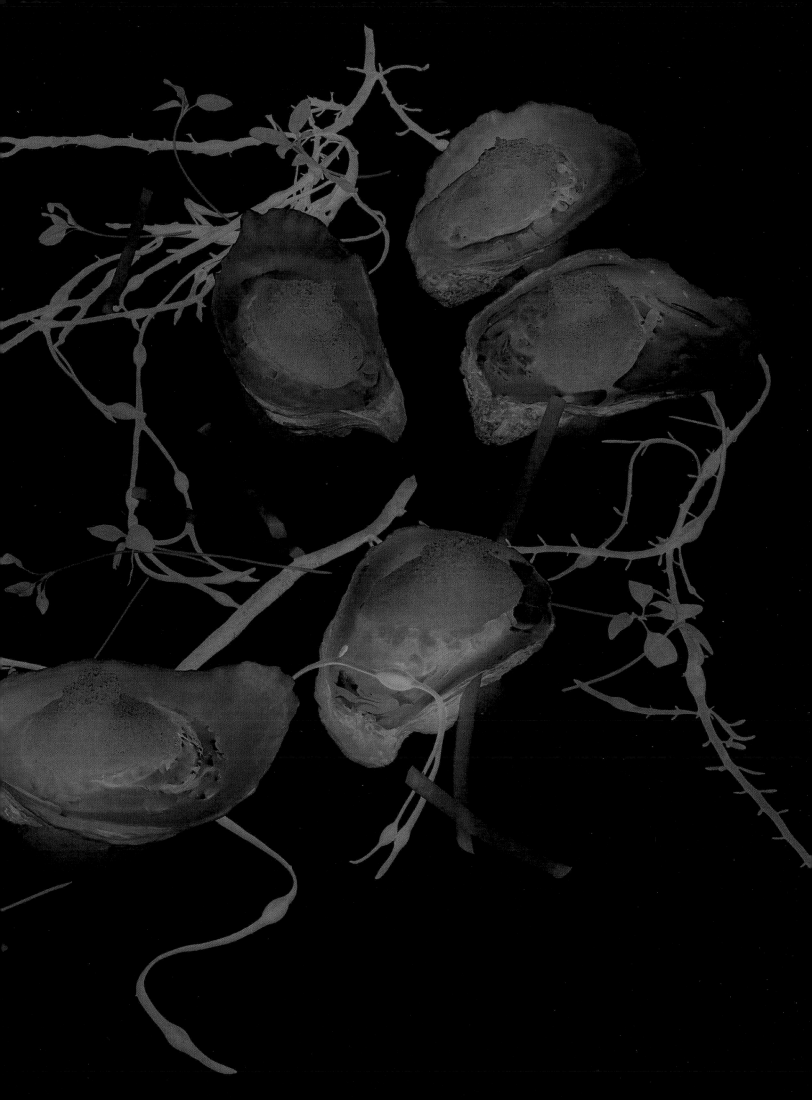

Oysters over a

Cucumber Roulade

SERVES 6   4 large English cucumbers, well washed and dried ■ 2 cups Citrus Vinaigrette (see page 235) ■ 2 tablespoons yuzu juice ■ ¼ cup sugar ■ 2 large red radishes, well washed, trimmed and julienned ■ ¼ cup mung bean sprouts ■ ¼ cup carrot julienne ■ ¼ cup English cucumber julienne ■ ¼ cup daikon radish julienne ■ Coarse salt and freshly ground white pepper ■ 1 watermelon radish, thinly sliced ■ 30 Malpeque oysters, shucked with juices reserved ■ 1 ounce Osetra caviar ■ 1 tablespoon yuzu powder ■ 2 cups micro-greens, well washed and dried

1 Trim each end from the cucumbers to make a neat even rectangular shape. Using a Japanese slicing machine or mandoline, cut the cucumbers, lengthwise, into paper-thin strips. You will need 30 pieces. Set aside.

2 Combine the Citrus Vinaigrette with the yuzu juice in a small bowl. Add the sugar and whisk until the sugar has dissolved. Set aside.

3 Combine the red radish julienne with the mung bean sprouts and the julienned carrot, cucumber and daikon in a mixing bowl. Add just enough of the reserved vinaigrette to lightly dress the vegetables. Season with salt and pepper and set aside.

4 Working with 1 slice at a time, wrap a small amount of the vegetable mixture in a cucumber slice, rolling it up cigar-fashion. Place on a chilled plate and continue making cucumber roulades until you have made 30.

5 Place 5 slices of watermelon radish on each of 6 luncheon plates. Place 5 cucumber roulades, upright, at the edge of each of the radish slices on each plate and then place an oyster on top of each roulade.

6 Add the caviar along with the reserved oyster juices to the remaining vinaigrette. Gently fold the caviar into the vinaigrette. Spoon the vinaigrette over the oysters and around the plate. Finish each plate with a light dusting of yuzu powder and a flourish of micro-greens.

Sunchoke Soup
with Potato Croutons
and Lemon Confit

Sweet Curry-Scented
Delicata Squash Soup
with Apple Dumplings

Shiitake Velouté with
Peanut Sabayon

Hot Soups

Shiitake Velouté with Peanut Sabayon

SERVES 6 1 cup unsalted butter ■ ¼ pound unsalted, skinless raw peanuts ■ 4 cups heavy cream ■ Coarse salt and freshly ground black pepper ■ 6 large egg yolks ■ 2 pounds shiitake mushrooms, cleaned, stemmed and quartered ■ 3 shallots, thinly sliced ■ 8 cups chicken stock ■ Freshly ground white pepper ■ 1 cup clarified butter ■ 1 cup thinly sliced shiitake mushroom caps ■ 2 tablespoons chile oil ■ 2 tablespoons chopped chives

1　Place ½ cup of the butter in a large saucepan pan over medium-low heat. Cook, stirring frequently, for about 5 minutes or just until the butter begins to color. Add the peanuts and sauté for about 10 minutes or until the peanuts are golden brown. Add the cream and season with salt and black pepper. Bring to a simmer and cook for 5 minutes.

2　Pour the peanut mixture into a blender and process to a smooth purée. Pour through a fine sieve into a clean container, discarding the solids. Taste, and, if necessary, adjust the seasoning with salt and black pepper.

3　Place the egg yolks in a small bowl and whisk about ½ cup of the peanut sauce into the eggs to temper them; then, whisk the egg mixture into the peanut sauce. Again, strain the mixture through a fine sieve. Pour into a foam canister and pressurize. Refrigerate until ready to use.

4　Heat the remaining ½ cup of butter in a large saucepan over medium heat. Add the quartered mushrooms and sauté for about 20 minutes or until the mushrooms are a deep golden brown. Add the shallots and continue to sauté for about 10 minutes or until they begin to caramelize. Add the chicken stock and season with salt and black pepper. Bring to a simmer and simmer for 10 minutes. Pour into a blender and process to a smooth purée. Taste and adjust the seasoning with a heavy accent of freshly ground white pepper.

5　Heat the clarified butter in a large sauté pan over medium-high heat. Add the sliced shiitakes and fry for about 5 minutes or until the mushrooms are light brown and crisp. Using a slotted spoon, remove the mushrooms from the butter and place on a double layer of paper towel to drain.

6　Return the velouté to a clean saucepan over medium heat and bring to a boil. If the soup seems too thick, thin slightly with additional chicken stock. Pour an equal portion of the velouté into each of 6 soup bowls. Squirt a small mound of Peanut Sabayon onto the velouté. Sprinkle the crisp mushrooms around the edge of the soup and dot with chile oil. Sprinkle with chives and serve.

Sunchoke Soup with Potato Croutons and Lemon Confit

SERVES 6 ■ Juice of ½ lemon ■ ½ pound sunchokes (Jerusalem artichokes) ■ 2 tablespoons unsalted butter ■ 2 parsnips, peeled, trimmed and chopped ■ 2 ribs celery, peeled, trimmed and chopped ■ 1 medium white onion, peeled and chopped ■ Coarse salt ■ 8 cups chicken stock ■ Lemon Confit Syrup ■ Freshly ground white pepper ■ Potato Croutons ■ Lemon Confit ■ 2 tablespoons chopped chives ■ 3 tablespoons argane oil

1 Combine the lemon juice with enough water to cover the sunchokes in a medium bowl. Peel the sunchokes and immediately place them in the acidulated water.

2 Heat the butter in a large saucepan over medium heat. Add the parsnips, celery and onion. Remove the sunchokes from the acidulated water, pat dry and chop. Season with salt and sauté for about 5 minutes or just until the vegetables have begun to sweat their liquid. Add the chicken stock and bring to a boil. Lower the heat and cook at a bare simmer for about 30 minutes or until the vegetables are very tender.

3 Remove the soup from the heat and process to a smooth purée. Pour through a fine sieve into a clean saucepan and season with salt and white pepper.

4 Place the soup over medium heat and cook for about 3 minutes or just until hot. Pour equal portions into each of 6 large shallow soup bowls. Sprinkle with Potato Croutons, Lemon Confit and chives. Drizzle the argane oil over the surface and serve.

POTATO CROUTONS

4 cups vegetable oil ■ **1 large Idaho potato, peeled and cut into a fine dice**

1 Heat the oil in a deep saucepan or deep-fat fryer over high heat to 300°F on an instant-read thermometer.

2 Add the diced potato and fry for about 1 minute or until just blanched. Using a slotted spoon, lift the potatoes from the oil and place on a double layer of paper towel to drain, leaving the oil on high heat.

3 Cook the oil until the temperature reaches 350°F on an instant-read thermometer. Return the blanched potatoes to the oil and fry for about 2 minutes or until golden brown. Using a slotted spoon, lift the potatoes from the oil and drain on a fresh layer of paper towel. Serve warm. (Potatoes may be made in advance of use and either reheated on a nonstick baking pan in a 500°F oven for a couple of minutes or refried just before serving. Whichever method is used, the potatoes should remain crisp.)

LEMON CONFIT AND SYRUP

2 lemons, well washed ■ **1 cup sugar** ■ **1 cup water**

1 Using a small knife or a zester, carefully remove the peel from the lemons, taking care not to remove any of the white pith. Cut the zest into a very small dice and set aside.

2 Juice the peeled lemons and then strain the juice through a fine sieve, discarding the solids. Set aside.

3 Bring a small saucepan of salted water to a boil over high heat. Add the lemon zest and blanch for 30 seconds. Drain well.

4 Combine the blanched zest with the sugar, water and reserved lemon juice in a small saucepan. Place over medium heat and bring to a boil. Lower the heat and simmer for about 30 minutes or until the lemon zest is very tender.

5 Remove from the heat and strain through a fine sieve, separately reserving the lemon zest and cooking syrup. Store, covered and refrigerated, until ready to use for up to 1 week. (Lemons may also be sliced paper thin and cooked to a confit in this same manner.)

Sweet Curry-Scented Delicata Squash Soup with Apple Dumplings

SERVES 6 1 tablespoon canola oil ■ 4 delicata squash, halved and seeded ■ 2 tablespoons unsalted butter ■ 2 Granny Smith apples, peeled, cored and chopped ■ 1 small white onion, peeled and chopped ■ 4 cups chicken stock ■ 3 cups Curry Stock ■ 1 banana, peeled and chopped ■ ½ vanilla bean, split lengthwise ■ ¼ cup pure maple syrup ■ Coarse salt and freshly ground pepper ■ 2 very thin slices prosciutto, cut into a fine julienne ■ Apple Dumplings ■ 2 tablespoons chopped chives ■ 3 tablespoons Curry Oil

1 Preheat the oven to 350°F. Lightly coat a nonstick baking pan with the canola oil. Place the squash, cut side down, on the oiled pan. Cover the entire pan with aluminum foil and place in the preheated oven. Bake for about 45 minutes or until the squash is easily pierced with the point of a small, sharp knife. Remove from the oven and uncover. Set aside until cool enough to handle. Scoop out and reserve the flesh. Set aside.

2 Heat the butter in a large saucepan over medium heat. Add the apples and onion and sauté for about 5 minutes or just until they have begun to soften but have not taken on any color. Add the chicken stock, Curry Stock and banana along with the reserved squash, stirring to blend. Bring to a simmer. Cook at a gentle simmer for 25 minutes. Scrape the vanilla bean seeds into the soup and whisk in the maple syrup.

3 Remove the soup from the heat. Pour into a blender and purée until smooth. Place in a clean saucepan and season with salt and pepper. Place over medium heat and bring to just a bare simmer.

4 Place the prosciutto in a small nonstick skillet over medium-high heat. Place in a stirring frequently, for about 4 minutes or just until the prosciutto is crisp. Fry, Using tongs, lift the prosciutto to a double layer of paper towel to drain.

5 Bring a large pot of salted water to a boil over high heat. Add the Apple Dumplings and boil for about 5 minutes or until all of the dumplings rise to the top and the dough is cooked through. Using a slotted spoon, lift the dumplings from the boiling water. Place 3 dumplings in each of 6 shallow soup bowls. Ladle equal portions of the soup into each bowl.

6 Sprinkle with chives and drizzle with Curry Oil. Rest a small mound of crisp prosciutto in the center of each bowl and serve.

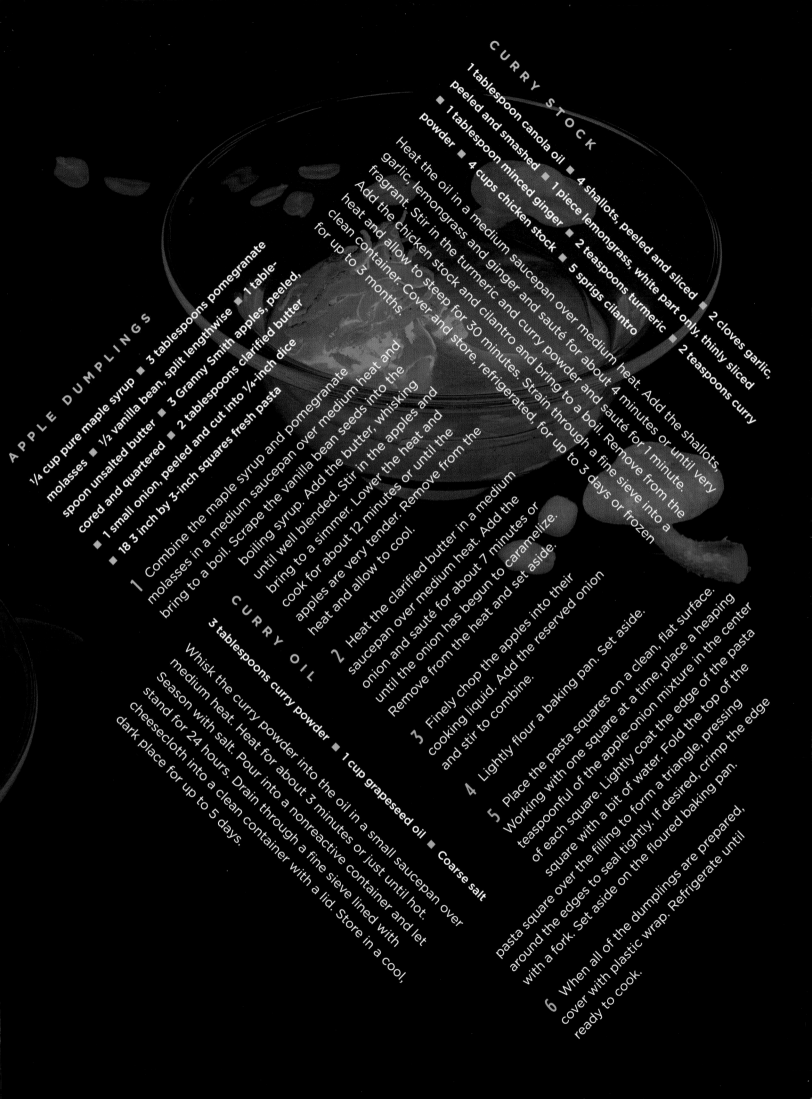

CURRY STOCK

- 1 tablespoon canola oil
- 4 shallots, peeled and sliced
- 1 piece lemongrass, white part only, thinly sliced
- 1 tablespoon minced ginger
- 2 cloves garlic, peeled and smashed
- 2 teaspoons turmeric
- 1 tablespoon minced ginger
- 2 teaspoons curry powder
- 4 cups chicken stock
- 5 sprigs cilantro

Heat the oil in a medium saucepan over medium heat. Add the shallots, garlic, lemongrass and ginger and sauté for about 4 minutes or until very fragrant. Stir in the turmeric and curry powder and sauté for 1 minute. Add the chicken stock and cilantro and bring to a boil. Remove from the heat and allow to steep for 30 minutes. Strain through a fine sieve into a clean container. Cover and store, refrigerated, for up to 3 days or frozen for up to 3 months.

APPLE DUMPLINGS

- ¼ cup pure maple syrup
- 3 tablespoons pomegranate molasses
- ½ vanilla bean, split lengthwise
- 1 tablespoon unsalted butter
- 2 tablespoons clarified butter
- 3 Granny Smith apples, peeled, cored and quartered
- 1 small onion, peeled and cut into ¼-inch dice
- 18 3 inch by 3-inch squares fresh pasta

1 Combine the maple syrup and pomegranate molasses in a medium saucepan over medium heat and bring to a boil. Scrape the vanilla bean seeds into the boiling syrup. Add the butter, whisking until well blended. Stir in the apples and bring to a simmer. Lower the heat and cook for about 12 minutes or until the apples are very tender. Remove from the heat and allow to cool.

2 Heat the clarified butter in a medium saucepan over medium heat. Add the onion and sauté for about 7 minutes or until the onion has begun to caramelize. Remove from the heat and set aside.

3 Finely chop the apples into their cooking liquid. Add the reserved onion and stir to combine.

4 Lightly flour a baking pan. Set aside.

5 Place the pasta squares on a clean, flat surface. Working with one square at a time, place a heaping teaspoonful of the apple-onion mixture in the center of each square. Lightly coat the edge of the pasta square with a bit of water. Fold the top of the pasta square over the filling to form a triangle, pressing around the edges to seal tightly. If desired, crimp the edge with a fork. Set aside on the floured baking pan.

6 When all of the dumplings are prepared, cover with plastic wrap. Refrigerate until ready to cook.

CURRY OIL

- 3 tablespoons curry powder
- 1 cup grapeseed oil
- Coarse salt

Whisk the curry powder into the oil in a small saucepan over medium heat. Heat for about 3 minutes or just until hot. Season with salt. Pour into a nonreactive container and let stand for 24 hours. Drain through a fine sieve lined with cheesecloth into a clean container with a lid. Store in a cool, dark place for up to 5 days.

Cold Soups

Chilled Corn and
Lemon Grass Soup

Chilled Carrot and Ginger Soup with Shrimp Ceviche

Chilled Sweet Pea Soup, Crab Salad and Rosemary Brioche Croutons

Chilled Sweet Pea Soup, Crab Salad and Rosemary Brioche Croutons

SERVES 6 2 pounds fresh English peas in their pods ■ 12 cups chicken stock ■ 2 branches rosemary, slightly bruised ■ 2 tablespoons unsalted butter ■ 2 shallots, peeled and thinly sliced ■ Coarse salt and freshly ground white pepper ■ Crab Salad ■ Lemon Sabayon ■ 1 ½ tablespoons lemon oil ■ Rosemary Brioche Croutons

1 Shell the peas, separately reserving the peas and half of the pods.

2 Combine the reserved pods with the chicken stock and rosemary in a large saucepan over medium heat. Bring to a simmer and cook for 15 minutes. Remove from the heat and pour into a blender (this may have to be done in batches) and process to a smooth purée. Strain through a fine sieve into a clean saucepan.

3 Bring a large pot of salted water to a boil over high heat. Add the reserved peas and blanch for 15 seconds to just set the color. Drain well and refresh under cold running water. Set aside.

4 Heat the butter in a medium sauté pan over medium heat. Add the shallots and sauté for about 4 minutes or just until the shallots have softened but not taken on any color.

5 Combine the peas and shallots in a blender. Add enough of the purée to make a smooth, slightly thick soup. It may be necessary to pour the soup from the blender and add additional stock purée to achieve the right consistency. (Do not discard the stock purée as the soup may require additional thinning after it has chilled.) Season with salt and white pepper. Pour the soup into a bowl and then place the bowl in a larger bowl of ice. Whisk constantly to cool the soup down as quickly as possible. Cover and refrigerate for at least 4 hours or until very well chilled.

6 Mound a generous serving of the Crab Salad in the center of each of 6 shallow soup bowls. Carefully ladle the chilled soup around the salad in each bowl, pouring so as not to disperse the salad. Squirt a mound of the Lemon Sabayon onto a plate and form it into a quenelle by moving and shaping it between 2 wet teaspoons. Place a quenelle beside the salad in each bowl. Continue making quenelles until all of the soup plates have one. Drizzle the soup with lemon oil and grind a bit of white pepper over all. Scatter a few Rosemary Brioche Croutons over the bowl and serve.

CRAB SALAD

½ pound lump crabmeat, picked clean ■ ¼ cup chopped chives ■ ½ cup fine-quality extra virgin olive oil ■ Coarse salt and freshly ground white pepper

Combine the crabmeat with the olive oil, chives and salt and pepper in a small bowl. Do not overmix. Cover with plastic wrap and refrigerate until ready to use.

LEMON SABAYON

- **3 large eggs**
- **2 ½ cups heavy cream**
- **3 tablespoons grated lemon zest**

1 Whisk the eggs together in a small bowl. Set aside.

2 Combine the cream and zest in a medium saucepan over medium heat. Cook, stirring frequently, for about 3 minutes or just until hot. Do not bring to a boil. Remove from the heat and allow to cool slightly. Pour through a fine sieve into a clean saucepan.

3 Whisk about ¼ cup of the hot cream into the reserved eggs. When well blended, whisk the egg mixture into the remaining cream. Place over medium-low heat and cook, whisking constantly, for about 5 minutes or just until the mixture is smooth and thick. Remove from the heat and cool slightly. Cover and place in the refrigerator for about one hour or until chilled.

4 When chilled, pour into a foam canister and pressurize. Refrigerate until ready to use.

ROSEMARY BRIOCHE CROUTONS

- **1 cup ¼-inch cubed brioche bread**
- **1 cup clarified butter**
- **2 tablespoons chopped rosemary**
- **Coarse salt and freshly ground pepper**

Combine the brioche with the clarified butter in a large sauté pan over medium heat. Fry, stirring and tossing, for about 5 minutes or until the bread is nicely browned on all sides. Add the rosemary and toss to coat evenly. Remove from the heat and, using a slotted spoon, transfer the toast cubes to a double layer of paper towel to drain. Season with salt and pepper.

Chilled Corn and Lemongrass Soup

SERVES 6 2 tablespoons unsalted butter ■ 2 shallots, peeled and thinly sliced ■ 1 stalk lemongrass, tender bottom part only, thinly sliced on the bias ■ 1 serrano chile, stemmed, seeded and thinly sliced ■ 2 tablespoons minced ginger ■ Coarse salt ■ 2 ½ cups (about 5 ears) fresh corn kernels ■ 3 kaffir lime leaves ■ 1 bay leaf ■ 1 teaspoon toasted coriander seed ■ 2 cups unsweetened coconut milk ■ 4 cups lobster stock ■ Freshly ground white pepper ■ Lobster Salad ■ 2 teaspoons Spicy Shrimp Oil ■ 1 teaspoon Lobster Roe Powder (see page 234) ■ 2 tablespoons chopped chives

1. Heat the butter in a large saucepan over medium heat. Add the shallots, lemongrass, serrano chile and ginger along with a pinch of salt. Sauté for about 7 minutes or just until the vegetables have sweat their liquid but have not taken on any color. Stir in the corn kernels, lime leaves, bay leaf and coriander seed. Add the coconut milk and bring to a simmer. Stir in the lobster stock and again bring to a simmer. Simmer, stirring occasionally, for 10 minutes. Remove from the heat and allow to rest for 15 minutes.

2. Pour the soup into a blender and process to a smooth purée. (This may have to be done in batches.) Pour the purée through a fine sieve into a clean bowl. Taste and adjust the seasoning with salt and white pepper. Place the soup down and whisk constantly to cool the soup down as quickly as possible. Cover with plastic wrap and refrigerate for at least 4 hours or until very well chilled.

3. When ready to serve, taste and, if necessary, adjust the seasoning with salt and white pepper. Place a mound of the Lobster Salad in the center of each of 6 shallow soup bowls. Carefully ladle the chilled soup around the salad in each bowl so as not to disperse the salad. Decorate the top with a few dots of Spicy Shrimp Oil and a sprinkling of Lobster Roe Powder. Sprinkle chives over all and serve.

4.

LOBSTER SALAD

■ 12 ounces cooked lobster meat, diced ■ 3 tablespoons Spicy Shrimp Oil ■ 3 tablespoons chopped chives ■ Coarse salt and freshly ground pepper

Place the lobster meat in a small bowl. Drizzle with the Spicy Shrimp Oil and toss to coat. Stir in the chives and season with salt and pepper. Cover with plastic wrap and refrigerate until ready to use.

SPICY SHRIMP OIL

15 shrimp shells ■ 2 tablespoons plus 2 cups grapeseed oil ■ 2 cloves garlic, peeled and thinly sliced ■ 5 kaffir lime leaves ■ 3 shallots, peeled and membrane removed, sliced ■ ½ jalapeño chile, seeds and membrane removed, sliced ■ 1 tablespoon thinly sliced lemongrass ■ 1 tablespoon chopped ginger ■ Coarse salt ■ 1 tablespoon tomato paste ■ 10 sprigs cilantro ■ 2 teaspoons toasted coriander seeds

1. Place the shrimp shells in a medium, nonstick sauté pan over medium heat and sauté for about 3 minutes or until bright red. Remove from the heat and set aside.

2. Heat 2 tablespoons of the oil in a medium saucepan over medium heat. Add the garlic and sauté for about 3 minutes or until golden. Add the shallots and sauté for an additional 2 minutes. Add the lime leaves, jalapeño, lemongrass and ginger along with a generous pinch of salt. Sauté for about 5 minutes or until very aromatic. Stir in the tomato paste and sauté for 1 minute. Add the cilantro and coriander. Stir to blend; then, add the reserved shrimp shells. Bring to 130°F on an instant-read thermometer and remove from the heat. Allow to cool to room temperature. Strain through a cheesecloth-lined fine sieve into a clean container, discarding the solids. Store, tightly covered and refrigerated, for up to 1 week. Bring to room temperature before serving.

2 cups of oil along with the reserved shrimp shells. Bring

Chilled Carrot and Ginger Soup with Shrimp Ceviche

SERVES 6 2 tablespoons unsalted butter ■ 1 medium onion, peeled and chopped ■ 2 tablespoons minced ginger ■ 5 large carrots, peeled, trimmed and grated ■ 1 cup carrot juice ■ 2 cups chicken stock ■ Coarse salt and freshly ground white pepper ■ 2 teaspoons toasted coriander seed ■ ¼ cup crème fraîche ■ Shrimp Ceviche ■ Crisp Ginger

1 Heat the butter in a large saucepan over medium heat. Add the onion and sauté for about 4 minutes or just until it has started to become translucent. Add the ginger and sauté for an additional 3 minutes or until the mixture is very fragrant. Add the carrots and sauté for another 3 minutes. Pour in the carrot juice and bring to a simmer. Add the chicken stock and again bring to a simmer. Season with salt and white pepper. Add the coriander. Simmer for 10 minutes.

2 Remove from the heat and transfer to a blender. Process to a smooth purée; then, pour through a fine sieve into a clean container. Place in an ice-water bath and cool, stirring from time to time. When cool, cover and refrigerate for about 3 hours or until the soup is well chilled and the flavors have blended.

3 Remove from the refrigerator and whisk in the crème fraîche. Pour an equal portion of soup into each of 6 large, shallow soup bowls. Mound some Shrimp Ceviche in the center of each bowl and garnish with Crisp Ginger. Serve cold.

SHRIMP CEVICHE

1 cup bay shrimp, cleaned ■ 5 sprigs cilantro ■ ½ cup freshly squeezed lime juice ■ 3 tablespoons olive oil ■ Coarse salt and freshly ground pepper

1 Combine the shrimp and cilantro in a shallow, nonreactive container. Set aside.

2 Combine the lime juice and olive oil in a small saucepan over medium heat and bring to a simmer. Immediately remove from the heat and season with salt and pepper. Pour over the shrimp and toss to coat well. Cover lightly with plastic wrap and set aside to cool slightly.

3 When just cool, transfer to the refrigerator. Chill, tossing from time to time, for about 3 hours or until the shrimp are opaque. (If the ceviche is made too far in advance, the shrimp will "cook" in the acid and begin to disintegrate.) Serve chilled.

CRISP GINGER

½ cup thinly sliced ginger ■ 1 cup sugar ■ Approximately 4 cups vegetable oil

1 Place the ginger in a small saucepan of cold water over high heat and bring to a boil. Drain well and repeat the blanching process. Drain well and pat dry.

2 Combine the blanched ginger and sugar in a small saucepan. Add cold water to cover by 1 inch. Place over medium-low heat and bring to a boil. Cook, at a bare simmer, for about 40 minutes or until the liquid is syrupy and the ginger has begun to candy.

3 Remove from the heat and drain well. Lay the candied ginger in a single layer on a clean, flat surface and allow to cool.

4 Heat the oil in a medium saucepan or deep-fat fryer over high heat to 365°F on an instant-read thermometer. Add the ginger, a few pieces at a time, and fry for about 45 seconds or until crisp. Using a slotted spoon, lift the ginger from the fat and place on a double layer of paper towel to drain. Continue frying until all of the ginger is crisp. Serve at room temperature.

THE ART OF AUREOLE

SALADS, VEGETABLES & GRAINS

Composed Salad
of Heirloom Tomatoes
with Crisp House-Cured
Pancetta

1 Slice the tomatoes into a variety of shapes, such as slices, quarters and chunks. Place in a mixing bowl and add just enough olive oil to lightly coat. Season with salt and pepper.

2 Place the dandelion greens in a mixing bowl and add just enough olive oil to lightly coat. Season with salt and pepper.

3 Place an equal portion of the seasoned tomatoes and dandelion greens on each of 6 luncheon plates. Garnish with pancetta rings. Spoon the Tomato Gelée around each plate and drizzle Basil Oil over all. Make 6 large quenelles of Tomato Sorbet by moving and shaping the sorbet between 2 wet tablespoons. Place one quenelle on top of each salad. Serve immediately.

SERVES 6   2 pounds mixed heirloom tomatoes (such as Brandywine, zebras, and sweet 100s), well washed and cored ■ ¼ cup extra virgin olive oil ■ Coarse salt and freshly ground pepper ■ 3 cups wild dandelion greens, well washed and dried ■ Crisp House-Cured Pancetta ■ Tomato Gelée ■ Basil Oil (see page 235) ■ Tomato Sorbet

CRISP HOUSE-CURED PANCETTA

◆ 1 pound fresh pork belly ■ Approximately 6 cups coarse salt ■ 2 tablespoons sel rose

1 Lightly season the pork belly with the sel rose. Line a glass baking dish with coarse salt and lay the seasoned pork belly in it. Add enough coarse salt to cover the pork belly. Tightly wrap in plastic wrap and refrigerate for 6 days.

2 Remove the cured pork from the refrigerator and, using a clean, damp kitchen towel, wipe off any salt.

3 Preheat the oven to 350°F.

4 Using an electric meat slicer, cut the cured pork belly, lengthwise, into very thin strips. Working with one strip at a time, wrap the cured meat around a length of 1½-inch-thick heatproof tubing (such as a copper pipe) cut to a size that will easily fit into the oven, leaving about ¼ inch between each circle.

5 Place a baking sheet on the bottom shelf of the preheated oven to catch the dripping fat. Place the tubing on the middle shelf of the oven and bake for about 15 minutes or until the pancetta rings are brown and crisp. Remove from the oven and place on a wire rack to cool. When cool enough to handle, gently push the rings off the tubing and store at room temperature until ready to use.

TOMATO GELÉE

- **2 pounds heirloom tomatoes, well washed, cored and chopped** ■ **1 tablespoon fleur de sel**
- **2 small sprigs basil** ■ **9 sheets gelatin** ■ **2 tablespoons chopped chives**

1 Combine the tomatoes with the fleur de sel in a blender and process to a smooth purée. Pour the purée into a clean kitchen towel and, using kitchen twine, tie the towel up and around the purée to make a bag. Hang or tie the bag over a deep bowl or pan. Slightly bruise the basil sprigs and place them in the bowl. Place the entire set-up in the refrigerator for about 12 hours or until all of the tomato water has dripped out.

2 Remove the bowl from the refrigerator and gently squeeze the bag to extract the last bit of liquid. Remove the bag, untie and discard the tomato pulp. Remove the basil from the tomato water and discard.

3 Place the tomato water in a medium nonstick saucepan over low heat and bring to a simmer, skimming off any impurities that rise to the top. Remove from the heat and set aside.

4 Place the gelatin in about 1/4 cup of warm water to dissolve. Whisk the dissolved gelatin into the tomato water, mixing until well blended. Pour into a shallow, glass baking dish and refrigerate for about 4 hours or until set.

5 When ready to serve, remove the gelée from the refrigerator and run a fork through it to loosen. Mix in the chives and serve immediately.

TOMATO SORBET

- **1 pound heirloom tomatoes, well washed, cored and chopped**
- **3 tablespoons citron vodka** ■ **2 teaspoons freshly grated horseradish**

1 Combine the tomatoes, vodka and horseradish in a blender and process to a smooth purée. To make sure that no seeds remain, pour through a medium sieve into a clean container.

2 Pour the mixture into the bowl of an ice cream machine and freeze according to the manufacturer's directions for sorbet.

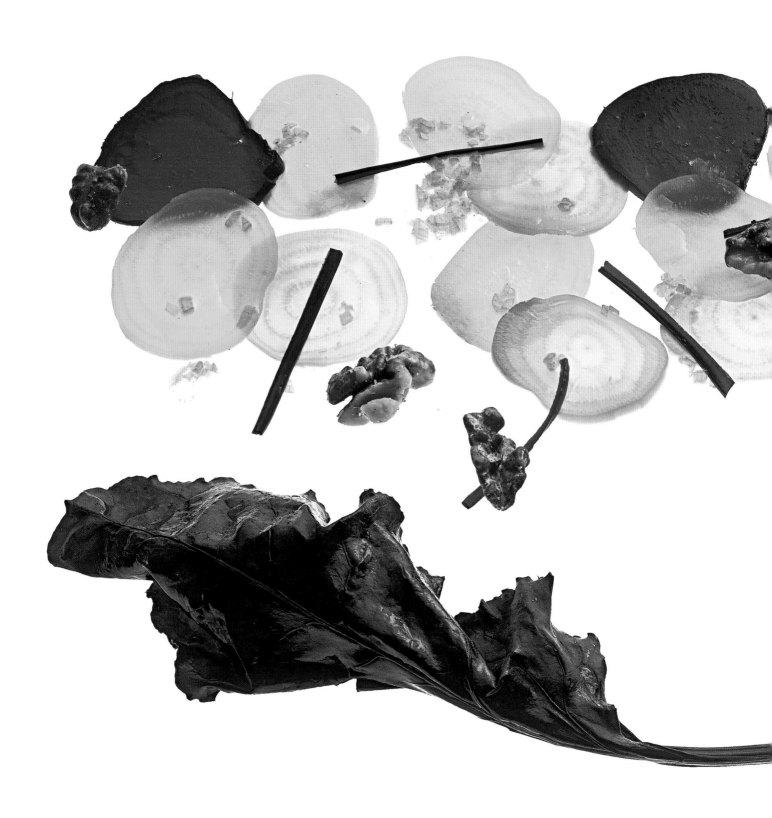

Beet Carpaccio,
Crottin de Chauvignol and Toasted Walnut
Vinaigrette

4 large beets (such as red, yellow, Chioggia or a combination)

■ ¼ cup grapeseed oil ■ Coarse salt ■ 6 Crottin de Chauvignol

■ 2 heads frisée, well washed, pulled apart and dried ■ 3 cups peppercress,
well washed and dried ■ 1 cup tiny celery leaves, well washed and dried

■ Toasted Walnut Vinaigrette ■ 1 cup toasted walnut pieces ■ Freshly
ground white pepper ■ ½ cup very thin, 1 ½-inch-long cooked beet sticks

■ Freshly ground black pepper

1 Preheat the oven to 325°F.

2 Generously coat the beets with the grapeseed oil and
season with salt. Wrap each beet in aluminum foil and place in
a baking dish. Place the dish in the preheated oven and roast the
beets for about 2 hours or until just tender when pierced with
the point of a small, sharp knife. Remove from the oven, unwrap
and set aside to cool.

3 When cool enough to handle, push off the beet skins and trim the root and stem end. Using a
mandoline, cut the beets, crosswise, into very thin rounds, keeping the slices in neat stacks. Using a
2-inch round cookie cutter, punch out 2-inch circles from the stacked beet thins. (Make beet sticks out of
the trimmings or reserve for another use, such as in a salad or as a chopped garnish on other vegetables.)

4 Preheat the oven to 350°F.

5 Place the cheese on a baking sheet in the preheated oven and bake for about 10 minutes or just
until warm through.

6 Combine the frisée, peppercress and celery leaves in a small bowl. Add just enough of the
vinaigrette to lightly coat the greens. Add about ½ cup of the toasted walnuts and season
with salt and white pepper. Toss to combine and set aside.

7 Make a circle of slightly overlapping beet rounds around the edge of each of
6 luncheon plates. Mound equal portions of the salad in the center of each
plate. Drizzle some of the remaining vinaigrette over each plate and
sprinkle with the remaining toasted walnuts and the beet sticks.
Place a warm cheese on top of each salad. Grind some
black pepper over all and serve.

TOASTED WALNUT VINAIGRETTE

2 teaspoons grapeseed oil ■ 3 tablespoons minced shallots ■ ¼ cup sherry wine vinegar ■ ¾ cup walnut oil ■ ¼ cup chopped toasted walnuts ■ Coarse salt and freshly ground pepper

1 Heat the oil in a small sauté pan over medium heat. Add the shallots and sauté for about 3 minutes or just until the shallots have softened. Remove from the heat.

2 Combine the shallots with the vinegar in a small bowl. Whisk in the oil and season with salt and pepper. Add the walnuts just before serving.

Mizuna Salad
with Crisp Chickpeas and
Tahini Vinaigrette

1　Heat the vegetable oil in a small saucepan over high heat to 365°F on an instant-read thermometer. Add the chickpeas and fry for about 2 minutes or until golden and crisp. Using a slotted spoon, lift the chickpeas from the oil and place on a double layer of paper towel to dry. Set aside.

2　Place the tahini and lemon juice in the small jar of a blender. Add the water and process to combine. Add the olive oil and process to emulsify. Season with salt and pepper and set aside.

3　Cut the cauliflower in half, lengthwise, reserving half for another use. Using a mandoline or Japanese vegetable slicer, cut one half of the cauliflower and the whole cucumber, lengthwise, into paper-thin slices.

4　Place equal portions of the mizuna in the center of each of 6 luncheon plates

5　Arrange an equal number of cauliflower and cucumber slices on each plate in a decorative pattern. Garnish each plate with chickpeas and Lemon Confit. Drizzle the reserved tahini vinaigrette over all. Sprinkle with parsley julienne and sesame seeds and serve.

SERVES 6　2 cups vegetable oil　■　1 cup cooked chickpeas, well drained and patted dry　■　3 tablespoons tahini　■　2 teaspoons freshly squeezed lemon juice ■　¼ cup cold water　■　3 tablespoons olive oil　■　Coarse salt and freshly ground pepper　■　1 small cauliflower, well washed and dried　■　1 English cucumber, well washed and dried　■　9 cups mizuna, well washed and dried ■　Lemon Confit (see page 55)　■　2 tablespoons flat-leaf parsley julienne　■　1 tablespoon toasted sesame seeds

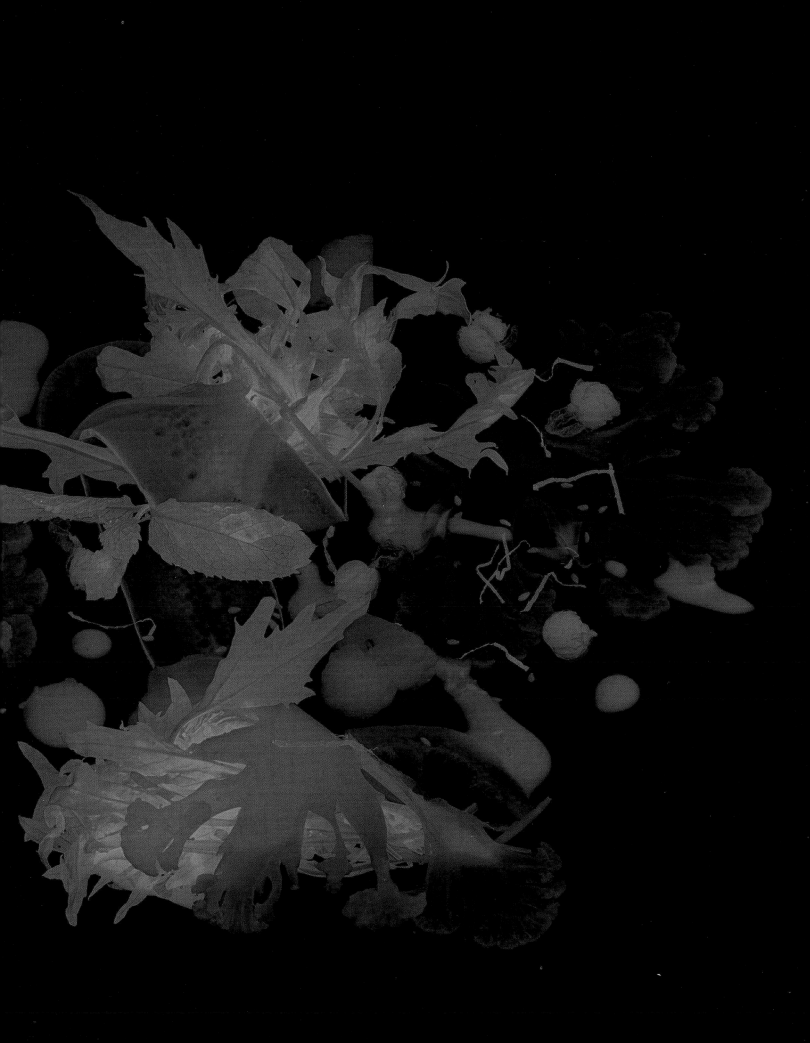

Soft-Boiled **Egg**
Topping a Truffled
Frisée Salad with
Braised Baby Leeks

SERVES 6   3 heads frisée, pulled apart, well washed, trimmed and dried ■ ¼ pound arugula, trimmed, well washed and dried ■ 1 cup baby spinach leaves, well washed and dried ■ ¼ cup chopped chives ■ 6 very fresh large eggs (plus a few extra to allow for breakage) ■ Braised Baby Leeks, warmed ■ 1½ cups Truffle Vinaigrette ■ Crisp Shallots ■ Fleur de sel ■ 12 small artichoke hearts, braised and split in half, lengthwise ■ 1 fresh black truffle

1 Toss the frisée, arugula, spinach leaves and chives together in a medium bowl. Set aside.

2 Line a baking sheet with a clean kitchen towel and set aside.

3 Bring a large saucepan of water to a boil over high heat. Carefully lower the eggs into the boiling water and boil for exactly 4 ½ minutes. Using a small sieve, one at a time, lift the eggs from the boiling water and place under cold running water until just cool enough to handle. Working very carefully, peel the shell from each egg (the egg will be quite soft) and place the peeled eggs on the prepared baking sheet. (The eggs can be prepared in advance and briefly reheated in 180°F water until the whites are just warm, taking care that the yolks do not cook.)

4 Place an equal portion of the warm leeks in the center of each of 6 plates to form a box shape with an empty center. Season the frisée mixture with just enough of the vinaigrette to lightly coat. Quickly toss in half of the Crisp Shallots and tightly mound the salad into the center of each leek box. Carefully place an egg on top of each salad and sprinkle the top with fleur de sel. Pile some of the remaining Crisp Shallots on top of each egg. Nestle a couple of artichoke halves into the arrangement. Drizzle the remaining vinaigrette around the edge of each plate. Slice fresh truffle over each salad just before serving.

BRAISED BABY LEEKS

24 baby leeks (or small spring onions) ■ 4 cups chicken stock ■ 5 sprigs thyme ■ 3 cloves garlic, peeled and crushed ■ 2 bay leaves ■ 3 tablespoons unsalted butter ■ Coarse salt and freshly ground pepper

1 Cut a piece of parchment paper to fit the top of a large, shallow, heavy-bottomed pan (such as a rondeau) and set aside.

2 Trim the dark green top leaves and root ends from the leeks (or onions). Slice each leek (or onion), lengthwise, to about 1 inch from the root end, leaving the leeks (or onions) intact. Individually place the leeks (or onions) under cold running water to rinse thoroughly. Shake off all excess water. Place the leeks in the large heavy-bottomed pan. Season with salt and pepper and place over medium heat. Cut the butter into pieces and add it to the stock, thyme, garlic and bay leaves. Cover with a lid and gently simmer for about 15 minutes or until the leeks (or onions) are fork-tender. Remove from the heat. Uncover and remove and discard the parchment. Allow the leeks (or onions) to cool in the cooking liquid. When cool, using a slotted spoon, transfer the leeks (or onions) to a plate. Strain the liquid through a fine sieve into a clean saucepan. When ready to serve, reheat the leeks (or onions) in the reserved cooking liquid until just barely warm.

80

TRUFFLE VINAIGRETTE

3 ounces truffle peelings ■ 1/2 cup Madeira ■ 1/2 cup plus 2 tablespoons olive oil ■ 1/4 cup chopped onions ■ 1/4 cup chopped carrots ■ 1/4 cup chopped celery ■ Sachet (see page 234) ■ 1/4 cup chicken stock ■ 1/4 cup sherry wine vinegar ■ 1/4 cup truffle oil ■ Coarse salt and freshly ground pepper ■ 2 teaspoons chopped chervil ■ 2 teaspoons chopped tarragon ■ 2 teaspoons chopped flat-leaf parsley ■ 2 teaspoons chopped chives

1. Combine the truffle peelings and Madeira in a small saucepan over medium heat. Bring to a simmer. Simmer for 5 minutes and then strain through a fine sieve, separately reserving the peelings and the liquid.

2. Heat 2 tablespoons of the olive oil in the same saucepan over medium heat. Add the onions, carrots, celery and Sachet and sauté for about 4 minutes or until the vegetables have just softened. Add the reserved truffle liquid and, using a wooden spoon, stir to deglaze the pan. Continue to simmer for about 3 minutes or until the liquid is almost dry. Add the stock and cook for about 4 minutes or until the liquid has reduced by half. Remove from the heat and immediately strain through a fine sieve into a heat-proof bowl, discarding the solids. Allow the liquid to cool.

3. Whisk in the vinegar and reserved truffle peelings; then, the remaining 1/2 cup of olive oil and the truffle oil. Season with salt and pepper. Stir in the chervil, parsley, tarragon and chives just before serving.

CRISP SHALLOTS

4 large shallots, peeled ■ 1 cup Wondra flour ■ Approximately 6 cups vegetable oil ■ Coarse salt

1. Using a Japanese vegetable cutter, cut the shallots, crosswise, into very thin slices. Pull the slices apart into individual rings.

2. Line a baking sheet with a triple layer of paper towel. Set aside.

3. Place the Wondra in a resealable plastic bag. Add the shallot rings and seal the bag. Shake and toss the bag to generously coat the shallots with flour. Transfer the coated shallots to a wire basket and shake vigorously to remove excess flour.

4. Heat the oil in a deep-fat fryer or deep saucepan over high heat to 350°F on an instant-read thermometer. Add the floured shallots and fry, turning occasionally so that all sides cook, for about 2 minutes, or until crisp and golden brown. Using a slotted spoon or a spider, transfer the shallots to the prepared baking sheet. Season with salt and set aside.

Hot Smoked
Rainbow Trout
with Fingerling
Potato Salad
and Marinated
Red Onions

1 Cut the potatoes, crosswise, into ¼-inch-thick rounds. Place in cold, salted water to cover over medium-high heat and bring to a boil. Lower the heat and simmer for about 10 minutes or just until tender. Remove from the heat and drain well. Place the potatoes out on a plate so that they cool quickly.

2 Cut the cucumbers, crosswise, into ¼-inch-thick half-moon shapes. Combine the cucumbers with the potatoes and half of the Marinated Red Onions. Add just enough of the Mustard Vinaigrette to lightly coat and toss with the chives. Taste and, if necessary, adjust the seasoning with salt and pepper.

3 Preheat the oven to 300°F.

4 Using your hands, lightly coat each trout fillet with the oil. Place the trout fillets on a nonstick baking pan in the preheated oven and bake for about 5 minutes or just until heated through.

5 Place equal portions of the potato salad in the center of each of 6 plates. Lay 2 warm trout fillets on top of each salad. Drizzle the remaining Mustard Vinaigrette and Verjus Reduction around the edge of each plate. Sprinkle the remaining Marinated Red Onions around each plate along with the mâche and dill.

SERVES 6 12 fingerling potatoes, well washed and dried ■ 1 English cucumber, peeled, seeded and halved, lengthwise ■ Marinated Red Onions ■ Mustard Vinaigrette ■ 1 tablespoon chopped chives ■ Coarse salt and freshly ground pepper ■ Smoked Rainbow Trout ■ 2 tablespoons canola oil ■ Verjus Reduction ■ 1 cup mâche leaves, well washed and dried ■ ¼ cup sprigs dill, well washed and dried

MARINATED RED ONIONS

1 large red onion, peeled ■ 2 cups port ■ 1 cup red verjus

1 Cut the onion into quarters. Cut each quarter into ¼-inch-thick slices, pulling each slice apart to make slivers.

2 Combine the wine and verjus in a small nonreactive saucepan over medium heat. Add the onion slivers and bring to a simmer. Simmer for about 5 minutes or until the onions are tender. Remove from the heat and allow the onions to cool in the liquid. Store, covered and refrigerated, until ready to use.

3 When ready to use, using a slotted spoon, lift the onions from the marinating liquid, reserving the liquid for reuse with another batch of onions, if desired.

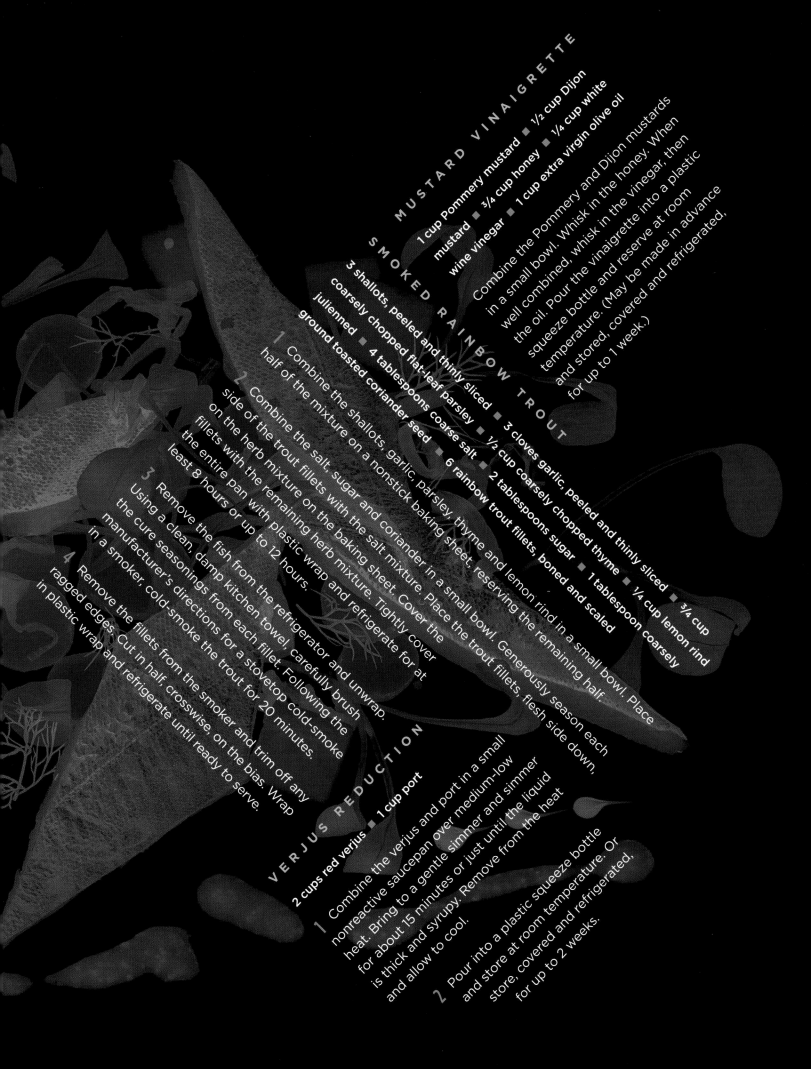

MUSTARD VINAIGRETTE

1 cup Pommery mustard ■ **½ cup Dijon mustard** ■ **¾ cup honey** ■ **¼ cup white wine vinegar** ■ **1 cup extra virgin olive oil**

Combine the Pommery and Dijon mustards in a small bowl. Whisk in the honey. When well combined, whisk in the vinegar, then the oil. Pour the vinaigrette into a plastic squeeze bottle and reserve at room temperature. (May be made in advance and stored, covered and refrigerated, for up to 1 week.)

SMOKED RAINBOW TROUT

3 shallots, peeled and thinly sliced ■ **3 cloves garlic, peeled and thinly sliced** ■ **¾ cup coarsely chopped flat-leaf parsley** ■ **½ cup coarsely chopped thyme** ■ **¼ cup lemon rind julienned** ■ **4 tablespoons coarse salt** ■ **2 tablespoons sugar** ■ **1 tablespoon ground toasted coriander seed** ■ **6 rainbow trout fillets, boned and scaled**

1 Combine the shallots, garlic, parsley, thyme and lemon rind in a small bowl. Place half of the mixture on a nonstick baking sheet, reserving the remaining half.

2 Combine the salt, sugar and coriander in a small bowl. Generously season each side of the trout fillets with the salt mixture. Place the trout fillets, flesh side down, on the herb mixture on the baking sheet. Cover the fillets with the remaining herb mixture. Tightly cover the entire pan with plastic wrap and refrigerate for at least 8 hours or up to 12 hours.

3 Remove the fish from the refrigerator and unwrap. Using a clean, damp kitchen towel, carefully brush the cure seasonings from each fillet. Following the manufacturer's directions for a stovetop cold-smoker, cold-smoke the trout for 20 minutes. in a smoker.

4 Remove the fillets from the smoker and trim off any ragged edges. Cut in half, crosswise, on the bias. Wrap in plastic wrap and refrigerate until ready to serve.

VERJUS REDUCTION

2 cups red verjus ■ **1 cup port**

1 Combine the verjus and port in a small nonreactive saucepan over medium-low heat. Bring to a gentle simmer and simmer for about 15 minutes or just until the liquid is thick and syrupy. Remove from the heat and allow to cool.

2 Pour into a plastic squeeze bottle and store at room temperature. Or store, covered and refrigerated, for up to 2 weeks.

Tuna Salad Niçoise with

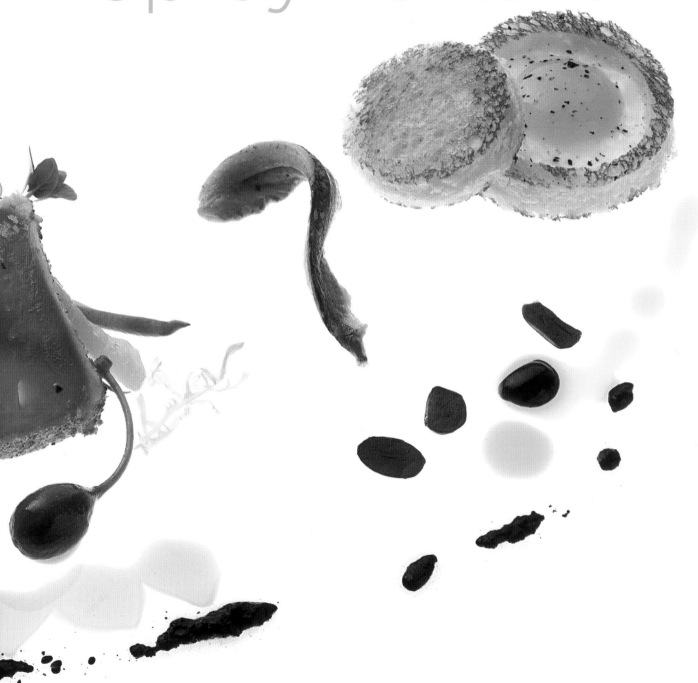

SERVES 6   2 tablespoons coarsely ground fennel seed ■ 1 tablespoon coarsely ground coriander seed ■ 1 tablespoon coarsely ground black peppercorns ■ 4 pounds center-cut tuna loin ■ 6 ½-inch-thick slices brioche bread ■ Coarse salt ■ 1 tablespoon canola oil ■ 2 tablespoons clarified butter ■ 6 quail eggs ■ Sel de Guerande ■ Freshly ground pepper ■ Niçoise Salad ■ 6 marinated white anchovy fillets ■ 6 caperberries ■ 2 tablespoons thinly sliced caperberries ■ ¼ cup Citrus Vinaigrette (see page 235) ■ Tapenade Vinaigrette ■ 1 cup micro-amaranth greens

1 Combine the coarsely ground fennel and coriander seeds with the coarsely ground black peppercorns on a plate. Set aside.

2 Cut the tuna into 6 long, square blocks about 2 inches high by 2 inches across, separately reserving the trimmings for other uses (such as for tuna tartare). Roll the tuna blocks in the spice mixture, taking care that all sides are evenly coated. Place on a plate and cover with plastic wrap. Refrigerate until ready to cook.

3 Using a doughnut cutter, cut a "doughnut" from each slice of brioche, discarding the pieces that have the crust, reserving the doughnut shaped rings and the "holes."

4 Remove the tuna from the refrigerator and season with salt to taste. Heat the canola oil in a large, nonstick sauté pan over medium-high heat. Add the tuna and sear, turning frequently, for about 6 minutes or until all sides are well seared. Remove from the heat and set aside.

5 Generously grease a nonstick griddle with the clarified butter. Place the 6 doughnut-shaped rings and their holes on the griddle and fry for about 2 minutes or until just lightly toasted. Turn and crack a quail egg into the center of each brioche ring and cook for about 3 minutes or just until the egg white has set. Using a spatula, lift the egg-filled rings from the griddle and season with sel de Guerande and pepper. Turn the "holes" so that each side is lightly toasted. Remove from the griddle and set aside.

6 Using a sharp slicing knife, cut each tuna block, crosswise, into ³/₈-inch-thick slices. Mound an equal portion of the Niçoise Salad in the center of each of 6 plates. Fan a sliced tuna block over the salad. Top with an anchovy fillet and sprinkle with sel de Guerande. Stand a caperberry up against the salad and sprinkle sliced caperberries around the plate. Set an egg-filled brioche ring off to the side and place the "hole" at the edge of the egg-filled opening. Drizzle the plate with Citrus Vinaigrette and Tapenade Vinaigrette and sprinkle with the micro-amaranth greens.

NIÇOISE SALAD

1 roasted red bell pepper, cored, seeded and cut into even strips ■ 1 roasted yellow bell pepper, cored, seeded and cut into even strips ■ 1 large red radish, well washed, trimmed and cut, crosswise, into paper-thin rounds ■ 1 head frisée, well washed, pulled apart and dried ■ 2 cups blanched, frenched, haricots vert ■ ¼ cup Niçoise olive slivers ■ ¼ cup Citrus Vinaigrette (see page 235) ■ Coarse salt and freshly ground pepper

1 Combine the peppers, radish, frisée, haricots vert and olive slivers in a medium bowl. Cover with plastic wrap and refrigerate until ready to serve.

2 When ready to serve, drizzle in the vinaigrette and season with salt and pepper. Toss to coat and serve immediately.

TAPENADE VINAIGRETTE

4 anchovy fillets, chopped ■ 1 tablespoon well-drained capers ■ ¾ cup pitted Niçoise olives ■ 1 tablespoon well-drained capers ■ ½ cup olive oil

Combine the anchovies, olives and capers in a small food processor fitted with the metal blade and process to a smooth purée. Transfer the purée to a small bowl and gently fold in the olive oil to form a "broken" vinaigrette. Cover and store at room temperature.

Shrimp-and-Cod-Stuffed Calamari with Arugula Salad and Sweet Red Pepper Sauce

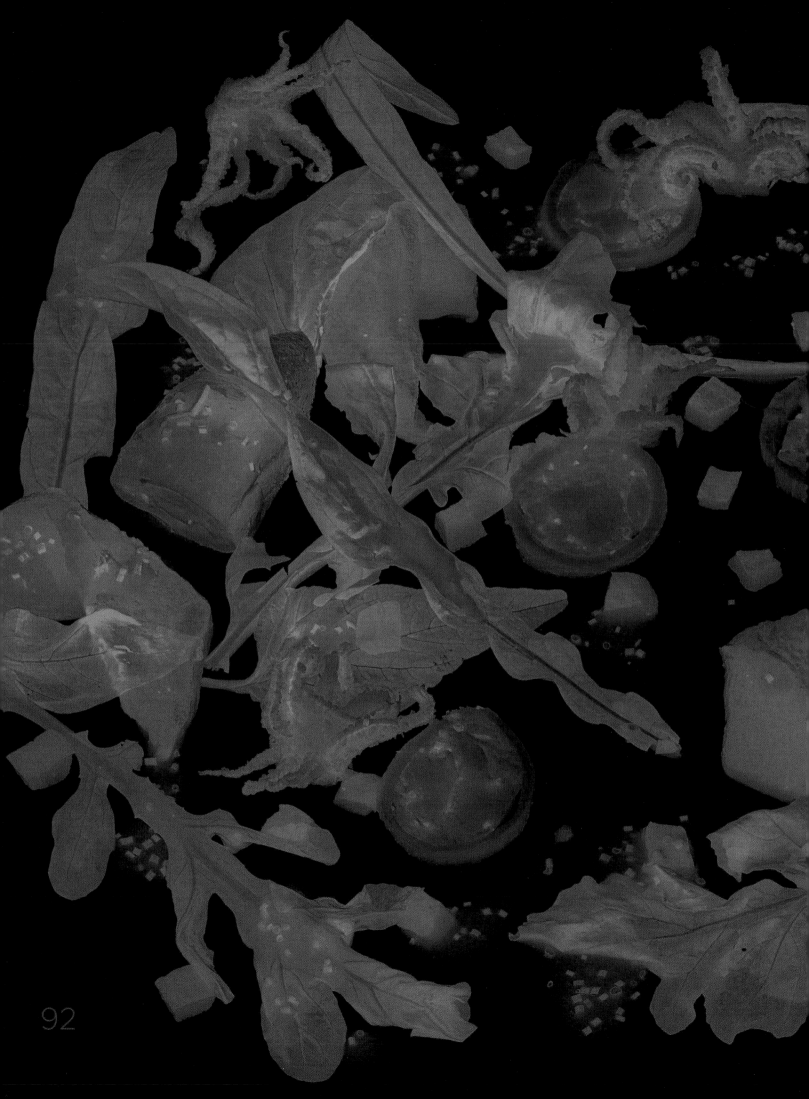

12 calamari, cleaned, bodies and tentacles separated ■ Shrimp-Cod Stuffing ■ Coarse salt and freshly ground pepper ■ 5 tablespoons olive oil ■ 1 cup dry white wine ■ ¼ cup unsalted butter ■ 3 shallots, peeled and minced ■ 2 cups chicken stock ■ 1 ½ cups Wondra flour ■ 3 roasted red bell peppers, peeled, cored, seeded, membrane removed and finely diced ■ ¼ cup basil chiffonade ■ Arugula Salad ■ 2 tablespoons chopped chives ■ ¼ cup extra virgin olive oil ■ Crisp Shallots (see page 81)

1 Fill each calamari body with Shrimp-Cod Stuffing. Secure the openings with toothpicks to hold them closed. Season the stuffed calamari with salt and pepper.

2 Preheat the oven to 350°F.

3 Heat 2 tablespoons of the olive oil in a large sauté pan over medium heat. Add the stuffed calamari to the hot oil and sear, carefully turning frequently, for about 4 minutes or until all sides are nicely seared. Using a slotted spoon, lift the seared calamari to a baking pan. Place in the preheated oven and bake for about 15 minutes or until piping hot and nicely colored.

4 Pour off any fat remaining in the sauté pan and return the pan to medium-high heat. Add the wine and bring to a boil, scraping the bottom of the pan with a wooden spoon to loosen any browned bits. Boil for about 5 minutes or until the wine has reduced by two-thirds. Add the butter, then the shallots and chicken stock and again bring to a boil. Boil for about 10 minutes or until a rich, thick sauce has formed.

5 While the sauce is reducing, fry the tentacles. Place the Wondra flour with salt and pepper in a plastic bag. Add the tentacles and toss to coat. Remove the tentacles from the seasoned flour and shake off any excess.

6 Heat the remaining 3 tablespoons of olive oil in a large sauté pan over medium-high heat. Add the tentacles and fry, turning frequently, for about 5 minutes or until golden and crisp. Remove from the heat and drain on a double layer of paper towel.

7 Stir the diced roasted bell peppers and basil chiffonade into the reduced sauce. Taste and, if necessary, adjust the seasoning with salt and pepper.

8 Remove the stuffed calamari from the oven. Remove and discard the toothpicks. Mound an equal portion of the Arugula Salad in the center of each of 6 plates. Place 2 stuffed calamari on top of each salad. Fold the chopped chives into the sauce and spoon it over and around the calamari on each plate. Drizzle with the extra virgin olive oil and top with the fried tentacles and Crisp Shallots.

SHRIMP-COD STUFFING

■ ½ cup unsalted butter ■ 1 cup finely diced onions ■ ½ pound shrimp, peeled, deveined and chopped ■ ¾ pound baked cod, flaked apart ■ 3 tablespoons chopped chives ■ Coarse salt and freshly ground pepper

Melt the butter in a large sauté pan over medium heat. Add the onions and sauté for about 5 minutes or just until the onions have sweat their liquid but have not taken on any color. Add the shrimp and continue to sauté for an additional 3 minutes or until the shrimp is just cooked. Remove from the heat and stir in the cod. Add the chives and season with salt and pepper. Transfer the mixture to a pastry bag fitted with a large, plain tip. Refrigerate until ready to use.

ARUGULA SALAD

■ 2 bunches baby arugula, well washed and dried ■ ¾ cup thinly sliced fennel bulb ■ ¼ cup Citrus Vinaigrette (see page 235)

1 Combine the arugula and fennel in a medium bowl and toss to mix well. Cover with plastic wrap and refrigerate until ready to use.

2 When ready to serve, unwrap the salad and drizzle with the vinaigrette. Toss to evenly coat. Serve immediately.

Soft Potato
Gnocchi with
Asparagus Butter

30 spears asparagus ■ 3 ½ cups chicken stock ■ Coarse salt and freshly ground pepper ■ 1 cup plus 3 tablespoons unsalted butter ■ 4 tightly packed cups spinach leaves ■ 60 Potato Gnocchi (see page 236) ■ Approximately 2 tablespoons olive oil ■ ½ pound heirloom tomatoes, well washed, cored and cut into slices, lengthwise ■ 1 ½ cups micro-amaranth ■ 3 tablespoons chopped chives ■ 3 tablespoons freshly grated Parmesan cheese or 12 Parmesan cheese curls ■ 1 tablespoon extra virgin olive oil

1 Peel the asparagus spears, reserving the peelings. Bring a large pot of salted water to a boil over high heat. Add the asparagus and blanch for about 1 minute or just until tender when pierced with the point of a small, sharp knife. Immediately drain and refresh under cold, running water. Pat dry.

2 Trim the fibrous end from each asparagus spear and cut the asparagus, on the bias, into 2-inch-long pieces. Set aside.

3 Combine the reserved asparagus peelings with 2 cups of the chicken stock in a medium saucepan over medium heat. Season with salt and pepper and bring to a simmer. Whisk in 1 cup of the butter. Add the spinach and bring to a boil. Remove from the heat and pour into a blender. Process to a smooth purée. Pour through a fine sieve into a bowl. Place the bowl in a larger bowl filled with ice and stir the purée to cool down as quickly as possible. When cool, remove from the ice bath. Transfer to a small saucepan and set aside.

4 Line a baking pan with parchment paper. Set aside.

5 Bring a large pot of salted water to a boil. Add the gnocchi and boil for about 5 minutes or until the gnocchi rise to the top and float. Using a slotted spoon, lift the gnocchi from the water and rinse under cold, running water. Place the slightly cool gnocchi in a bowl and toss with just enough olive oil to lightly coat. Transfer to the lined baking pan and set aside.

6 Combine the tomatoes and micro-amaranth and set aside.

7 Place the reserved asparagus butter over low heat to just warm.

8 Combine the remaining 1 ½ cups of chicken stock and 3 tablespoons butter in a large sauté pan over medium heat. Season with salt and pepper and bring to a boil, whisking constantly until the butter is emulsified into the stock. Add the reserved asparagus and gnocchi and gently toss to coat with the sauce.

9 Place a pool of asparagus butter in each of 6 large, shallow soup bowls. Using a slotted spoon, place equal portions of the asparagus-gnocchi mixture evenly over the asparagus butter in each bowl. Sprinkle with chives and Parmesan cheese.

10 Toss the reserved tomatoes and micro-amaranth with the extra virgin olive oil, season with salt and pepper and serve on the side.

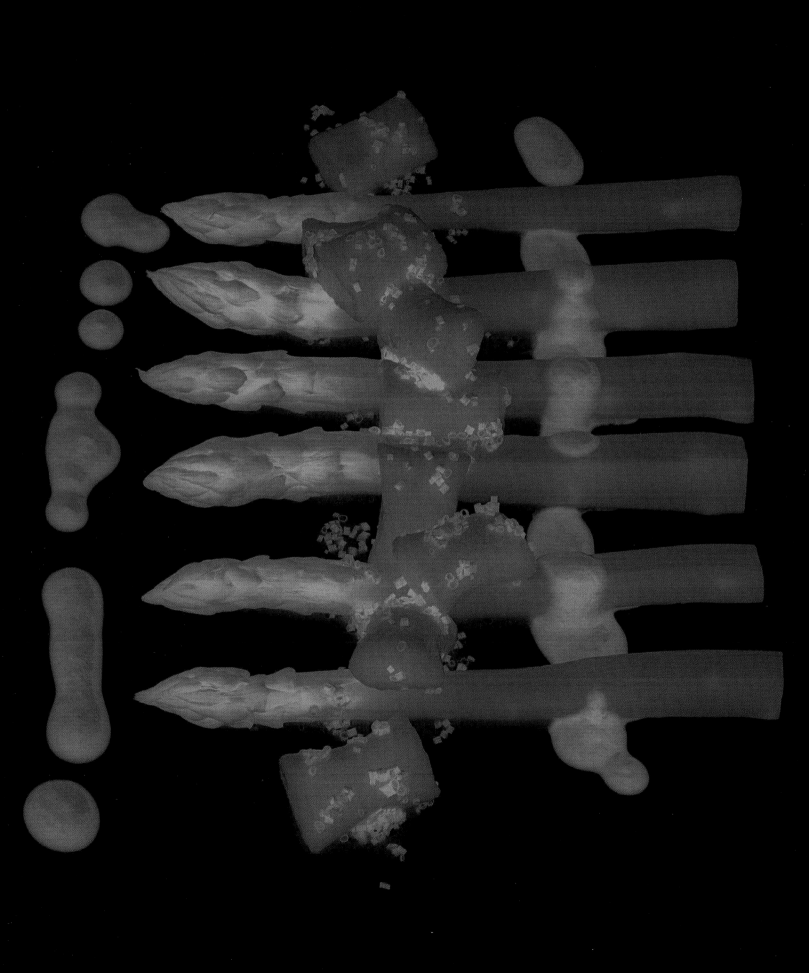

Robiola Cheese
Agnolotti with
Sweet Corn Broth

SERVES 6   2 ½ to 3 cups all-purpose flour   ■   Pinch coarse salt plus
more   ■   5 large egg yolks   ■   1 large whole egg   ■   1 ½ tablespoons extra
virgin olive oil   ■   ½ tablespoon milk   ■   3 cups riced cooked potatoes
■   ½ cup robiola cheese   ■   3 tablespoons truffle oil   ■   3 tablespoons
minced chives   ■   Freshly ground white pepper   ■   Sweet Corn Broth
■   24 chive points   ■   3 ears baby corn, cut into paper-thin slices
lengthwise   ■   1 fresh black truffle, cut into paper-thin slices

1   Combine the flour and a pinch of salt and form into a small mound on a clean, flat surface. Make a well in the center of the flour and add the egg yolks and the egg. Using a fork, lightly mix the eggs together. Add the oil and milk to the eggs and again lightly mix. Using your fingers, work the liquid into the flour using a circular motion to pull the ingredients together. Gather the dough into a ball and knead by hand for about 10 minutes or until smooth and elastic. Form the dough into a ball, wrap in plastic wrap and refrigerate for at least 4 hours or up to 12 hours.

2   Combine the potatoes with the cheese in a mixing bowl. Beat in the truffle oil and the chives. Season with salt and pepper. Cover with plastic wrap and refrigerate until ready to use.

3   Divide the pasta dough into 8 pieces. Working with one piece at a time and using a pasta machine, roll each piece into sheets thin enough to see your hand through, keeping the remaining pieces wrapped in plastic wrap to prevent drying. If the dough tears when passing through the pasta machine, it may need additional flour. If so, simply dust it with extra flour.

4   Cut the dough into sixty 4-inch circles. Remove the filling from the refrigerator and place a heaping teaspoonful of filling in the center of each pasta circle. Working with one circle at a time, fold the pasta around the filling, pressing on the edges to tightly seal the pasta around the filling. Using a ridged pastry cutter, trim each end of the filled pasta on the bias.

5   Bring a large pot of salted water to a boil. Add the agnolotti and boil for about 4 minutes or until still al dente. Using a slotted spoon, lift the pasta from the water and place 10 agnolotti in each of 6 large, shallow soup bowls. Pour equal portions of Sweet Corn Broth into each bowl and garnish with chive points, baby corn slices and truffles.

SWEET CORN BROTH

6 ears fresh corn ■ **2 tablespoons unsalted butter** ■ **2 leeks, white parts only, well washed and chopped** ■ **2 ribs celery, well washed, trimmed and halved** ■ **1 large carrot, peeled, trimmed and halved** ■ **6 cups water** ■ **Coarse salt and freshly ground pepper**

1 Holding the cobs upright, cut the kernels from the corn, separately reserving the kernels and the cobs. Cut the cobs into quarters and set aside.

2 Heat the butter in a large saucepan over medium heat. Add the leeks, celery and carrot and sauté for 4 minutes. Add the reserved corn cobs and sauté for 2 minutes. Add the water and bring to a boil. Add the corn kernels and lower the heat to a simmer. Simmer for about 30 minutes or until the broth has taken on a sweet corn flavor. Season with salt and pepper and remove from the heat.

3 Using tongs, remove and discard the celery, carrot and corn cobs. Transfer the broth to a blender and process to a smooth purée. Pour through a fine sieve into a clean saucepan. Place over medium heat and cook for about 3 minutes or until hot. Remove from the heat and serve. (Alternately, prepare the soup up to 2 days in advance and store, covered and refrigerated. Reheat just before serving.)

Napa Cabbage
Stuffed with
Red Pepper Tabbouleh

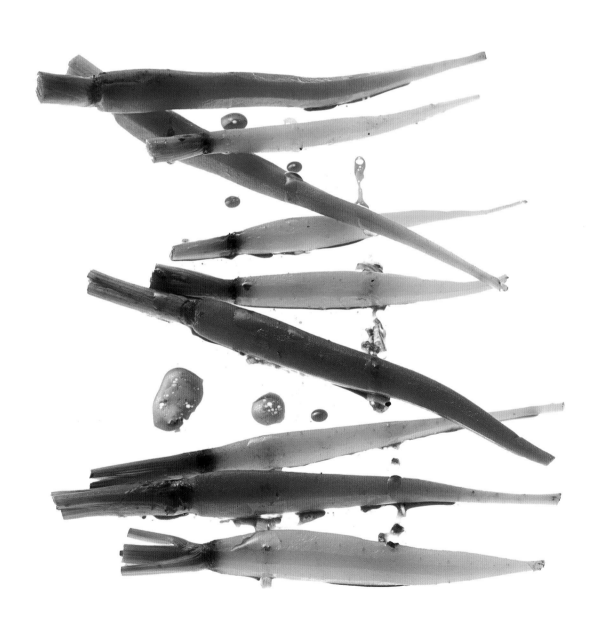

1 Cut the morels, crosswise, into thick rings. Place on a steamer rack over boiling water and steam for 5 minutes. Remove from the heat and allow to cool.

2 Combine the vegetable stock with ¼ cup of the olive oil in a medium nonstick saucepan over high heat. Generously season with salt and pepper and bring to a boil. Immediately add the bulgur and remove from the heat. Cover and let stand for about 15 minutes or until all of the liquid has been absorbed. Transfer to a mixing bowl and fluff with a fork. Toss in the bell pepper strips and diced onion. Taste and, if necessary, adjust the seasoning with additional salt and pepper.

3 Lay the cabbage leaves on a clean, flat surface. Place an abundant amount of the tabbouleh in the center of each leaf and loosely wrap to enclose, allowing some tabbouleh to spill out of the ends. Place 2 leaves, closed side down, on each of 6 plates.

4 Using the remaining olive oil, lightly dress the baby carrots, seasoning with salt and pepper. Arrange 3 each of the red and yellow carrots on each plate. Drizzle each plate with a generous amount of vinaigrette. Sprinkle sliced morels and micro-amaranth around each plate and serve.

SERVES 6 ¼ pound morel mushrooms, brushed clean of all debris ■ 4 cups vegetable stock ■ ¼ cup plus 3 tablespoons extra virgin olive oil ■ Coarse salt and freshly ground pepper ■ 2 cups medium bulgur wheat ■ 1 roasted red pepper, peeled, cored, seeded and cut into ¼-inch-thick strips ■ 1 roasted yellow bell pepper, peeled, cored, seeded and cut into ¼-inch-thick strips ■ ¼ cup finely diced red onion ■ 12 large napa cabbage leaves, lightly blanched ■ 18 baby red carrots, 1½-inch stem left on, peeled and blanched ■ 18 baby yellow carrots, 1½-inch stem left on, peeled and blanched ■ 2 cups Sherry-Shallot Vinaigrette (see page 236) ■ 2 cups micro-amaranth greens

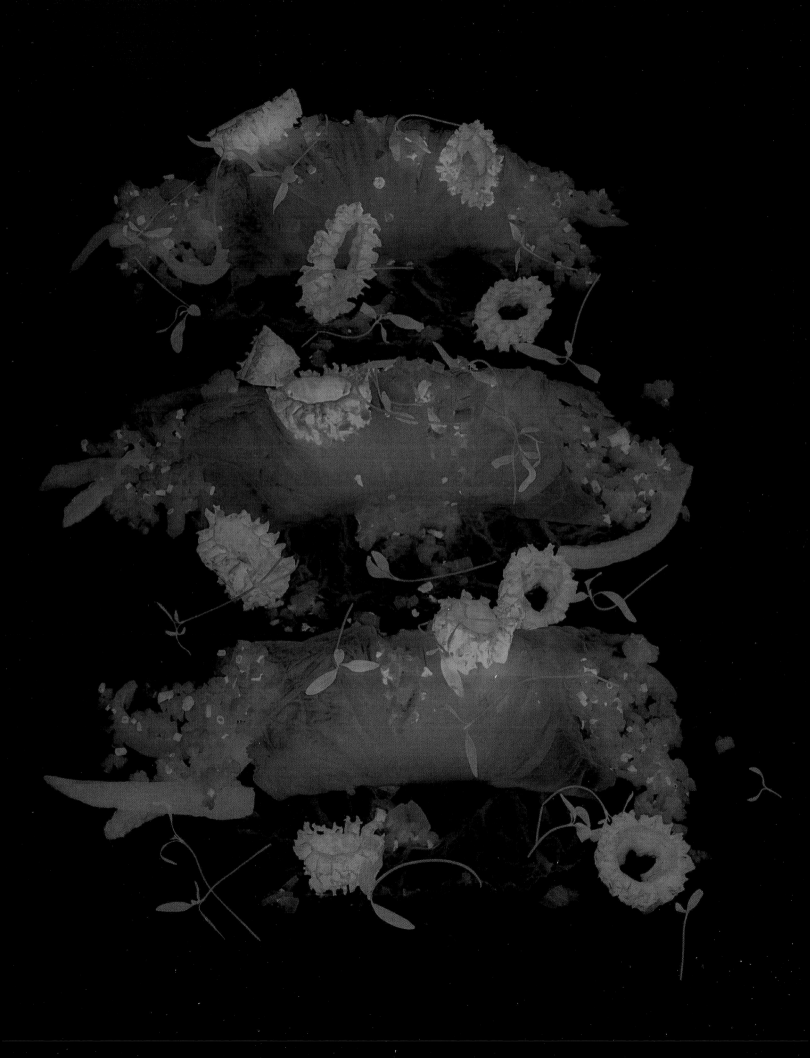

Summer
Vegetable
Pistou

2 leeks, white part only, well washed and chopped ▪ 2 carrots, peeled, trimmed and chopped ▪ 2 ripe tomatoes, well washed, cored and chopped ▪ 2 ribs celery, well washed, trimmed and chopped ▪ 1 turnip, peeled and chopped ▪ 1 onion, peeled and chopped ▪ 1 clove garlic, peeled and chopped ▪ ½ teaspoon peppercorns ▪ Coarse salt ▪ 1 tablespoon chopped flat-leaf parsley ▪ 1 tablespoon chopped basil ▪ 1 teaspoon chopped thyme ▪ 1 teaspoon chopped rosemary ▪ An assortment of baby vegetables such as asparagus, zucchini, yellow squash, yellow beets, red onions, Yukon gold potatoes, carrots and fennel and/or fava beans, spring onions and snap peas, blanched and/or raw tiny tomatoes, micro-fennel and/or thinly sliced watermelon, icicle or black radishes

1 Place the chopped leeks, carrots, tomatoes, celery, turnip, onion and garlic along with the peppercorns and salt in a large, shallow crueset-type pan. The bottom should be wide enough to hold the vegetables in an even layer; they should not be piled high in the pan. Add water to just barely cover the vegetables and place over medium-low heat. Bring to a simmer and then cook at a bare simmer for 15 minutes or until the vegetables are very aromatic but remain vibrantly colored. Set aside to cool. (This broth may be made with various thyme and rosemary. Remove from the heat and stir in the parsley, basil, vegetable trimmings and odds and ends. The type of vegetable is not as important as the clean, garden-fresh taste required with the brief simmer and herb infusion.)

2 Strain the cooled broth through a fine sieve lined with cheesecloth into a clean saucepan. Lift the cheesecloth from the sieve and twist to extract all of the liquid. Discard the solids. Taste and, if necessary, adjust the seasoning with salt and pepper.

3 Place the broth over medium heat and add the blanched vegetables. Cook until just warm; do not boil. Ladle equal portions of the soup into each of 6 large, shallow soup bowls. Add any raw vegetables and serve.

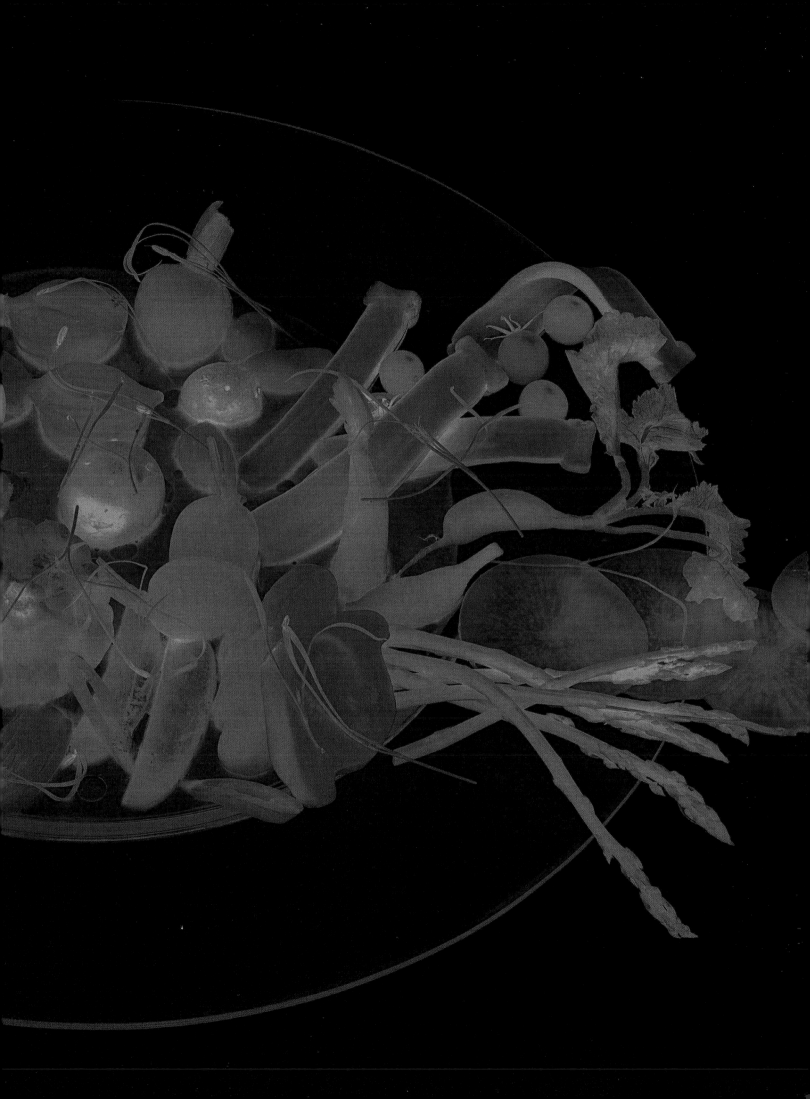

THE ART OF AUREOLE

POULTRY, MEAT & GAME

Truffled Chicken
for TWO with
Truffle Gnocchi

SERVES 6 1 cup unsalted butter, at room temperature ■ ¼ cup chopped truffles ■ Three 4-pound chickens, head and feet attached ■ 2 fresh black truffles, brushed clean ■ 1 cup vegetable oil ■ Coarse salt and freshly ground pepper ■ Caramelized Onion Sauce ■ ½ cup marjoram leaves ■ Caramelized Root Vegetables and Wild Mushrooms ■ Truffle Gnocchi

1. Preheat the oven to 350°F.

2. Combine the butter with the chopped truffles in a small mixing bowl.

3. Remove and discard the head and neck from each chicken. Using your fingertips, carefully detach the skin from the breasts and thighs on each chicken and liberally coat the breast and thigh meat with truffle butter.

4. Using a sharp knife or a truffle slicer, cut the truffles into thin slices. Evenly place the truffle slices over the truffle butter on the breasts and thighs of each bird. Wrap the feet with aluminum foil to keep them from burning while the chickens are roasting. Insert a metal skewer into the thigh joints on each bird so that the heat can penetrate and encourage even cooking with the breast meat. Liberally season the birds with salt and pepper. Place the birds, breast side up, on wire racks in roasting pans (or on baking sheets with sides) in the preheated oven and roast, basting occasionally, for about 1 hour or until the skin is golden brown and an instant-read thermometer inserted into the thickest part reads 160°F. Remove from the oven, cut the trussing string and remove the skewers as well as the foil from the feet. Allow to rest for 10 minutes.

5. Place the Caramelized Onion Sauce on low heat and stir the marjoram into it. As soon as the sauce is warm, remove it from the heat.

6. Arrange an equal portion of the Caramelized Root Vegetables and Wild Mushrooms in the center of each of 6 warm dinner plates. Cut each chicken into 2 breast halves and two thighs. (Reserve the remaining meat for another use or for stock.) Place a thigh on top of the vegetables on each plate and lean a breast into each thigh. Spoon an equal portion of the Caramelized Onion Sauce over the chicken and around the edge of each plate. Place a ramekin of Truffle Gnocchi on each plate and serve.

CARAMELIZED ONION SAUCE

3 tablespoons clarified butter ■ 3 cups chopped onions ■ 4 cups dark chicken stock ■ 4 sprigs thyme ■ ½ cup unsalted butter, at room temperature ■ Coarse salt and freshly ground pepper

1. Heat the clarified butter in a large, heavy-bottomed sauté pan over medium heat. Add the onions and cook, stirring frequently, for about 20 minutes or until the onions are nicely caramelized. Drain off all of the butter and return to medium-high heat. Add the stock and thyme sprigs and bring to a boil. Lower the heat and simmer for about 30 minutes or until the stock has reduced by half. Remove from the heat and strain the sauce through a fine sieve into a clean small saucepan, discarding the solids.

2. Return the pan to medium heat and bring to a bare simmer. Beat in the room-temperature butter until well incorporated and the sauce has taken on a nice sheen. Taste and adjust the seasoning with salt and pepper and serve. (The sauce may be made early in the day and reheated before serving. If so, place the sauce in the top half of a double boiler over boiling water to reheat.)

CARAMELIZED ROOT VEGETABLES AND WILD MUSHROOMS

2 tablespoons canola oil ■ 12 baby carrots, well washed, peeled and trimmed to 1 inch of stem ■ 12 baby turnips, well washed, peeled and trimmed to 1 inch stem ■ 2 cups 1-inch-dice rutabagas ■ ¼ cup unsalted butter ■ 3 cups wild mushrooms, brushed clean and any tough stems removed ■ Coarse salt and freshly ground pepper ■ 3 shallots, peeled and minced

1 Heat the oil in a large sauté pan over medium heat. Add the carrots, turnips and rutabaga and cook, tossing constantly, for about 5 minutes or until the vegetables are lightly caramelized. Add the butter and continue to cook for about 4 minutes or until the butter is nicely colored and very aromatic, taking care that it does not burn. Lay the mushrooms in the pan, covering the vegetables. Using a spatula, slowly incorporate the mushrooms into the vegetables. Season with salt and pepper and continue to sauté for about 7 minutes or until the mushrooms are golden brown. Add the shallots and sauté for an additional 3 minutes or just until the shallots have sweat their liquid but have not taken on any color.

2 Remove from the heat. Taste and, if necessary, adjust the seasoning with salt and pepper. Tent lightly with aluminum foil to keep warm until ready to use.

TRUFFLE GNOCCHI

2 tablespoons unsalted butter ■ 10 peppercorns ■ 2 cups heavy cream ■ 1 tablespoon truffle juice from canned truffles ■ Potato Gnocchi (see page 236) ■ ¼ cup finely diced black truffles ■ Coarse salt and freshly ground white pepper ■ 3 tablespoons freshly grated Parmesan cheese ■ 3 shallots, peeled and minced ■ 3 sprigs thyme

1 Preheat the oven to 375°F.

2 Lightly butter 6 shallow 6-ounce ramekins. Set aside. Heat the butter in a medium saucepan over medium heat. Add the shallots and sauté for 3 minutes or until the shallots have sweat their liquid but have not taken on any color. Add the thyme and peppercorns and sauté for an additional 2 minutes or until the mixture is very aromatic. Add the cream and bring to a simmer. Whisk in the truffle juice. Return the cream to low heat and stir in the gnocchi and diced truffles. Season with salt and cook at a bare simmer for about 15 minutes or until the cream has reduced by one-fourth.

3 Remove from the heat and strain through a fine sieve into a clean saucepan. Spoon an equal portion of the creamy gnocchi into each of the prepared ramekins. Season with salt and pepper. Sprinkle an equal portion of the Parmesan cheese over the top of each ramekin. (The gnocchi can be made up to this point early in the day and baked just before serving.) Place in the preheated oven and bake for about 15 minutes or until the sauce is thick and bubbling and the top is golden brown.

4 Raise the oven temperature to broil. Remove the gnocchi from the oven and place under the broiler for about 3 minutes or until the top is slightly crisp and well browned. Remove from the broiler and serve.

Barbecued Quail

with Chipotle Glaze and
Tart Apple-Onion Soubise

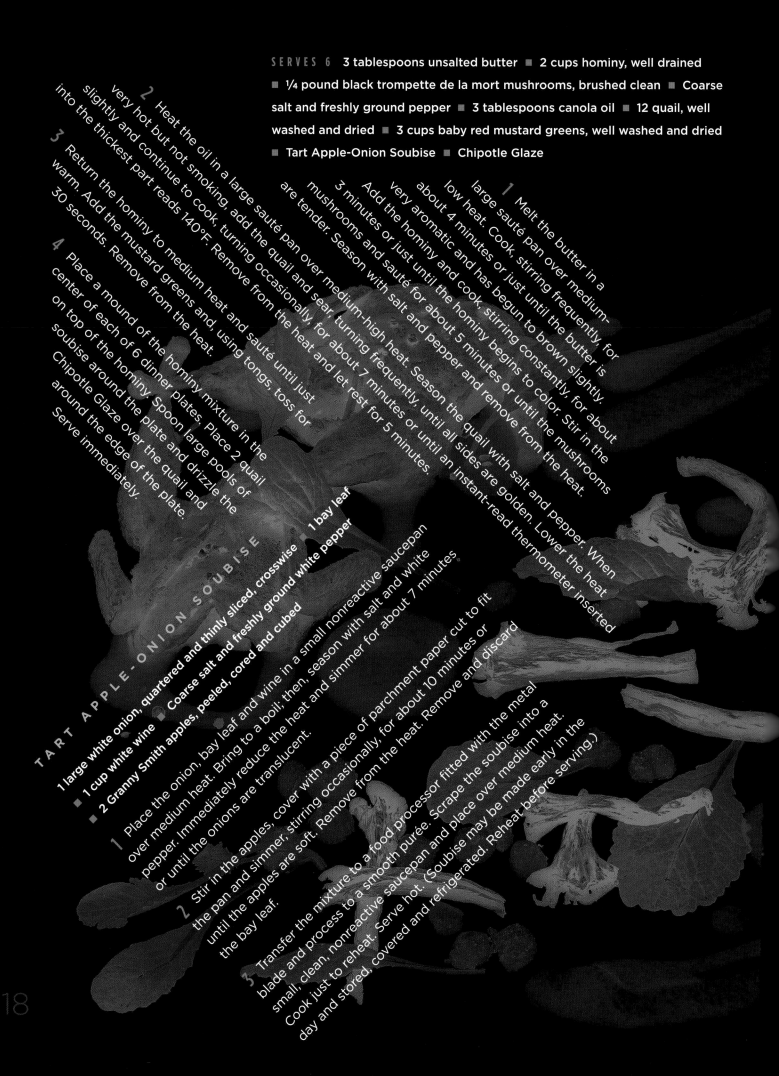

SERVES 6   3 tablespoons unsalted butter ■ 2 cups hominy, well drained ■ ¼ pound black trompette de la mort mushrooms, brushed clean ■ Coarse salt and freshly ground pepper ■ 3 tablespoons canola oil ■ 12 quail, well washed and dried ■ 3 cups baby red mustard greens, well washed and dried ■ Tart Apple-Onion Soubise ■ Chipotle Glaze

1 Melt the butter in a large sauté pan over medium-low heat. Cook, stirring frequently, for about 4 minutes or just until the butter is very aromatic and has begun to brown slightly. Add the hominy and cook, stirring constantly, for about 5 minutes or until the hominy begins to color. Stir in the mushrooms and sauté for about 3 minutes or just until the mushrooms are tender. Season with salt and pepper and remove from the heat.

2 Heat the oil in a large sauté pan over medium-high heat. Season the quail with salt and pepper. When very hot but not smoking, add the quail and sear, turning occasionally, for about 7 minutes or until all sides are golden. Lower the heat slightly and continue to cook, turning frequently, until an instant-read thermometer inserted into the thickest part reads 140°F. Remove from the heat and let rest for 5 minutes.

3 Return the hominy to medium heat and, using tongs, toss for 30 seconds. Remove from the heat. Add the mustard greens and, sauté until just warm.

4 Place a mound of the hominy mixture in the center of each of 6 dinner plates. Place 2 quail on top of the hominy. Spoon large pools of soubise around the plate and drizzle the Chipotle Glaze over the quail and around the edge of the plate. Serve immediately.

TART APPLE-ONION SOUBISE

1 large white onion, quartered and thinly sliced, crosswise ■ 1 bay leaf ■ 1 cup white wine ■ Coarse salt and freshly ground white pepper ■ 2 Granny Smith apples, peeled, cored and cubed

1 Place the onion, bay leaf and wine in a small nonreactive saucepan over medium heat. Bring to a boil; then, season with salt and white pepper. Immediately reduce the heat and simmer for about 7 minutes or until the onions are translucent.

2 Stir in the apples, cover with a piece of parchment paper cut to fit the pan and simmer, stirring occasionally, for about 10 minutes or until the apples are soft. Remove from the heat. Remove and discard the bay leaf.

3 Transfer the mixture to a food processor fitted with the metal blade and process to a smooth purée. Scrape the soubise into a small, clean, nonreactive saucepan and place over medium heat. Cook just to reheat. Serve hot. (Soubise may be made early in the day and stored, covered and refrigerated. Reheat before serving.)

CHIPOTLE GLAZE

- 3 strips fine-quality smoked bacon
- ½ cup diced red onion
- ½ cup diced celery
- 2 tablespoons honey
- 2 tablespoons tomato paste
- ¼ cup cider vinegar
- 1 chipotle chile pepper
- 1 cup veal demi-glace
- 1 cup dark chicken stock
- Coarse salt
- 1 teaspoon toasted coriander seed
- 1 teaspoon toasted cumin seed
- 1 teaspoon toasted coriander seed
- and freshly ground pepper

1   Combine the bacon, red onion and celery in a medium saucepan over medium heat. Sauté for about 7 minutes or until the bacon is crisping and the vegetables are beginning to caramelize. Add the honey and cook, stirring frequently, for about 6 minutes or until the caramelization has reached a deep, golden brown. Add the vinegar and, using a wooden spoon, stir to deglaze the pan. Simmer for about 4 minutes or until the liquid has reduced by two-thirds. Stir in the tomato paste and cook, stirring constantly, for 3 minutes.

2   Raise the heat and add the chipotle, demi-glace, stock, cumin and coriander. Bring to a boil; then, lower the heat and simmer for about 45 minutes or until the liquid is shiny and thick. Remove from the heat and strain through a fine sieve into a clean saucepan. Season with salt and pepper.

3   Return to medium heat just to reheat. Serve hot. (Glaze may be made up to 1 week in advance of use and stored, covered and refrigerated. Reheat before serving.)

Duck Breast
Poached in Bouillon
with Duck Cracklings
and Coddled Quail Egg

SERVES 6 3 ducks ▪ 1 carrot, peeled and chopped ▪ 1 large onion, peeled and chopped ▪ 1 rib celery, well washed, trimmed and chopped ▪ Coarse salt and freshly ground pepper ▪ 12 cups rich chicken stock ▪ 1 tomato, peeled, cored and cubed ▪ 1 medium onion, peeled and cubed ▪ 1 carrot, peeled, trimmed and cubed ▪ 1 rib celery, well washed, trimmed and cubed ▪ 3 large egg whites ▪ ¾ cup Madeira ▪ 8 whole sage leaves ▪ 18 braised baby beets, peeled ▪ 3 burdock roots, peeled, cut, on the bias, into ⅛-inch pieces, and blanched ▪ ¼ cup sage leaf julienne ▪ 12 quail eggs, coddled

1 Preheat the oven to 375°F.

2 Using a boning knife, carefully remove and reserve the breasts from each duck. Trim off the legs and thighs and reserve for another use, such as confit. Chop the remaining carcasses and place them in a roasting pan along with the chopped carrot, onion and celery. Season with salt and pepper and place in the preheated oven and roast for about 30 minutes or until nicely browned. Remove from the oven and drain off all fat. Add the roasted duck bones and vegetables and bring to a boil. Lower the heat and simmer for about 45 minutes or until the duck flavor has nicely infused the chicken stock. Remove from the heat and strain through a fine sieve lined with cheesecloth into a clean saucepan. Place the saucepan in a large bowl of ice and, stirring frequently, allow the broth to cool so that the fat will rise to the top. Skim off all fat.

3 Place the chicken stock in a large saucepan over medium-high heat.

4 Combine the cubed tomato, onion, carrot and celery in a food processor fitted with the metal blade and process to slightly chop. Add the egg whites and process to just blend, leaving the vegetables coarsely chopped.

5 Place the defatted broth over medium heat. Cook for about 4 minutes or just until beginning to warm. Whisk in the chopped vegetable mixture and bring to a simmer, stirring and scraping the bottom of the pan from time to time. (Do not allow the egg to stick to the bottom of the pan or it will begin to burn.) Once the broth comes to a boil, do not stir. Simmer for about 30 minutes or until the egg foam begins to rise and cover the surface of the pan. As the foam begins to firm, using a gentle motion, poke a small hole in the center of the crust with the end of a wooden spoon. Lower the heat and cook at a bare simmer for another 30 minutes or until the egg mixture has formed a dense, solid crust on top of the broth.

6 Line a fine sieve with a double layer of damp cheesecloth. Remove the pan from the heat and very gently push an opening in the crust with a wooden spoon. Using a cup or a ladle, carefully pour the broth through the cheesecloth-lined sieve into a clean saucepan, discarding the solids. You should have about 8 cups of liquid. Taste and adjust the seasoning with salt. (Bouillon made be made up to 3 days in advance of use and stored, covered and refrigerated.)

7 Place the Madeira in a small saucepan over medium heat. Bring to just a simmer, remove from the heat and carefully ignite the alcohol with a match. Allow the flame to burn out and then add the Madeira to the clarified bouillon. Set aside.

8 Working carefully with a small knife, gently remove the skin from each duck breast. Set the skin aside. Trim any sinew or remaining fat from the breast meat and cut each breast into two halves. Place the trimmed breasts on a plate, cover with plastic wrap and refrigerate until ready to use.

9 Lightly season the skin with salt and pepper. Place the seasoned skin in a heavy-bottomed sauté pan over low heat. Lay another sauté pan or a heavy lid small enough to fit into the larger sauté pan and press down on the skin to hold it flat. Cook, turning once, for about 45 minutes or until the skin has become crackling crisp and golden brown. Transfer the cracklings to a double layer of paper towel to drain. When well drained, break into pieces and set aside. (Cracklings may be made up to 1 day in advance of use and stored in a tightly sealed container on a double layer of paper towel. Place in a preheated 350°F to reheat.)

10 Transfer 2 cups of the reserved bouillon to a large sauté pan with a lid. Add the sage leaves and the trimmed duck breasts. Place over medium heat and bring the liquid to 185°F on an instant-read thermometer. Lower the heat to maintain that temperature and poach the duck breasts for about 12 minutes or until an instant-read thermometer reads 135°F when inserted into the thickest part. (The breasts will continue cooking as they rest.) Using a slotted spoon, lift the breasts from the poaching liquid to a warm plate. Tent lightly with aluminum foil and keep warm

11 Place the reserved bouillon over medium heat and bring to a simmer. Pour equal portions into each of 6 shallow soup plates. Working with one at a time, slice each duck breast, crosswise on the bias, into ¼-inch-thick pieces. Slightly fan a duck breast half in the center of each plate. Garnish each soup plate with an equal portion of the beets, burdock and sage leaf julienne. Gently place 2 quail eggs on top of the sliced duck, sprinkle duck cracklings over all and serve.

Baby Pheasant with

Sweet Potato Shepherd's Pie
and Apple Cider-Foie Gras Sauce

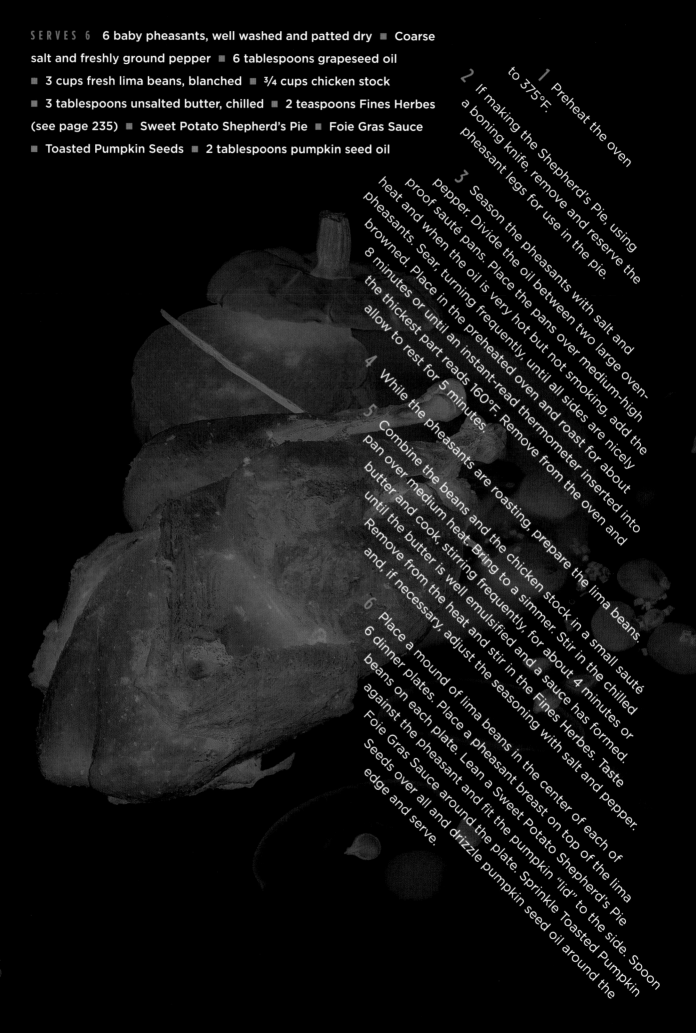

SERVES 6 6 baby pheasants, well washed and patted dry ■ Coarse salt and freshly ground pepper ■ 6 tablespoons grapeseed oil ■ 3 cups fresh lima beans, blanched ■ ¾ cups chicken stock ■ 3 tablespoons unsalted butter, chilled ■ 2 teaspoons Fines Herbes (see page 235) ■ Sweet Potato Shepherd's Pie ■ Foie Gras Sauce ■ Toasted Pumpkin Seeds ■ 2 tablespoons pumpkin seed oil

1. Preheat the oven to 375°F.

2. If making the Shepherd's Pie, using a boning knife, remove and reserve the pheasant legs for use in the pie.

3. Season the pheasants with salt and pepper. Divide the oil between two large oven-proof sauté pans. Place the pans over medium-high heat and when the oil is very hot but not smoking, add the pheasants. Sear, turning frequently, until all sides are nicely browned. Place in the preheated oven and roast for about 8 minutes or until an instant-read thermometer inserted into the thickest part reads 160°F. Remove from the oven and allow to rest for 5 minutes.

4. While the pheasants are roasting, prepare the lima beans. Combine the beans and the chicken stock in a small sauté pan over medium heat. Bring to a simmer. Stir in the chilled butter and cook, stirring frequently, for about 4 minutes or until the butter is well emulsified and a sauce has formed. Remove from the heat and stir in the Fines Herbes. Taste and, if necessary, adjust the seasoning with salt and pepper.

5.

6. Place a mound of lima beans in the center of each of 6 dinner plates. Place a pheasant breast on top of the lima beans on each plate. Lean a Sweet Potato Shepherd's Pie against the pheasant and fit the pumpkin "lid" to the side. Spoon Foie Gras Sauce around the plate. Sprinkle Toasted Pumpkin Seeds over all and drizzle pumpkin seed oil around the edge and serve.

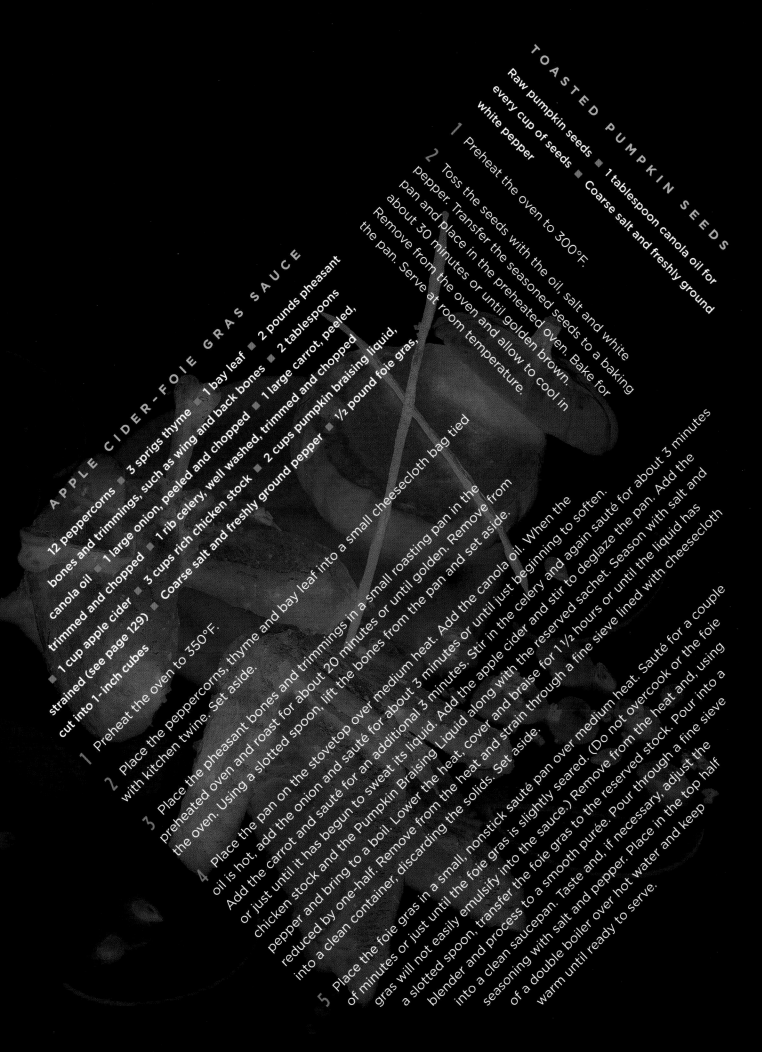

TOASTED PUMPKIN SEEDS

Raw pumpkin seeds ■ 1 tablespoon canola oil for every cup of seeds ■ Coarse salt and freshly ground white pepper

1 Preheat the oven to 300°F.

2 Toss the seeds with the oil, salt and white pepper. Transfer the seasoned seeds to a baking pan and place in the preheated oven. Bake for about 30 minutes or until golden brown. Remove from the oven and allow to cool in the pan. Serve at room temperature.

APPLE CIDER-FOIE GRAS SAUCE

12 peppercorns ■ 3 sprigs thyme ■ 1 bay leaf ■ 2 pounds pheasant bones and trimmings, such as wing and back bones ■ 2 tablespoons canola oil ■ 1 large onion, peeled and chopped ■ 1 large carrot, peeled, trimmed and chopped ■ 1 rib celery, well washed, trimmed and chopped ■ 2 cups pumpkin braising liquid, ■ 1 cup apple cider ■ 3 cups rich chicken stock ■ Coarse salt and freshly ground pepper ■ ½ pound foie gras, strained (see page 129) ■ cut into 1-inch cubes

1 Preheat the oven to 350°F.

2 Place the peppercorns, thyme and bay leaf into a small cheesecloth bag tied with kitchen twine. Set aside.

3 Place the pheasant bones and trimmings in a small roasting pan in the preheated oven and roast for about 20 minutes or until golden. Remove from the oven. Using a slotted spoon, lift the bones from the pan and set aside.

4 Place the pan on the stovetop over medium heat. Add the canola oil. When the oil is hot, add the onion and sauté for about 3 minutes or until just beginning to soften. Add the carrot and sauté for an additional 3 minutes. Stir in the celery and again sauté for about 3 minutes or just until it has begun to sweat its liquid. Add the apple cider and stir to deglaze the pan. Add the chicken stock and the Pumpkin Braising Liquid along with the reserved sachet. Season with salt and pepper and bring to a boil. Lower the heat, cover and braise for 1½ hours or until the liquid has reduced by one-half. Remove from the heat and strain through a fine sieve lined with cheesecloth into a clean container, discarding the solids. Set aside.

5 Place the foie gras in a small, nonstick sauté pan over medium heat. Sauté for a couple of minutes or just until the foie gras is slightly seared. (Do not overcook or the foie gras will not easily emulsify into the sauce.) Remove from the heat and, using a slotted spoon, transfer the foie gras to the reserved stock. Pour into a blender and process to a smooth purée. Pour through a fine sieve into a clean saucepan. Taste and, if necessary, adjust the seasoning with salt and pepper. Place in the top half of a double boiler over hot water and keep warm until ready to serve.

SWEET POTATO SHEPHERD'S PIE

- ¼ cup canola oil ■ 12 pheasant legs ■ Coarse salt and freshly ground black pepper ■ 12 cups rich chicken stock ■ 2 large sweet potatoes, well washed and dried ■ ¾ cup plus 2 tablespoons unsalted butter ■ ½ vanilla bean, split ■ Freshly ground white pepper ■ 6 baby pumpkins
- 2 leeks, white part only, well washed, dried and chopped ■ 1 cup diced shiitake mushroom caps ■ 2 teaspoons Fines Herbes (see page 235) ■ Approximately 3 tablespoons Natural Sauce (see page 234)

1 Heat 2 tablespoons of the canola oil in a large crueset-style pan over medium-high heat. Season the pheasant legs with salt and black pepper and place in the hot pan. Sear, turning frequently, for about 5 minutes or until nicely browned on all sides. Drain the excess fat from the pan. Return to medium heat and add 4 cups of the stock. Cover and bring to a boil. Lower the heat and simmer for about 45 minutes or until the meat is almost falling off the bone. Remove from the heat and allow the meat to cool in the braising liquid.

2 When the legs are cool enough to handle, remove the legs from the liquid. Remove the skin and pull the meat from the bones. Cut the meat into a fine dice and set aside.

3 Preheat the oven to 350°F.

4 Using about 2 tablespoons of the canola oil, lightly coat the sweet potatoes. Place on the middle rack of the oven and bake for about 1 hour or until very soft when pierced with the end of a small, sharp knife. Remove from the oven. Peel and cut into cubes. Place on a plate in a warm spot to dry slightly.

5 Push the sweet potatoes through a food mill into a clean bowl. Beat in 4 tablespoons of the butter. Scrape the vanilla beans from the pod, separately reserving the pod, into the sweet potato and season with salt and white pepper. Set aside.

6 Using a sharp knife, carefully and neatly cut the stem end from each pumpkin to make a "lid." Using a grapefruit spoon (or other serrated spoon), scoop out the seeds and any fiber, leaving a clean cavity. (If making the Toasted Pumpkin Seeds, separately reserve the seeds in a small bowl.) Place 1 tablespoon of butter in each cavity and season with salt and white pepper to taste. Cover with the pumpkin "lid."

7 Place the cleaned, covered pumpkins in a heavy-bottomed crueset-style pan with a cover large enough to hold them in a single layer. Add the remaining 8 cups of chicken stock along with the reserved vanilla pod and place over high heat. Bring to a simmer; then, lower the heat, cover and braise for about 20 minutes or until just barely tender. (Do not allow the pumpkins to become too soft or they will be unfillable.) Using a slotted spoon, lift the pumpkins from the braising liquid and set aside on a wire rack. (If making the Foie Gras Sauce, reserve the braising liquid.)

8 Heat 2 tablespoons of the butter in a medium sauté pan over medium heat. Add the leeks and lower the heat so that the leeks are just barely cooking in their juices for about 20 minutes or until they have almost melted. Add the reserved diced leg meat to the leeks and stir to combine. Remove from the heat and set aside.

9 Heat the remaining 2 tablespoons of butter in a small sauté pan over medium heat. Cook, stirring frequently, for about 4 minutes or just until the butter is very aromatic and has begun to brown slightly. Add the shiitakes and sauté for about 5 minutes or until the mushrooms are tender and golden brown. Scrape the mushrooms into the leg-meat mixture. Stir in the Fines Herbes and add just enough of the Natural Sauce to moisten the mixture. Remove from the heat; then, taste and adjust the seasoning with salt and black pepper.

10 Spoon the leg-meat mixture into each of the pumpkins, packing down to tightly fill the pumpkins about three-quarters full. Spoon the sweet potatoes on top of the leg-meat filling in each pumpkin to completely fill the pumpkin cavity.

11 When ready to serve, preheat the oven to 350°F. Place the filled pumpkins into the preheated oven and bake for about 20 minutes or until heated through. Raise the oven heat to broil. Place the hot pumpkins under the broiler and broil for about 1 minute or until the tops are lightly browned. Remove from the broiler and serve with the lids balanced at the side.

12 Place the

Caramelized Partridge
with Chanterelle Roulade
and Pommery Mustard Jus

2 tablespoons canola oil ■ 6 partridge breasts, skin on, with the wing-joint handles exposed ■ Coarse salt and freshly ground pepper ■ 6 sprigs thyme ■ 6 tablespoons unsalted butter ■ 36 pearl onions, peeled ■ ¼ pound chanterelle mushrooms, brushed clean and trimmed of any dry parts ■ 3 tablespoons chicken stock ■ 1 teaspoon thyme leaves ■ Chanterelle Roulade ■ Sweet and Sour Red Cabbage ■ Caraway Potato Cakes (or Potato-Shallot Cakes [see page 226]) ■ Pommery Mustard Jus ■ 1 tablespoon fennel seeds

1. Heat the oil in a large, oven-proof sauté pan over medium-high heat. Season the partridge breasts with salt and pepper and place, skin side down, into the hot pan. Sear, turning frequently, for about 5 minutes or until nicely browned on all sides. Add the thyme sprigs to the pan. Roast, basting occasionally, for about 10 minutes or until an instant-read thermometer inserted into the thickest part reads 160°F and the skin is golden and crisp. Remove from the oven and let rest for 5 minutes.

2. While the partridge is roasting, heat 3 tablespoons of the butter in a large sauté pan over medium heat. Add the pearl onions and season with salt and pepper. Sauté for 6 minutes or until nicely caramelized.

3. While the onions are caramelizing, heat the remaining 3 tablespoons of butter in a small sauté pan over medium heat. Add the chanterelles and sauté for 4 minutes. Scrape the mushrooms into the onions and stir to combine. Add the chicken stock, raise the heat and cook, stirring frequently, for about 2 minutes or until the onions are nicely glazed. Remove from the heat, stir in the thyme and keep warm.

4. Set a roulade across the top of each of 6 dinner plates. Mound some of the Sweet and Sour Red Cabbage just under the roulade on each plate. Prop a Caraway Potato Cake against the roulade and then set a partridge breast on top of the cake so that it is half on the cake and half on the cabbage on each plate. Spoon some of the chanterelle-onion mixture on the other side of the breast. Drizzle the Pommery Mustard Jus around the plate and serve, sprinkled with fennel seeds.

2 tablespoons canola oil ■ 6 partridge legs, skin on ■ Coarse salt and freshly ground pepper ■ 6 cups chicken stock ■ 2 tablespoons unsalted butter ■ 1 cup chopped chanterelle mushrooms ■ 1 boneless, skinless chicken breast, cut into cubes ■ 1 large egg 1 large egg yolk ■ ½ cup heavy cream ■ ½ teaspoon freshly ground nutmeg ■ 2 tablespoons roasted garlic purée ■ 1 tablespoon Fines Herbes (see page 235) ■ 1 tablespoon mustard oil 6 large green cabbage leaves, well washed and blanched ■ 1 tablespoon olive oil

1 Heat the canola oil in a large crueset-style pan over medium-high heat. Season the partridge legs with salt and pepper and place in the hot pan. Sear, turning frequently, for about 5 minutes or until nicely browned on all sides. Drain the excess fat from the pan. Return to medium heat and add the stock. Cover and bring to a boil. Lower the heat and simmer for about 45 minutes or until the meat is almost falling off the bone. Remove from the heat and allow the meat to cool in the braising liquid.

2 When the legs are cool enough to handle, remove the legs from the liquid, discarding the liquid. Remove the skin and pull the meat from the bones. Cut the meat into a fine dice and place in a mixing bowl. Set aside.

3 Heat the butter in a small sauté pan over medium heat. Add the chanterelles and season with salt and pepper. Sauté for about 4 minutes or just until tender. Remove from the heat and cool. When cool, add to the diced leg meat.

4 Place the diced chicken meat in a food processor fitted with the metal blade and process until finely minced. Add the whole egg and egg yolk and continue processing to a smooth purée. With the motor running, slowly add the cream. When well incorporated, add the nutmeg along with salt and pepper. Add the chicken mousse to the leg-meat mixture. Stir in the roasted garlic purée, Fines Herbes and mustard oil. When well blended, taste and, if necessary, adjust the seasoning with salt and pepper. (This makes much more mousse than is required for the roulades. Bake the leftover mousse in a well-buttered terrine and, when cool, freeze for later use as an hors d'oeuvre or appetizer.)

5 Lay the cabbage leaves out on a clean, flat surface. Place a generous portion of the leg-meat mixture in the center of each leaf. Working with one leaf at a time, fold in the edges and then roll the top of the cabbage over the filling. Roll the leaf up and over the filling to make a neat cylinder.

6 Place each cabbage cylinder in the center of a piece of plastic wrap large enough to enclose it completely. Drizzle a bit of olive oil over the cabbage and wrap the plastic wrap around it to tightly seal. (The roulades may be made up to this point and refrigerated for up to 1 day.)

7 When ready to serve, place the roulades in a steamer basket over boiling water. Cover and steam for about 12 minutes or until heated through. Serve hot.

SWEET-AND-SOUR RED CABBAGE

¼ cup honey ■ 1 large onion, peeled and diced ■ ½ large head red cabbage, well washed, quartered and cut, lengthwise, into ¼-inch-thick slices ■ 1 bay leaf ■ Coarse salt and freshly ground white pepper ■ 2 tablespoons red wine ■ ¼ cup red wine vinegar

1 Preheat the oven to 275°F.

2 Place the honey in a medium, heavy-bottomed, crueset-style pan with a lid over medium-low heat. Cook, stirring frequently, for about 5 minutes or until the honey is beginning to caramelize. Add the onion and sauté for an additional 5 minutes or until the onion is very tender. Add the cabbage and toss to coat. Add the vinegar, wine and bay leaf. Season with salt and white pepper. Place in the preheated oven and braise, uncovering and stirring from time to time, for about 1½ hours or until the cabbage is very soft. If the moisture evaporates before the cabbage is soft, add a bit of water to the pan. Remove from the oven, remove and discard the bay leaf and serve hot. (The cabbage may be made up to 3 days in advance of use and stored, covered and refrigerated. Reheat before serving.)

CARAWAY POTATO CAKES

2 large Idaho potatoes, peeled ■ Coarse salt ■ 1 tablespoon lightly toasted caraway seeds ■ Approximately 1 cup clarified butter

1 Using a mandoline or Japanese vegetable slicer, cut the potatoes, lengthwise, into long, thin strands. Place in a clean kitchen towel and pull the towel up and around the potatoes to completely enclose them. Tighten the towel around the potato strands and wring out excess liquid.

2 Place the potato strands in a large bowl. Add the caraway seeds and salt and toss to coat.

Heat about 2 tablespoons of the butter in a medium, non-stick sauté pan over medium-high heat. Toss a small handful of potato strands into the hot butter, spreading them out to form an open-weave circle. Fry for 2 minutes or until golden; then, turn and fry the other side until golden. Remove from the pan and place on a double layer of paper towel to drain. Continue making potato cakes until you have 6 nearly identical cakes. Serve hot or, alternately, prepare early in the day and store at room temperature. Reheat in a preheated 375°F oven for about 5 minutes.

POMMERY MUSTARD JUS

2 pounds partridge bones and trimmings ▪ Coarse salt and freshly ground pepper ▪ 1 large carrot, peeled and chopped ▪ 1 large onion, peeled and chopped ▪ 1 rib celery, well washed, trimmed and chopped ▪ ¼ cup white wine ▪ 4 cups rich chicken stock ▪ ¼ cup Pommery mustard ▪ 1 table- spoon minced chives

1 Preheat the oven to 350°F.

2 Place the bones and trimmings in a small roasting pan. Season with salt and pepper and place in the preheated oven. Roast for 15 minutes or until nicely browned. Add the carrot, onion and celery and stir to combine. Roast for an additional 10 minutes or until the vegetables begin to caramelize. Add the wine and stir to deglaze the pan.

3 Remove from the oven and place on the stovetop over medium heat. Add the chicken stock and bring to a boil. Lower the heat and simmer for about 30 minutes or until the liquid has reduced by one-half. Remove from the heat and strain through a fine sieve into a clean saucepan. Place in an ice-water bath and quickly chill, removing any fat that rises to the top.

4 Place the sauce over medium heat and bring to a boil. Lower the heat and simmer for about 15 minutes or until the liquid has reduced by one-third. Add the Pommery mustard and chives. Taste and, if necessary, adjust the seasoning with salt and pepper. Serve hot. (The sauce may be made early in the day and stored, covered and refrigerated. Reheat before serving. Do not add the chives until just before serving.)

Guinea Fowl
with Fennel Purée
and Savory Pasty

SERVES 6　3 guinea fowl, well washed and patted dry ■ Coarse salt and freshly ground pepper ■ ¼ cup canola oil ■ 4 cups rich chicken stock ■ Fennel Purée (see page 140) ■ Savory Pasty ■ Fennel Confit (see page 141) ■ Fennel Chips (see page 141)

1　Using a boning knife, remove the legs and thighs from the guinea fowl, separately reserving the breasts and, if making the Savory Pasties, the legs. Reserve the thighs for another use.

2　Using a boning knife, cut the breasts in half, making 6 guinea breast halves. Place on a plate, cover with plastic wrap and refrigerate until ready to roast.

3　If making the Savory Pasties, season the legs with salt and pepper. Heat 2 tablespoons of the oil in a heavy-bottomed crueset-style pan over medium-high heat. Add the legs and sear, turning occasionally, for about 5 minutes or until nicely browned on all sides. Add the chicken stock and bring to a boil. Lower the heat, cover and braise for about 1½ hours or until the meat is almost falling off the bone. Remove from the heat and let cool in the braising liquid.

4　When the legs are cool enough to handle, remove them from the braising liquid, reserving the liquid. Push off the skin and pull the meat from the bones. Cut the meat into a fine dice. Place in a small bowl, cover and refrigerate until ready to use in the pasties. Set aside and keep warm.

5　Strain the braising liquid through a fine sieve into a clean saucepan. Place over medium heat and bring to a boil. Lower the heat and simmer for about 20 minutes or until reduced by half and slightly thick. Set aside and keep warm.

6　Preheat the oven to 375°F.

7　Heat the remaining oil in a large, ovenproof saute pan over medium-high heat. Season the reserved guinea breasts with salt and pepper and place skin side down, into the hot pan. Sear for about 4 minutes or until the skin is golden. Transfer to the preheated oven and roast for about 10 minutes or until an instant-read thermometer inserted into the thickest part reads 140°F. Remove from the oven and allow to rest for 5 minutes.

8　Using a chef's knife, carve the breast meat off the bone, keeping the meat, skin on, in one piece. Ladle a pool of Fennel Purée into the center of each of 6 dinner plates. Place a guinea breast half in the center of each plate with a Savory Pasty at its side. Crisscross the batons of Fennel Confit around the plate. Whisk the warm braising liquid and drizzle it around the edge of the plate. Garnish with Fennel Chips and serve. (If desired, streaks of white and green Fennel Purée may be swirled on the plate.)

SAVORY PASTY

3¾ cups all-purpose flour ▪ 1½ teaspoons salt ▪ 1 cup unsalted butter, cubed and chilled ▪ 5 tablespoons lard, cubed and chilled ▪ ⅓ cup ice water ▪ 1 tablespoon olive oil ▪ ½ cup minced onion ▪ 2 tablespoons minced celery ▪ 2 cups finely diced braised guinea leg meat (see page 138) ▪ Coarse salt and freshly ground pepper ▪ 1 large egg ▪ 2 tablespoons water ▪ 1 tablespoon fennel seeds

1 Combine the flour and salt in a food processor fitted with the metal blade. With the motor running, add the butter and lard and process to large crumbs. With the motor running, pour in the ice water and process just until the dough comes together. Scrape the dough from the bowl and form into a disk. Wrap in plastic wrap and refrigerate for at least 1 hour to chill thoroughly.

2 Heat the olive oil in a small sauté pan over medium heat. Add the onion and celery and sauté for about 4 minutes or until the vegetables have sweat their liquid but not taken on any color. Remove from the heat and combine with the leg meat. Season with salt and pepper.

3 Combine the egg and water in a small bowl. Set aside.

4 Preheat the oven to 350°F.

5 Line a baking sheet with parchment paper and set aside.

6 Remove the dough from the refrigerator. Unwrap and roll out on a lightly floured surface to about ⅛ inch thick. Using a sharp knife, cut out six 5-inch dough circles, reserving the remaining dough for another use.

7 Mound a generous portion of the leg-meat mixture in the center of each of the dough circles. Bring one side of the dough up and over the filling to make a half circle, pressing around the edges to seal. Using a pastry brush, lightly coat each pasty with the reserved egg wash. Sprinkle the top with fennel seeds. (Pasties may be made up to this point and stored, covered and refrigerated, for up to 1 day or tightly sealed and frozen, for up to 2 months. If frozen, do not thaw before baking; increase the baking time by about 10 minutes.)

8 Transfer the pasties to the parchment-lined baking sheet. Place in the preheated oven and bake for about 20 minutes or until golden brown. Remove from the oven and serve hot.

FENNEL PURÉE

- 1 large bulb fennel with fronds attached, well washed
- 2 tablespoons butter
- ½ cup chicken stock
- Approximately ¼ cup grapeseed oil
- Coarse salt and freshly ground pepper

1 Cut the fronds from the fennel bulb and set aside. Trim off and discard (or reserve for another use such as stock) the fibrous stalks. If pithy, tough and/or damaged, remove the outer sections. Cut the bulb in half, lengthwise, remove the center root section and dice the remaining fennel. Set aside.

2 Bring a small saucepan of water to a boil over high heat. Add the fennel fronds and blanch for 20 seconds. Immediately drain and refresh under cold running water. Place in a blender and process to a smooth purée, drizzling in just enough grapeseed oil to emulsify. Set aside.

3 Heat the butter in a medium sauté pan over medium-low heat. Add the diced fennel and sauté for about 4 minutes or just until wilted. Add the chicken stock and season with salt and pepper. Simmer for about 10 minutes or until the fennel is very tender. Transfer to a blender. Process to a smooth purée, drizzling in just enough grapeseed oil to emulsify. Transfer to a small nonstick saucepan. Place over medium heat and cook until just warmed through. Add the reserved green frond purée. Taste and, if necessary, adjust the seasoning with salt and pepper. (If desired, separate out about ⅓ cup of each purée before mixing to use as a plate garnish.)

FENNEL CONFIT

- 1 teaspoon black peppercorns ■ 1 teaspoon fennel seeds ■ 1 teaspoon coriander seeds
- 1 large fennel bulb, well washed ■ 2 cups mildly flavored olive oil ■ 1 clove garlic, peeled

1 Place the peppercorns, fennel and coriander in a cheesecloth bag tied closed with kitchen twine. Set aside.

2 Trim the fronds, fibrous stalk and any pithy, tough and/or damaged outer layers from the fennel bulb. Cut the bulb in half, lengthwise, and then into batons about 2 inches long and 1/4 inch in diameter.

3 Place the olive oil in a medium saucepan. Add the fennel along with the garlic and the reserved sachet. Place over medium-low heat and bring to a simmer. Lower the heat and cook at a bare simmer for about 15 minutes or until the fennel is very tender. Remove from the heat and allow to cool. Store the fennel in the oil until ready to use.

(If storing for longer than one day, cover and refrigerate. Bring to room temperature before serving. When all of the fennel has been used, the remaining oil can be used for seasoning vegetables and vinaigrettes or for sautéing fish or poultry.)

FENNEL CHIPS

- 1 cup water ■ 1 cup sugar ■ ½ large fennel bulb, well washed and trimmed

1 Combine the water and sugar in a small saucepan over medium heat. Bring to a simmer and simmer just until the sugar has dissolved. Remove from the heat and allow to cool.

2 Preheat the oven to 300°F.

3 Line a baking sheet with parchment paper.

4 Using a mandoline or Japanese vegetable slicer, cut the fennel into paper-thin slices. Working with one piece at a time, dip the slices into the cooled sugar syrup and then place them in a single layer on the prepared baking sheet. Place another baking sheet on top of the fennel-covered baking sheet to hold the fennel flat as it bakes. Place in the preheated oven and bake for about 20 minutes or until the fennel is golden and crisp. Remove from the oven and cool on wire racks. Serve at room temperature.

Squab
with Roasted Figs
and Crisp Salsify

6 squab, well washed and patted dry ■ ¼ cup grapeseed oil ■ 1 onion, peeled and diced ■ 1 carrot, peeled, trimmed and diced ■ 2 ribs celery, well washed, dried and diced ■ 1 medium ripe tomato, cored and chopped ■ Approximately 6 cups chicken stock ■ Sachet (see page 234) ■ Coarse salt ■ 2 cloves roasted garlic ■ 9 sprigs thyme ■ 1 bay leaf ■ Freshly ground pepper ■ 3 tablespoons clarified butter ■ Roasted Figs, warmed ■ Braised Salsify ■ Crisp Salsify

1 Preheat the oven to 300°F.

2 Using a sharp knife, carefully remove the breasts and legs (keeping the thighs attached) from the squab. Cut the breasts in half, leaving the meat on the bone. Place them on a small plate, cover with plastic wrap and refrigerate. Neatly slit open each thigh to reveal the bone and then carefully remove the thigh bone. Coarsely chop the squab carcasses along with the neck, back and wing bones. Set aside.

3 Heat 2 tablespoons of the oil in a large, shallow, ovenproof saucepan over medium heat. Add the carcass pieces and sear, turning frequently, until nicely browned. Add the onion and carrot and sauté for about 7 minutes or until the vegetables begin to caramelize. Add the celery and tomato and sauté for about 4 minutes or until they have begun to sweat their liquid. Add 3 cups of the chicken stock along with the Sachet, season with salt and bring to a simmer. Immediately cover and place in the preheated oven and braise for 45 minutes. Remove the pan from the oven, uncover and strain the liquid through a fine sieve, pressing on the solids to extract all of the juice. Discard the solids. Place the pan juices in a medium saucepan over medium heat and bring to a simmer. Simmer, skimming off any fat or impurities that rise to the top, for about 20 minutes or until reduced by half and beginning to thicken. Remove from the heat, place in the top half of a double boiler over hot water and keep warm.

4 Heat the remaining 2 tablespoons of oil in a large, heavy-bottomed, ovenproof saucepan over medium heat. Add the squab legs and sear, turning frequently, until the skin is golden brown. Add enough of the chicken stock (about 3 cups) to cover the meat by two-thirds. Add the roasted garlic and then 3 sprigs of the thyme and the bay leaf and bring to a simmer. Season with salt and pepper and immediately transfer to the hot oven. Braise, uncovered, for about 25 minutes or until the meat is fork-tender. Remove from the oven and set aside to cool in the cooking liquid. When the meat is cool, carefully lift the legs to a clean ovenproof pan. Strain the cooking liquid through a fine sieve into the pan with the legs. Set aside.

5 Preheat the broiler and, if necessary, the oven to 375°F. (If the broiler is part of the oven, just preheat to broil.)

6 Remove the breasts from the refrigerator. Heat the clarified butter in a large sauté pan over medium-high heat. Add the breasts and sear, turning frequently, for about 8 minutes or until nicely browned on all sides. Add the remaining 6 thyme sprigs and season with salt and pepper. Cook, basting with the butter and thyme, for about 3 minutes or until an instant-read thermometer reads 150°F when inserted into the thickest part for medium-rare. Remove the breasts from the pan and place on a wire rack placed in a baking pan. Tent lightly with aluminum foil to keep warm.

7 While the breasts are cooking, reheat the reserved legs in their cooking juices over medium-high heat. When hot, transfer to the broiler for about 3 minutes or until the skin is slightly crisp.

8 Place an equal portion of the warm Roasted Figs in the center of each of 6 dinner plates. Arrange a breast and a leg on top. Drizzle the jus around the center and lightly over the top. Arrange equal portions of the Braised Salsify along with 2 pieces of Crisp Salsify on each plate and serve immediately.

ROASTED FIGS

- 9 ripe fresh figs, well washed and dried
- 3 whole star anise
- 1 teaspoon cardamom
- 2 whole cloves
- One 3-inch cinnamon stick
- ¼ cup unsalted butter

1. Preheat the oven to 350°F.

2. Cut the figs in half, lengthwise. Set aside.

3. Place the butter in a large, heavy-bottomed, ovenproof sauté pan over medium-low heat. Cook, stirring occasionally, for about 5 minutes or until the butter is very aromatic and has begun to turn a golden brown. Add the figs, cut side down, and sear for about 3 minutes or until the flesh has begun to caramelize.

4. Add the star anise, cloves, cinnamon and cardamom to the pan and cook for about 2 minutes or until the spices are quite fragrant and lightly toasted. Place the pan in the preheated oven and roast for about 10 minutes or until the figs are quite soft and well caramelized. Remove from the oven and, using a slotted spoon, carefully transfer the figs from the pan to a baking pan. Discard the spices and drizzle the cooking juices over the top of the figs. Serve warm or at room temperature. (To reheat, place in a preheated 350°F oven for 5 minutes.)

BRAISED SALSIFY

- 4 large salsify
- Coarse salt and freshly ground pepper
- 3 tablespoons unsalted butter
- ¼ cup chicken stock

1. Bring a medium saucepan of salted water to a boil over high heat. Add the salsify and cut into thin sticks about 2 inches long. Peel the salsify and cut into thin sticks to the boiling water and blanch for about 1 minute. Drain well and pat dry.

2. When ready to serve, heat the butter in a medium sauté pan over medium heat. Add the salsify and sauté for 3 minutes. Add the chicken stock and season with salt and pepper. Cook, stirring occasionally, for about 3 minutes or until a slightly thick pan sauce has formed. Remove from the heat and serve.

CRISP SALSIFY

- 2 large salsify
- Approximately 3 cups grapeseed or canola oil
- Coarse salt

1. Peel and trim the salsify. Using a vegetable peeler, peel, from the stem to the root end, long, thin shavings from each salsify.

2. Heat the oil in a medium saucepan over medium-high heat until it registers 365°F on an instant-read thermometer.

3. Add the salsify shavings, a few at a time, into the hot oil. Fry for about 2 minutes or until golden and crisp. Using a slotted spoon, remove the crisps from the oil and place on a double layer of paper towels to drain. Continue frying and draining until all of the salsify has been fried. Season with salt. Serve warm or at room temperature. (If necessary, store in an airtight container and reheat in a preheated 200°F oven for about 5 minutes.)

If making Potato Crisps, use Idaho potatoes and cut the paper-thin slices, lengthwise, into thirds. Heirloom potatoes may also be used for a variety of shapes and colors.

note: Any root vegetable or potato may be crisped in this same fashion.

Charcoal-Grilled
Filet of Beef
with Oxtail Crepinettes
and Fava Beans

1 Preheat the oven to 350°F.

2 Season each filet with salt and pepper.

3 Heat 3 tablespoons of the butter in a large, ovenproof sauté pan over medium heat. Add the filets and sear, turning once, for about 6 minutes or until both sides are nicely colored. Sprinkle with the parsley, thyme and rosemary and place in the preheated oven for 5 minutes or until an instant-read thermometer inserted into the thickest part registers 135°F for rare. (The filet will continue to cook as it rests so it will reach 140°F, the correct internal temperature for rare beef.) Remove from the oven and allow to rest for about 5 minutes.

4 Combine the Red Wine Sauce with the reserved oxtail-braising liquid in a small saucepan over medium heat. Bring to a simmer, then lower the heat to just keep hot.

5 Remove the crepinettes from the refrigerator. Place a large nonstick skillet over medium heat. When hot, but not smoking, add the crepinettes, smooth side down, and sear for about 3 minutes or until beginning to brown. Using a slotted spatula, working with one at a time, place a crepinette on top of each piece of Crisp Polenta on the baking pan. Place in the oven and bake for about 5 minutes or until heated through. Remove from the oven and keep warm.

6 Heat the remaining 2 tablespoons of butter and the chicken stock in a medium sauté pan over medium heat. Add the fava beans and sauté for about 5 minutes or until nicely coated with the butter-stock emulsion. Remove from the heat and keep warm.

7 Slice the beef, slightly on the bias, keeping each filet intact. Fan a single filet out on each of 6 dinner plates. Place a crepinette-topped polenta circle slightly off-center on each plate. Stir the savory into the fava beans and arrange an equal portion on each plate. Drizzle the sauce over the crepinette and filet and around the edge of the plate. Garnish the crepinette with Crispy Leeks and serve immediately.

SERVES 6   Six 8-ounce, 1½-inch-thick filet mignons ▪ Coarse salt and freshly ground pepper ▪ 5 tablespoons unsalted butter ▪ 1 tablespoon minced flat-leaf parsley ▪ 2 teaspoons minced thyme ▪ 2 teaspoons minced rosemary ▪ Red Wine Sauce ▪ Reserved oxtail-braising liquid ▪ Oxtail Crepinettes ▪ Crisp Polenta ▪ ¼ cup chicken stock ▪ 3 cups fresh fava beans, blanched and peeled ▪ 1 teaspoon savory ▪ Crispy Leeks (see page 234)

RED WINE SAUCE

1 tablespoon olive oil ▪ 4 shallots, peeled and thinly sliced ▪ ½ cup chopped button mushrooms ▪ 3 cups red wine ▪ 8 cups veal stock ▪ Sachet (see page 234) ▪ 8 black peppercorns ▪ Coarse salt and freshly ground pepper

1 Heat the olive oil in a large saucepan over medium heat. Add the shallots and mushrooms and sauté for 5 minutes or until the vegetables have sweat most of their liquid. Add the wine, Sachet and peppercorns. Raise the heat and bring to a boil. Lower the heat and simmer for about 25 minutes or until the pan is almost dry.

2 Add the stock, again raise the heat and bring to a boil. Lower the heat and simmer, stirring occasionally and skimming off any fat or impurities that rise to the top, for about 1 hour or until the liquid has reduced to 3 cups. Remove from the heat and strain through a fine sieve into a small saucepan, discarding the solids. Season with salt and pepper. Set aside until ready to serve. (The sauce may be made up to 3 days in advance of use and stored, covered and refrigerated.)

- 2 tablespoons canola oil ■ 1 oxtail, cut into 4 pieces ■ 1 large onion, peeled and chopped ■ 1 large carrot, peeled and chopped ■ 2 ribs celery, well washed, dried and chopped ■ 2 tomatoes, well washed, cored and chopped ■ 2 cups Madeira ■ 1 cup red wine ■ 6 cups veal stock ■ Sachet (see page 234) ■ Coarse salt and freshly ground pepper ■ 5 tablespoons unsalted butter ■ 4 leeks, white part only, well washed and finely diced ■ 1 pound assorted wild mushrooms, cleaned, trimmed and sliced ■ 3 tablespoons chopped black truffles ■ 3 tablespoons truffle oil ■ 2 tablespoons Fines Herbes (see page 235) ■ Six 5-inch-square pieces caul fat

1 Preheat the oven to 350°F.

2 Place the oil in a Dutch oven over medium heat. Add the oxtail and sear, turning frequently, until all sides are nicely browned. Add the onion and carrot and sauté about 7 minutes or until the vegetables are golden brown. Add the celery and tomatoes and sauté for 4 minutes. Add the Madeira and red wine and stir to deglaze the pan. Bring to a simmer and cook for about 30 minutes or until the liquid has reduced by half. Stir in the veal stock and Sachet and season with salt and pepper. Cover and transfer to the preheated oven. Braise, uncovering and stirring occasionally, for about 3 hours or until the meat is falling-off-the-bone tender. Remove from the oven and allow to cool. When the meat is cool enough to handle, using a slotted spoon, lift the oxtail from the cooking liquid and strain the cooking liquid through a fine sieve into a clean saucepan, discarding the solids. Using your fingertips, push off as much of the meat as possible. Coarsely chop the meat and set aside. Place the liquid over high heat and bring to a simmer. Lower the heat and simmer, skimming off any fat, foam or impurities that rise to the top, for about 45 minutes or until reduced by half and slightly thick. Remove from the heat and set aside.

3 Heat 2 tablespoons of the butter in a medium sauté pan over medium-low heat. Add the leeks and sauté for about 6 minutes or just until the leeks have softened and sweat their liquid but have not taken on any color. Using a slotted spoon, remove the leeks from the pan and set aside. Return the pan to medium heat and add the remaining 3 tablespoons of butter. Cook, stirring frequently, for about 6 minutes or until the butter is light brown but not burned. Add the mushrooms and sauté for about 10 minutes or until golden brown and slightly crisp. Add the reserved leeks and season with salt and pepper. Remove from the heat and stir in the reserved oxtail meat along with the truffles, truffle oil and Fines Herbes. Taste and, if necessary, adjust the seasoning with salt and pepper.

4 Lay the caul fat out in a single layer on a clean, flat surface. Working with one piece at a time, lay the caul fat down into a 2½-inch ring mold, pushing the fat against the edge of the mold. Spoon enough of the oxtail mixture into the ring mold to make a solid filling. Fold the fat over the filling to make a neat package. Carefully remove the crepinette from the ring mold and set aside. Continue making crepinettes until all of the caul fat is used. (You may have some stuffing remaining.) Place the crepinettes on a plate, cover with plastic wrap and refrigerate until ready to cook.

CRISP POLENTA

4 cups milk ■ **2 cups instant polenta** ■ **2 cups truffle juice** ■ **1 cup freshly grated Parmesan cheese** ■ **Coarse salt and freshly ground pepper** ■ **2 tablespoons olive oil**

Place the milk in a medium nonstick saucepan over medium heat. Bring to a boil and immediately whisk in the polenta. Cook, stirring constantly, for about 8 minutes or until the polenta is very thick. Whisk in the truffle juice and Parmesan cheese. When well incorporated, taste and adjust the seasoning with salt and pepper. Pour the polenta into a nonstick baking pan and, using a spatula, smooth the top. Set aside to cool and firm. When cool, cut into 2½-inch rounds. Heat the oil in a large sauté pan over medium heat. Add the polenta rounds and fry, turning occasionally, for about 5 minutes or until crisp and golden

Duo of Aged Sirloin and Red Wine–Braised with Mustard

Short Ribs
Greens and Honeyed Turnips

SERVES 6 Six 4-ounce, 1½-inch-thick aged sirloin steaks ▪ Coarse salt and freshly ground pepper ▪ Red Wine–Braised Short Ribs ▪ 3 tablespoons unsalted butter ▪ 3 tablespoons minced shallots ▪ 4 cups roughly chopped, blanched mustard greens ▪ 2 tablespoons mustard oil ▪ Pommes Purée ▪ 2 tablespoons minced chives ▪ 18 Potato Crisps (see page 145) ▪ Honeyed Turnips ▪ 1 cup baby spinach leaves, well washed and dried ▪ Fleur de sel

1 Preheat and oil the grill.

2 Season the steaks with salt and pepper. Place on the preheated grill and grill, turning occasionally, for about 8 minutes or until an instant-read thermometer inserted into the thickest part reads 135°F for rare. (The steak will continue to cook as it rests so it will reach 140°F, the correct internal temperature for rare beef.) Remove from the grill and place on a wire rack to rest for 3 minutes.

3 While the steak is grilling, return the short ribs to medium heat and bring to a simmer. Lower the heat to just keep the short ribs hot.

4 Heat the butter in a large sauté pan until very fragrant and beginning to color. Add the shallots and sauté for 2 minutes. Add the mustard greens, season with salt and pepper and, using tongs, toss and turn the greens for about 5 minutes or until wilted and tender. Season with the mustard oil and remove from the heat.

5 Form a large quenelle of Pommes Purée by moving and shaping the potatoes between 2 wet tablespoons. Place a quenelle in the center of each of 6 dinner plates. Sprinkle with chives and insert 3 Potato Crisps into the quenelle. Nestle 2 turnip disks into the quenelle on each plate and then set an equal portion of short ribs on the turnips. Place a mound of mustard greens on each plate. Slice each steak, keeping it intact, and place a steak on each mound of mustard greens. Spoon the braised short rib sauce around the edge of the plate. Garnish with baby spinach leaves and fleur de sel and serve.

POMMES PURÉE

2 pounds Yukon gold potatoes, peeled and cubed ▪ ⅓ cup very warm heavy cream ▪ Coarse salt and freshly ground pepper ▪ ¼ cup unsalted butter, chilled and diced

Place the potatoes in a medium saucepan over medium heat with cold, salted water to cover. Bring to a boil, then lower the heat and simmer for about 20 minutes or until the potatoes are tender. Remove from the heat and drain well. Pass through a ricer or food mill into a clean, nonstick saucepan. Using a wooden spoon, beat in the butter and then the warm cream. Season with salt and pepper. Return to low heat and, beating constantly, cook to just heat through. (Alternately, place the potatoes in the top half of a double boiler over boiling water, cover and reheat.)

HONEYED TURNIPS

Approximately 3 pounds white turnips ▪ 2 cups white wine vinegar ▪ 2 cups honey

1 Peel and trim the turnips. Using a small, sharp knife, cut the turnips into 12 disks, 1½ inches round by ½ inch thick, reserving all of the trimmings. Set the disks aside.

2 Place the trimmings in a medium saucepan over high heat with about 5 cups of lightly salted water. Bring to a boil, then lower the heat and simmer for 15 minutes or until tender. Using a slotted spoon, lift the turnip disks from the cooking liquid and place on a plate to cool. Continue to simmer the cooking liquid for about 1 hour or until slightly thick and a light caramel color. (Turnips may be prepared to this point up to 2 days in advance of serving.)

Remove from the heat and allow to cool. When cool, strain through a fine sieve into a clean saucepan. Add the reserved turnip disks along with the vinegar and honey and place over medium heat. Bring to a boil, then lower the heat and simmer for about 15 minutes or until tender. Using a slotted spoon, lift the turnip disks from the

3 When ready to serve, place the reduced cooking liquid in a large sauté pan. Add the turnip disks and place over medium heat. Bring to a simmer and cook, turning frequently, for about 15 minutes or until the liquid is almost evaporated and the disks are a beautiful caramel color. Serve hot.

RED WINE-BRAISED SHORT RIBS

- ¼ cup canola oil ◆ 4 cloves garlic, peeled and minced
- and thinly sliced ◆ Coarse salt ◆ 5 sprigs thyme ◆ 2 bay leaves ◆ 3 shallots, peeled
- black peppercorns ◆ 2 carrots, peeled, trimmed and diced ◆ 3 beef short ribs, trimmed of excess fat ◆ 1 tablespoon
- ground pepper ◆ 1 medium onion, peeled and diced ◆ 4 cups veal stock ◆ 2 ribs celery, well washed, trimmed and
- diced ◆ 4 cups red wine ◆ Sachet (see page 234) ◆ Freshly

1 Heat 2 tablespoons of the oil in a large saucepan over medium heat. Add the garlic and shallots along with a pinch of salt and sauté for 3 minutes. Add the thyme, bay leaves and peppercorns and sauté for about 4 minutes or until the vegetables have sweat most of their liquid but have not taken on any color and the mixture is very aromatic. Add the wine, then raise the heat and bring to a boil. Remove from the heat and allow to cool.

2 Place the short ribs in a nonreactive bowl or baking dish large enough to hold them in a single layer. Pour the cooled red wine marinade over the ribs, cover with plastic wrap and refrigerate for at least 12 hours or up to 2 days.

3 Using tongs, lift the short ribs from the marinade and set aside. Strain the marinade through a fine sieve into a clean saucepan. Place over medium-high heat and bring to a boil. Lower the heat and simmer for about 40 minutes or until the liquid has reduced by half. Remove from the heat and set aside.

4 Preheat the oven to 350°F.

5 Heat the remaining 2 tablespoons of oil in a Dutch oven over medium-high heat. Season the short ribs with salt and pepper and place in the Dutch oven. Sear, turning frequently, for about 5 minutes or until all sides are nicely browned. Using tongs, lift the ribs from the pan and set aside.

6 Immediately add the carrots, celery and onion to the pan and sauté for about 6 minutes or until the vegetables are caramelized. Return the ribs to the pan along with the veal stock, Sachet, salt and pepper and the reserved, reduced red wine marinade. Braise for about 2 hours or until the rib meat is almost falling off the bones. Remove from the oven and place in the preheated oven. Braise for about 2 hours or until the rib meat is almost falling off the bones. Remove from the oven and allow to rest until the meat is cool enough to handle.

7 Using a slotted spoon, lift the ribs from the cooking liquid. Place the ribs in a shallow dish, cover with plastic wrap and refrigerate for about 2 hours or until nicely chilled.

8 Strain the cooking liquid through a fine sieve into a clean saucepan. Place over medium-high heat and bring to a boil. Lower the heat and simmer, skimming off any fat or impurities that rise to the top, for about 45 minutes or until the liquid has reduced to a saucelike consistency. Remove from the heat and allow to cool.

9 Remove the chilled ribs from the refrigerator. Carefully pull the meat from the bones, keeping the shape whole. Trim off any excess fat and cartilage and cut the rib meat in half, crosswise. Add the trimmed rib meat to the reduced sauce. (Recipe may be prepared up to this point and stored, covered and refrigerated, for up to 3 days.) If serving the short ribs on their own, return to medium heat and cook until just heated through. If using as a component in the Whole Aged Sirloin Short Ribs recipe, follow directions for reheating in the master recipe on page 152.

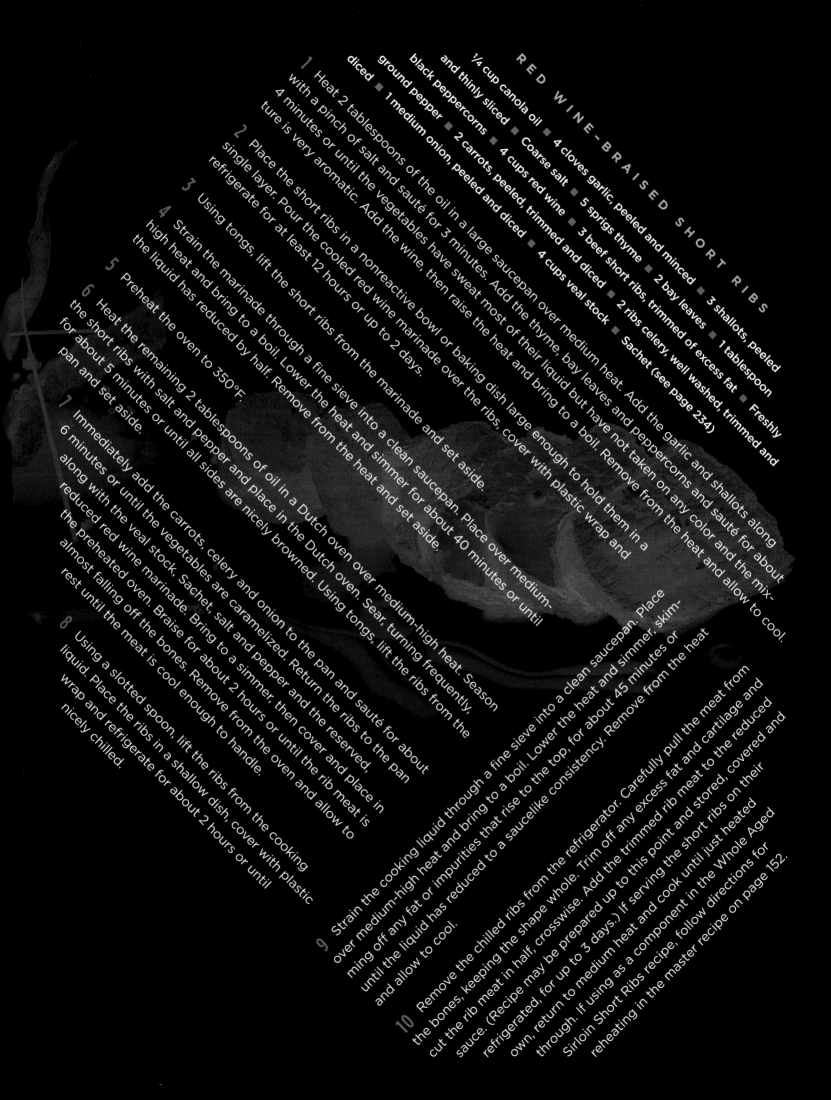

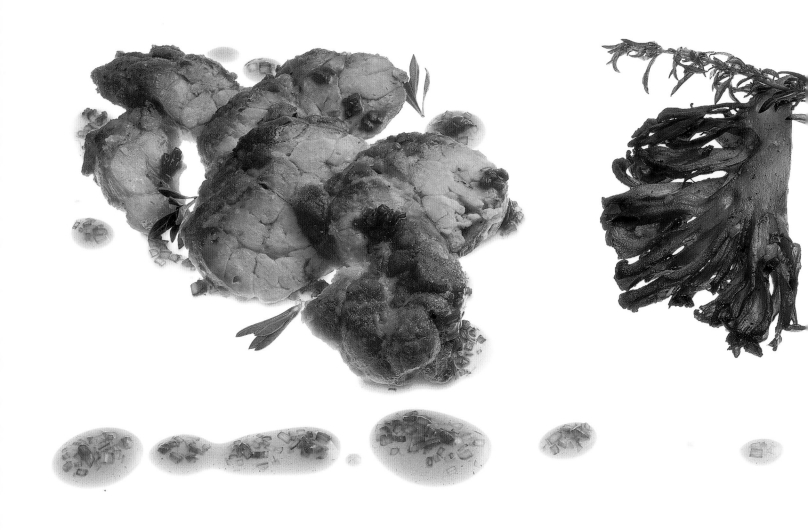

Veal Short Ribs and Sautéed Sweetbreads
with Brown Butter Mushrooms

1 ½ pounds veal sweetbreads ■ 1 tablespoon coarse salt plus more ■ Approximately 5 cups cold milk ■ 1 cup Wondra flour ■ 1 teaspoon ground cloves ■ 6 tablespoons clarified butter ■ Freshly ground pepper ■ Brown Butter Mushrooms ■ Veal Short Ribs ■ 1 tablespoon lemon zest ■ Sherry-Shallot Natural Sauce ■ Pommes Soufflés

1 Place the sweetbreads in a bowl with ice water to cover. Add 1 tablespoon of the salt. Lightly cover with plastic wrap and refrigerate for at least 2 hours or up to 12 hours.

2 Rinse the sweetbreads under cold running water for 5 minutes. Place in a deep saucepan with cold milk to cover by 1 inch. Season with salt and place over medium-low heat and slowly bring to a boil. Boil for 90 seconds, then lift the sweetbreads from the milk and allow to cool.

3 Cover a large plate with a clean kitchen towel. Set aside.

4 Using a sharp knife, trim any veins, sinew or fat from the sweetbread lobes. Divide into 6 equal portions, keeping the pieces as large as possible. Place the cleaned sweetbreads on the prepared plate and fold the towel up and over to enclose the meat. Invert another plate on top and lay a heavy weight (such as a small cast-iron skillet) on top. Refrigerate for at least 8 hours.

5 Combine the flour and cloves in a large, shallow bowl. Place 1 cup of milk in another shallow bowl. Dip the sweetbreads into the milk and then lightly dredge in the flour mixture. Set aside.

6 Heat the clarified butter in a large sauté pan over medium-low heat. Add the sweetbreads and season with salt and pepper. Fry for about 3 minutes or until golden; turn, and fry the remaining side for 2 minutes or until golden. Using a slotted spatula, transfer the sweetbreads to a double layer of paper towels to drain.

BROWN BUTTER MUSHROOMS

■ ½ cup unsalted butter ■ ½ pound hen-of-the-woods mushrooms, brushed clean and sliced into ½-inch-thick pieces ■ 2 tablespoons minced shallots ■ 1 tablespoon summer savory leaves ■ 3 tablespoons chicken stock ■ Coarse salt and freshly ground pepper

1 Heat the butter in a large sauté pan over medium heat. Cook, stirring occasionally, for about 4 minutes or until the butter is very aromatic and beginning to color. Add the mushrooms and toss to coat. Fry, shaking the pan from time to time to redistribute the butter and keep the mushrooms from sticking, for about 5 minutes or until the mushrooms are nicely colored. Watch the heat carefully so that the butter does not burn.

2 Add the shallots and savory and allow them to sizzle in the butter. Add the stock and shake the pan to emulsify the butter into the stock so that it creates a light sauce. Season with salt and pepper and serve hot.

SHERRY-SHALLOT NATURAL SAUCE

■ 3/4 cup sherry wine vinegar ■ ½ teaspoon coarsely ground pepper ■ ½ cup minced shallots ■ ½ cup chicken stock, if needed ■ 1 cup veal demi-glace ■ 3 tablespoons Lemon Confit (see page 55) ■ 2 tablespoons Lemon

Combine the vinegar, shallots and pepper in a small saucepan over medium heat. Bring to a boil, then lower the heat and simmer until the pan is almost dry. Add the demi-glace and bring just until the flavors have blended. If the sauce reduces too quickly or tastes sharp, add 1 tablespoon of the stock at a time until the sauce is nicely balanced. Stir in the Lemon Confit and serve hot.

1 Place an equal portion of the Brown Butter Mushrooms in the center of each of 6 dinner plates. Place a portion of sweetbreads on top of the mushrooms on each plate. Nestle a veal short rib next to the sweetbreads and sprinkle a bit of lemon zest over the rib. Drizzle the Sherry-Shallot Natural Sauce around the plate and over the sweetbreads. Place 2 Pommes Soufflés into the center and serve.

POMMES SOUFFLÉS

1 large Idaho potato, peeled ◆ **Approximately 2 quarts vegetable oil**

1 Trim the potato into a long rectangle. Using a mandoline or Japanese vegetable slicer, cut the potato rectangle, lengthwise, into 1/16-inch-thick slices. (This recipe requires 2 Pommes Soufflés per person but you can make as many as you like by increasing the number of potatoes.)

2 Heat 4 cups of the oil in a medium saucepan (or deep-fat fryer) over low heat to 250°F on an instant-read thermometer.

3 Heat the remaining 4 cups of oil in another medium saucepan (or deep-fat fryer) over high heat to 350°F on an instant-read thermometer.

4 Blanch the potato slices, stirring constantly, in the 250°F oil for about 3 minutes or until just softening.

5 Using a slotted spoon, immediately transfer the blanched potatoes to the hotter oil and fry, stirring constantly, for about 1 minute or until golden brown, puffed and crisp. Serve hot. (Potatoes may be souffléd with a brief fry and then removed from the fat and placed on a paper towel–lined baking sheet until ready to serve. When ready to serve, reheat the oil to 350°F and fry for about 1 minute or until golden brown, puffed and crisp.)

VEAL SHORT RIBS

6 shallots, peeled and sliced ◆ **6 cloves garlic, peeled and sliced** ◆ **Freshly grated zest of 1 lemon** ◆ **2 tablespoons chopped flat-leaf parsley** ◆ **2 tablespoons chopped thyme** ◆ **2 teaspoons toasted, crushed coriander seed** ◆ **2 tablespoons coarse salt** ◆ **Two 3-rib veal short ribs, trimmed of excess fat** ◆ **4 cups duck fat**

1 Combine the shallots, garlic, lemon zest, parsley, thyme, coriander and salt in a small mixing bowl. When well combined, sprinkle half of the mixture on the bottom of a large, glass baking pan. Place the short ribs in a single layer on top of the cure mixture in the pan. Sprinkle the remaining cure mixture on top of the ribs. Tightly cover with plastic wrap and refrigerate for 24 hours.

2 Remove the ribs from the refrigerator. Unwrap and, using a damp, clean kitchen towel, brush the cure from the meat. Place the ribs in a heavy-bottomed, crueset-style pan. Add duck fat to cover the meat and place over medium heat. Bring to a simmer, then cover and cook at a bare simmer for about 2 ½ hours or until the meat is fork-tender. Remove from the heat and allow to cool in the fat.

3 When cool, cover and refrigerate for at least 24 hours or up to 5 days.

4 When ready to serve, remove the ribs from the fat and cut into 6 separate ribs. Trim off any excess fat. Return the ribs to the fat and place over medium heat. Cook for about 5 minutes or until just heated through. Using tongs, lift the ribs from the fat and serve hot.

Roasted Lamb with Crisp Lamb

Brics and Blackberries

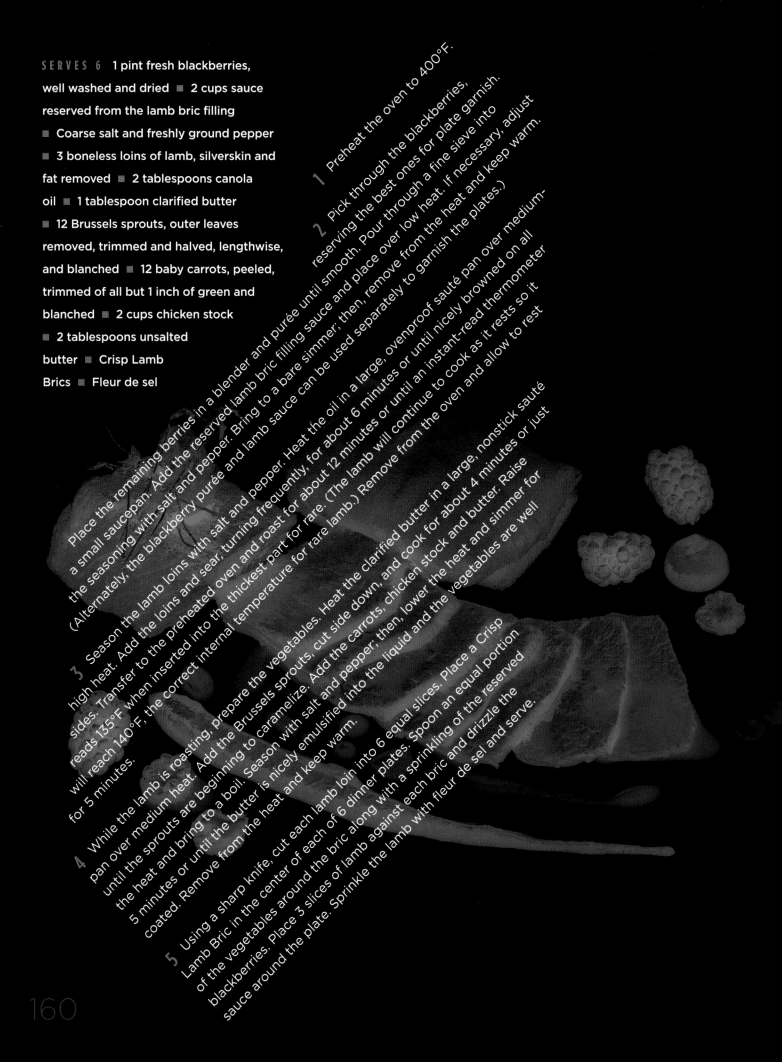

SERVES 6   1 pint fresh blackberries, well washed and dried ■ 2 cups sauce reserved from the lamb bric filling ■ Coarse salt and freshly ground pepper ■ 3 boneless loins of lamb, silverskin and fat removed ■ 2 tablespoons canola oil ■ 1 tablespoon clarified butter ■ 12 Brussels sprouts, outer leaves removed, trimmed and halved, lengthwise, and blanched ■ 12 baby carrots, peeled, trimmed of all but 1 inch of green and blanched ■ 2 cups chicken stock ■ 2 tablespoons unsalted butter ■ Crisp Lamb Brics ■ Fleur de sel

1   Preheat the oven to 400°F.

2   Pick through the blackberries, reserving the best ones for plate garnish. Place the remaining berries in a blender and purée until smooth. Pour through a fine sieve into a small saucepan. Add the reserved lamb bric filling sauce and place over low heat. If necessary, adjust the seasoning with salt and pepper. Bring to a bare simmer; then, remove from the heat and keep warm. (Alternately, the blackberry purée and lamb sauce can be used separately to garnish the plates.)

3   Season the lamb loins with salt and pepper. Heat the oil in a large, ovenproof sauté pan over medium-high heat. Add the loins and sear, turning frequently, for about 6 minutes or until nicely browned on all sides. Transfer to the preheated oven and roast for about 12 minutes or until an instant-read thermometer reads 135°F when inserted into the thickest part for rare. (The lamb will continue to cook as it rests so it will reach 140°F, the correct internal temperature for rare lamb.) Remove from the oven and allow to rest for 5 minutes.

4   While the lamb is roasting, prepare the vegetables. Heat the clarified butter in a large, nonstick sauté pan over medium heat. Add the Brussels sprouts, cut side down, and cook for about 4 minutes or just until the sprouts are beginning to caramelize. Add the carrots, chicken stock and butter. Raise the heat and bring to a boil. Season with salt and pepper; then, lower the heat and simmer for 5 minutes or until the butter is nicely emulsified into the liquid and the vegetables are well coated. Remove from the heat and keep warm.

5   Using a sharp knife, cut each lamb loin into 6 equal slices. Place a Crisp Lamb Bric in the center of each of 6 dinner plates. Spoon an equal portion of the vegetables around the bric along with a sprinkling of the reserved blackberries. Place 3 slices of lamb against each bric and drizzle the sauce around the plate. Sprinkle the lamb with fleur de sel and serve.

CRISP LAMB BRICS

1 tablespoon canola oil ■ 1½ pounds boneless lamb shoulder, trimmed of fat and diced ■ Coarse salt and freshly ground pepper ■ 3 ribs celery, well washed, dried and finely diced ■ 2 large carrots, peeled, trimmed and finely diced ■ 1 large onion, peeled and finely diced ■ 4 cups Pinot Noir ■ 8 cups chicken stock ■ Sachet (see page 234) ■ 1 cup freshly grated Parmesan cheese ■ 2 tablespoons crème fraîche ■ 2 tablespoons Fines Herbes (see page 235) ■ 1 large egg ■ 1 tablespoon cold water ■ 6 pieces bric pastry ■ Approximately 6 cups vegetable oil

1 Preheat the oven to 350°F.

2 Heat the canola oil in a roasting pan over medium-high heat. Add the lamb and season with salt and pepper. Sear, turning frequently, for about 10 minutes or until the lamb is nicely browned. Add the celery, carrots and onion and sauté for about 10 additional minutes or until the vegetables have begun to caramelize. Add the wine and bring to a boil. Lower the heat and simmer for about 20 minutes or until the liquid has reduced by two-thirds. Add the chicken stock and Sachet and again bring to a boil. Cover and transfer to the preheated oven. Braise for about 1 hour or until the lamb is fork-tender. Remove from the oven and allow the meat to cool in the liquid.

3 Using a slotted spoon, lift the lamb from the liquid and set aside. Remove from the heat and simmer for about 2 hours or until reduced to a saucelike consistency. Remove from the heat and set aside.

4 Strain the liquid into a clean saucepan, discarding the solids, and place over high heat. Bring to a boil; then, lower the heat and simmer for about 2 hours or until reduced to a saucelike consistency. Set aside.

5 Shred the lamb into a bowl. Add the Parmesan, crème fraîche and Fines Herbes and stir to combine. Set aside.

6 Combine the egg and water in a small bowl and whisk to blend well. Set aside.

7 Place the bric pastry on a clean, flat surface. Place an equal portion of the lamb filling in the center of each piece of pastry. Using a pastry brush, lightly coat the edge of each pastry piece with the egg wash. Pull the edges up and over so that the pastry tightly encloses the filling. Place on a nonstick baking sheet, sealed side down. Cover with plastic wrap and refrigerate until ready to fry.

8 When ready to serve, heat the vegetable oil in a deep-fat fryer over medium-high heat to 365°F. Remove the brics from the refrigerator and place them into the hot fat and fry, carefully turning from time to time, for about 6 minutes or until crisp and golden. Transfer to a double layer of paper towel to drain. (If necessary, reheat in a preheated 350°F oven for 5 minutes.)

Prosciutto-Wrapped
Pork Loin with
Summer Truffle
Pan Sauce

SERVES 6 **3 pork tenderloins, trimmed of all fat and silverskin ▪ 1 medium summer truffle, scrubbed and thinly sliced plus an additional truffle, thinly sliced for garnish ▪ 16 slices prosciutto ▪ 3 tablespoons canola oil ▪ ¼ cup clarified butter ▪ 24 fingerling potato wedges, blanched in vegetable oil ▪ Coarse salt and freshly ground pepper ▪ Sautéed Wild Asparagus, Bluefoot Mushrooms, and Pearl Onions ▪ Chive Maximes**

1 Using a sharp knife, cut each tenderloin in half, crosswise; then, fit the 2 halves together with the tail end against the fattest part of the loin to make 3 even pieces. Fit an equal portion of the truffle slices into the seam where the 2 halves fit together. Tightly wrap prosciutto slices around each piece of tenderloin to cover. Wrap in plastic wrap and refrigerate for at least an hour.

2 When ready to serve, preheat the oven to 375°F.

3 Remove the tenderloins from the refrigerator and unwrap. Heat the oil in a large ovenproof sauté pan over medium-high heat. Place the tenderloins into the hot pan and sear, turning frequently, for about 4 minutes or until evenly colored all around. Transfer the pan to the preheated oven and roast for about 12 minutes or until an instant-read thermometer inserted into the thickest part reads 150°F. Remove from the oven and allow to rest for 5 minutes.

4 While the pork is roasting, heat the clarified butter in a medium sauté pan over medium-high heat. Add the fingerling potatoes and fry for about 6 minutes or until golden brown and crisp. Using a slotted spoon, lift the potatoes from the pan and place on a double layer of paper towel to drain. Season with salt and pepper.

5 Using a sharp knife, cut the tenderloins into 12 equal portions. Make a circle of the asparagus-onion mixture in the center of each of 6 dinner plates. Lay 2 slices of pork on top. Place 4 fingerling potato wedges around the pork. Rest 2 Chive Maximes in the meat, scatter a few slices of summer truffle around the edge, and serve.

164

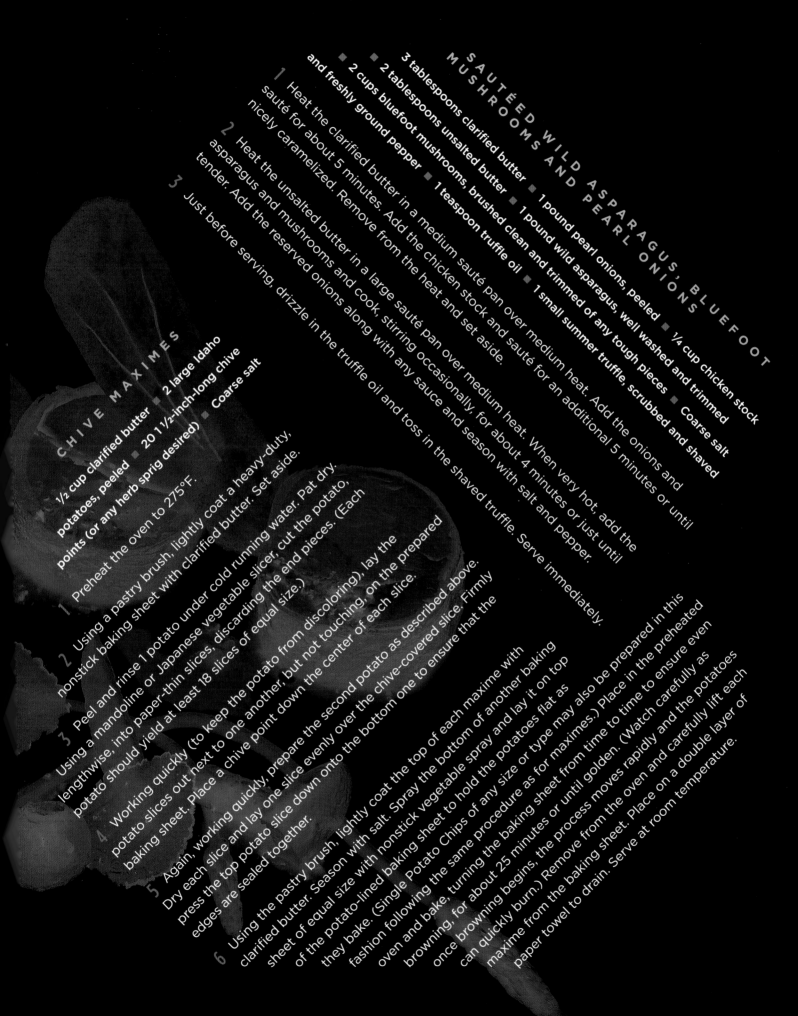

SAUTÉED WILD ASPARAGUS, BLUEFOOT MUSHROOMS AND PEARL ONIONS

- **3 tablespoons clarified butter** ▪ **1 pound pearl onions, peeled** ▪ **¼ cup chicken stock**
- **2 tablespoons unsalted butter** ▪ **1 pound wild asparagus, well washed and trimmed**
- **2 cups bluefoot mushrooms, brushed clean and trimmed of any tough pieces** ▪ **Coarse salt and freshly ground pepper** ▪ **1 teaspoon truffle oil** ▪ **1 small summer truffle, scrubbed and shaved**

1 Heat the clarified butter in a medium sauté pan over medium heat. Add the onions and sauté for about 5 minutes. Add the chicken stock and sauté for an additional 5 minutes or until nicely caramelized. Remove from the heat and set aside.

2 Heat the unsalted butter in a large sauté pan over medium heat. When very hot, add the asparagus and mushrooms and cook, stirring occasionally, for about 4 minutes or just until tender. Add the reserved onions along with any sauce and season with salt and pepper.

3 Just before serving, drizzle in the truffle oil and toss in the shaved truffle. Serve immediately.

CHIVE MAXIMES

½ cup clarified butter ▪ **2 large Idaho potatoes, peeled** ▪ **20 1½-inch-long chive points (or any herb sprig desired)** ▪ **Coarse salt**

1 Preheat the oven to 275°F.

2 Using a pastry brush, lightly coat a heavy-duty, nonstick baking sheet with clarified butter. Set aside.

3 Peel and rinse 1 potato under cold running water. Pat dry. Using a mandoline or Japanese vegetable slicer, cut the potato, lengthwise, into paper-thin slices, discarding the end pieces. (Each potato should yield at least 18 slices of equal size.)

4 Working quickly (to keep the potato from discoloring), lay the potato slices out next to one another, but not touching, on the prepared baking sheet. Place a chive point down the center of each slice.

5 Again, working quickly, prepare the second potato as described above. Dry each slice and lay one slice evenly over the chive-covered slice. Firmly press the top potato slice down onto the bottom one to ensure that the edges are sealed together.

6 Using the pastry brush, lightly coat the top of each maxime with clarified butter. Season with salt. Spray the bottom of another baking sheet of equal size with nonstick vegetable spray and lay it on top of the potato-lined baking sheet to hold the potatoes flat as they bake. (Single Potato Chips of any size or type may also be prepared in this fashion following the same procedure as for maximes.) Place in the preheated oven and bake, turning the baking sheet from time to time to ensure even browning, for about 25 minutes or until golden. (Watch carefully as once browning begins, the process moves rapidly and the potatoes can quickly burn.) Remove from the oven and carefully lift each maxime from the baking sheet. Place on a double layer of paper towel to drain. Serve at room temperature.

Rabbit
Four
Ways

Prepare the Crisp Rabbit Flank, the Braised Rabbit Leg, the Confit Rack of Rabbit and the Rabbit Loin Sauté and place each one, along with its garnish, in a separate section on each of 6 large dinner plates. Garnish the plates with sprigs of lavender (or other edible flowers or herbs) and serve. (Please note that each component can also be served separately.)

CRISP RABBIT FLANK

6 rabbit flanks ■ Coarse salt and freshly ground pepper ■ ¼ cup canola oil ■ 4 cups dark chicken stock ■ 1 large egg ■ 1½ cups all-purpose flour ■ 1½ cups bread crumbs ■ 3 endives, well washed, trimmed and cut, lengthwise, into quarters ■ 1 cup Citrus Vinaigrette (see page 235) ■ 1 teaspoon sugar ■ 2 ripe but firm apricots, well washed and cut, lengthwise, into thin slices ■ 1½ cups frisée, well washed and dried ■ ½ cup endive julienne ■ 1 cup Red Wine Vinaigrette (see page 236)

1 Season the flanks with salt and pepper. Heat 1 tablespoon of the oil in a heavy braising pan over medium heat. Add the seasoned flanks and sear, turning occasionally, for about 4 minutes or until nicely colored. Remove the flanks from the pan and drain off all oil.

2 Return the flanks to the pan along with the stock. Place over medium-high heat and bring to a simmer. Cover, lower the heat and simmer for about 30 minutes or until the meat is fork-tender. Remove from the heat and allow to come to room temperature in the cooking liquid. When cool, lift the flanks from the liquid and trim off the edges to make rather abstract triangles.

3 Place the egg in a small bowl and whisk to blend. Place the flour on a plate, season with salt and pepper and place next to the egg. Place the bread crumbs on another plate and place it next to the flour.

4 One at a time, dip the flank pieces into the egg, then the seasoned flour and finally the bread crumbs to lightly coat. Place on a clean plate, cover with plastic wrap and place in the refrigerator for at least 30 minutes or up to 6 hours to chill and firm up.

5 Place the endives, Citrus Vinaigrette and sugar in a medium sauté pan over medium heat. Bring to a simmer, then cover and braise for about 15 minutes or until very tender. Remove from the heat and allow to cool.

6 Heat the remaining 3 tablespoons of oil in a large sauté pan over medium-high heat. Remove the breaded flanks from the refrigerator, uncover and place in the hot pan. Fry, turning occasionally, for about 10 minutes or until the flanks are golden. Remove from the heat and drain on a double layer of paper towels.

7 Combine the reserved braised endive with the apricots, frisée and endive julienne. Add just enough Red Wine Vinaigrette to lightly coat and toss to combine. Mound equal portions of the salad on each of 6 plates. Place a breaded flank on top, drizzle a bit of the remaining Red Wine Vinaigrette over the top and serve.

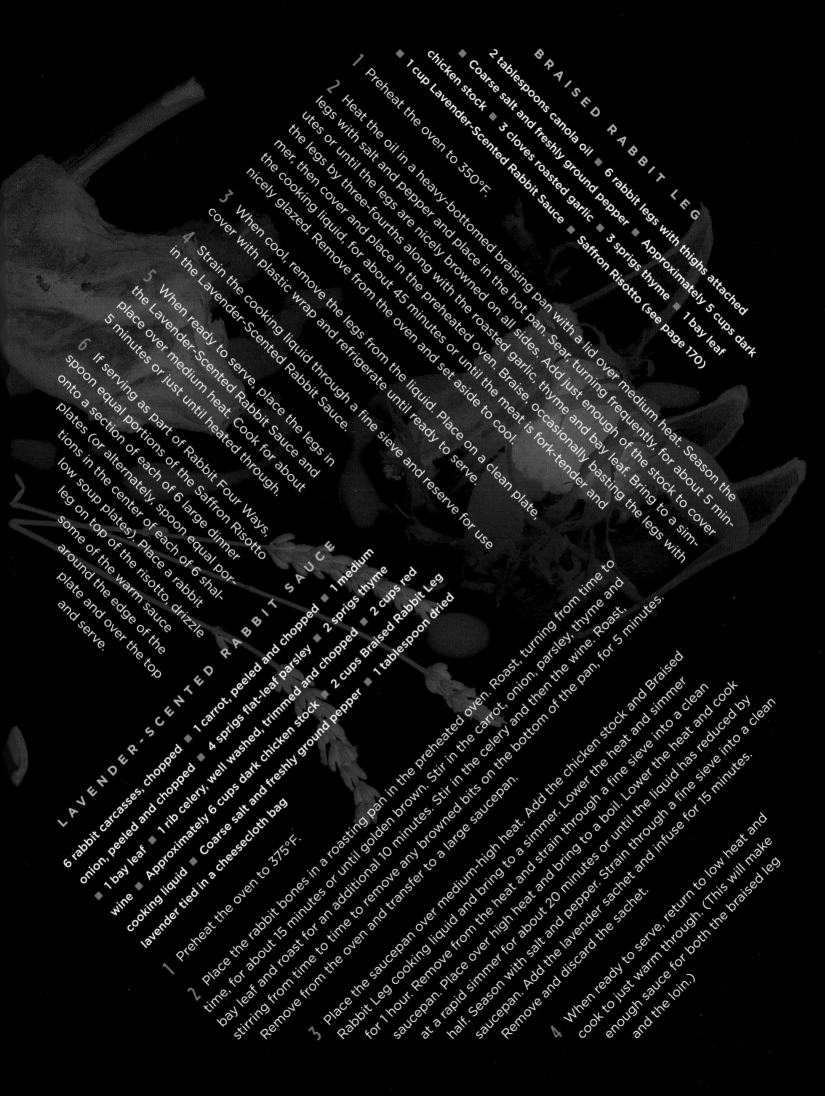

BRAISED RABBIT LEG

- 2 tablespoons canola oil
- 6 rabbit legs with thighs attached
- Coarse salt and freshly ground pepper
- 3 cloves roasted garlic
- 3 sprigs thyme
- Approximately 5 cups dark chicken stock
- 1 cup Lavender-Scented Rabbit Sauce
- Saffron Risotto (see page 170)
- 1 bay leaf

1 Preheat the oven to 350°F.

2 Heat the oil in a heavy-bottomed braising pan with a lid over medium heat. Season the legs with salt and pepper and place in the hot pan. Sear, turning frequently, for about 5 minutes or until the legs are nicely browned on all sides. Add just enough of the stock to cover the legs by three-fourths along with the roasted garlic, thyme and bay leaf. Bring to a simmer, then cover and place in the preheated oven. Braise, occasionally basting the legs with the cooking liquid, for about 45 minutes or until the meat is fork-tender and nicely glazed. Remove from the oven and set aside to cool. Place on a clean plate,

3 When cool, remove the legs from the liquid. Place on a clean plate, cover with plastic wrap and refrigerate until ready to serve.

4 Strain the cooking liquid through a fine sieve and reserve for use in the Lavender-Scented Rabbit Sauce.

5 When ready to serve, place the legs in the Lavender-Scented Rabbit Sauce and place over medium heat. Cook for about 5 minutes or just until heated through.

6 If serving as part of Rabbit Four Ways, spoon equal portions of the Saffron Risotto onto a section of each of 6 large dinner plates (or alternately, spoon equal portions in the center of each of 6 shallow soup plates). Place a rabbit leg on top of the risotto, drizzle some of the warm sauce around the edge of the plate and over the top and serve.

LAVENDER-SCENTED RABBIT SAUCE

- 6 rabbit carcasses, chopped
- 1 carrot, peeled and chopped
- 1 medium onion, peeled and chopped
- 4 sprigs flat-leaf parsley
- 2 sprigs thyme
- 1 bay leaf
- 1 rib celery, well washed, trimmed and chopped
- 2 cups red wine
- Approximately 6 cups dark chicken stock
- 2 cups Braised Rabbit Leg cooking liquid
- Coarse salt and freshly ground pepper
- 1 tablespoon dried lavender tied in a cheesecloth bag

1 Preheat the oven to 375°F.

2 Place the rabbit bones in a roasting pan in the preheated oven. Roast, turning from time to time, for about 15 minutes or until golden brown. Stir in the carrot, onion, parsley, thyme and bay leaf and roast for an additional 10 minutes. Stir in the celery and then the wine. Roast, stirring from time to time to remove any browned bits on the bottom of the pan, for 5 minutes. Remove from the oven and transfer to a large saucepan.

3 Place the saucepan over medium-high heat. Add the chicken stock and Braised Rabbit Leg cooking liquid and bring to a simmer. Lower the heat and simmer for 1 hour. Remove from the heat and strain through a fine sieve into a clean saucepan. Place over high heat and bring to a boil. Lower the heat and cook at a rapid simmer for about 20 minutes or until the liquid has reduced by half. Season with salt and pepper. Strain through a fine sieve into a clean saucepan. Add the lavender sachet and infuse for 15 minutes. Remove and discard the sachet.

4 When ready to serve, return to low heat and cook to just warm through. (This will make enough sauce for both the braised leg and the loin.)

SAFFRON RISOTTO

1½ cups white wine ▪ ¼ teaspoon saffron threads ▪ 6 cups chicken stock ▪ 3 tablespoons unsalted butter ▪ 1 medium onion, peeled and finely diced ▪ ¾ cup Arborio rice ▪ Coarse salt and freshly ground pepper

1 Place the wine in a small saucepan over low heat. Cook for about 3 minutes or just until warm.

2 Place the saffron in a small nonstick pan over low heat. Toast, stirring frequently, for about 2 minutes or until very aromatic and slightly colored. Remove from the heat and transfer to the wine. Set aside to steep for 1 hour.

3 Place the stock in a saucepan over medium heat and bring to a simmer. Lower the heat and keep at a bare simmer.

4 Heat the butter in a heavy-bottomed saucepan over medium-low heat. Add the onion and cook, stirring frequently, for about 4 minutes or until the onion is soft but has not taken on any color. Stir in the rice and cook, stirring frequently, for about 5 minutes or until the rice is glistening and has deepened in color to become almost chalky-looking. Stir in the wine and cook, stirring constantly, for about 10 minutes or until the liquid has been absorbed.

5 Ladle in 1 cup of the hot stock and cook, stirring constantly, for about 7 minutes or until the liquid has been absorbed. Continue adding the hot stock, 1 cup at a time, and stirring until the rice is creamy and tender yet still al dente. Remove from the heat and season with salt and pepper. Serve hot. (If desired, half of the liquid may be used and then the risotto spread out on a baking sheet and stored, covered and refrigerated, for up to 2 days. When ready to serve, remove from the baking sheet and return to a saucepan. Reheat the remaining stock and finish cooking).

CONFIT RACK OF RABBIT

6 racks of rabbit ▪ 6 sprigs thyme ▪ 6 sprigs flat-leaf parsley ▪ 2 sprigs rosemary ▪ 1 teaspoon black peppercorns ▪ Approximately 4 cups duck fat ▪ Grilled Marinated Onions (see page 171)

1 Preheat the oven to 300°F.

2 Place the racks, thyme, parsley, rosemary and peppercorns in a large, heavy-bottomed pan with a lid. Add enough duck fat to cover the racks and place over medium heat. Bring to a simmer, then cover and transfer to the preheated oven and braise for about 1½ hours or until fork-tender. Remove from the oven and allow the racks to cool in the fat. Do not discard the fat.

3 When cool, using a boning knife, carefully cut the meat from the rack bones to french the bones.

4 When ready to serve, return the racks to the fat and reheat over medium heat. For the Rabbit Four Ways presentation, place 1 rack onto its section of each of 6 large dinner plates. Garnish with Grilled Marinated Onions scattered over the rack.

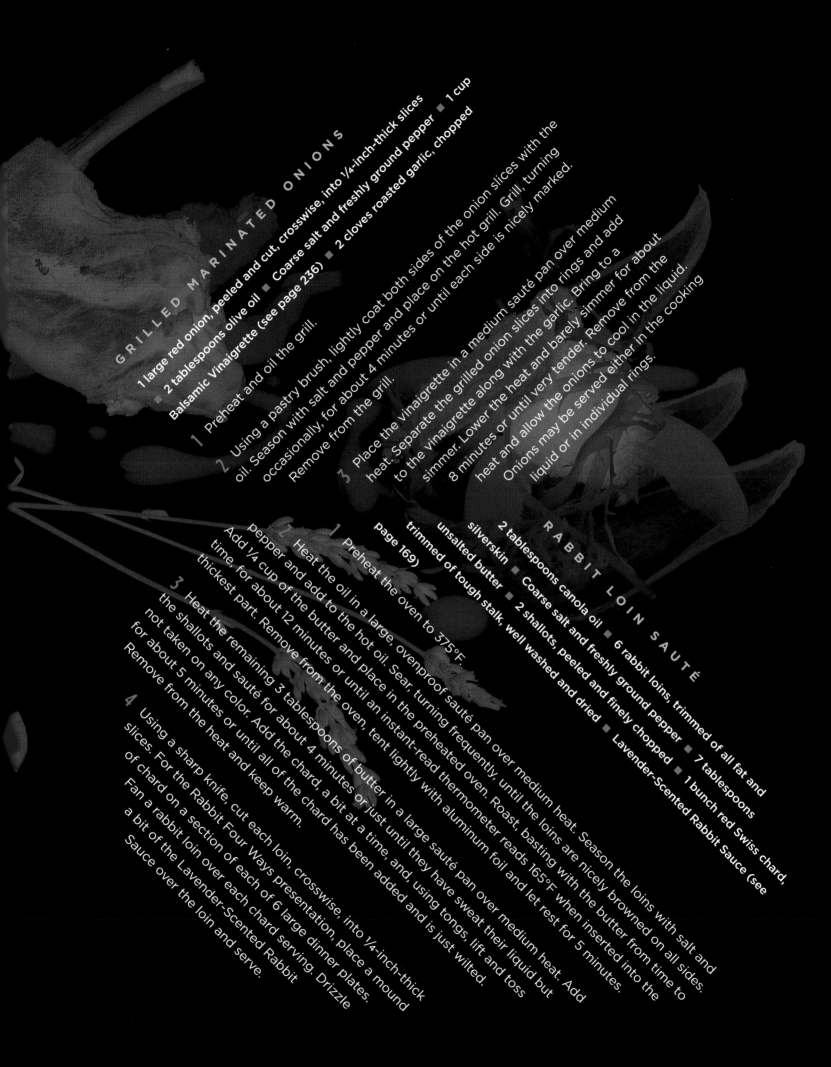

GRILLED MARINATED ONIONS

- 1 large red onion, peeled and cut, crosswise, into ¼-inch-thick slices
- 2 tablespoons olive oil
- Coarse salt and freshly ground pepper
- 1 cup Balsamic Vinaigrette (see page 236)
- 2 cloves roasted garlic, chopped

1 Preheat and oil the grill.

2 Using a pastry brush, lightly coat both sides of the onion slices with the oil. Season with salt and pepper and place on the hot grill. Grill, turning occasionally, for about 4 minutes or until each side is nicely marked. Remove from the grill.

3 Place the vinaigrette in a medium sauté pan over medium heat. Separate the grilled onion slices into rings and add to the vinaigrette along with the garlic. Bring to a simmer. Lower the heat and barely simmer for about 8 minutes or until very tender. Remove from the heat and allow the onions to cool in the liquid. Onions may be served either in the cooking liquid or in individual rings.

RABBIT LOIN SAUTÉ

- 2 tablespoons canola oil
- 6 rabbit loins, trimmed of all fat and silverskin
- Coarse salt and freshly ground pepper
- 7 tablespoons unsalted butter
- 2 shallots, peeled and finely chopped
- Lavender-Scented Rabbit Sauce (see page 169)
- 1 bunch red Swiss chard, trimmed of tough stalk, well washed and dried

1 Preheat the oven to 375°F.

2 Heat the oil in a large, ovenproof sauté pan over medium heat. Season the loins with salt and pepper and add to the hot oil. Sear, turning frequently, until the loins are nicely browned on all sides. Add ¼ cup of the butter and place in the preheated oven. Roast, basting with the butter from time to time, for about 12 minutes or until an instant-read thermometer reads 165°F when inserted into the thickest part. Remove from the oven, tent lightly with aluminum foil and let rest for 5 minutes.

3 Heat the remaining 3 tablespoons of butter in a large sauté pan over medium heat. Add the shallots and sauté for about 4 minutes or just until they have sweat their liquid but not taken on any color. Add the chard, a bit at a time, and, using tongs, lift and toss for about 5 minutes or until all of the chard has been added and is just wilted. Remove from the heat and keep warm.

4 Using a sharp knife, cut each loin, crosswise, into ¼-inch-thick slices. For the Rabbit Four Ways presentation, place a mound of chard on a section of each of 6 large dinner plates. Fan a rabbit loin over each chard serving. Drizzle a bit of the Lavender-Scented Rabbit Sauce over the loin and serve.

Venison Loin
with Chestnut-Brioche
Charlotte and Cranberry–
Red Currant Coulis

SERVES 6 2 tablespoons canola oil ■ 2 ¼ pounds venison loin, trimmed of all fat and silverskin ■ Coarse salt and freshly ground pepper ■ ½ cup unsalted butter ■ 1 tablespoon minced shallots ■ 2 teaspoons Fines Herbes (see page 235) ■ 18 cooked fresh chestnuts ■ Chestnut-Brioche Charlottes ■ Cranberry–Red Currant Coulis ■ Fleur de sel ■ Venison Sauce ■ 1 cup fresh red currants, well washed and dried ■ 1 cup micro-greens

1 Preheat the oven to 400°F.

2 Heat the oil in an oven-proof sauté pan over high heat. Season the venison with salt and pepper and place it in the hot pan. Sear, turning occasionally, until all sides are nicely browned. Transfer to the preheated oven. Add ¼ cup of the butter along with the shallots and Fines Herbes and roast, basting frequently with the melted butter mixture, for about 15 minutes or until an instant-read thermometer reads 150°F when inserted into the thickest part. Remove from the oven and allow to rest for 5 minutes.

3 While the venison is roasting, prepare the chestnuts. Heat the remaining ¼ cup of butter in a small sauté pan over medium heat. Add the chestnuts and sauté for about 5 minutes or until the butter is very aromatic and light brown and the chestnuts are golden. Season with salt and pepper. Remove from the heat and, using a slotted spoon, lift the chestnuts from the butter to a double layer of paper towels to drain.

4 Place a warm Chestnut-Brioche Charlotte in the center of each of 6 dinner plates. Slice the venison, crosswise, into ¼-inch-thick slices. Fan equal portions of the venison around the charlotte on each plate. Spoon Cranberry–Red Currant Coulis around the venison and arrange 3 chestnuts on the venison. Drizzle Venison Sauce around the edge of the plate, garnish with fresh currants and micro-greens and serve.

VENISON SAUCE ■ 2 pounds venison bones, cracked ■ 1 carrot, peeled and chopped ■ 1 onion, peeled and chopped ■ 1 rib celery, well washed, trimmed and chopped ■ ½ cup red wine ■ 6 cups dark chicken stock ■ One 4-inch cinnamon stick ■ 1 tablespoon freshly grated orange zest ■ 1 teaspoon juniper berries ■ 1 teaspoon black peppercorns ■ ½ teaspoon whole cloves ■ Coarse salt and freshly ground pepper

1 Preheat the oven to 375°F.

2 Place the bones in a roasting pan in the preheated oven and roast, turning occasionally, for about 15 minutes or until nicely browned. Stir in the carrot, onion and celery and roast for an additional 10 minutes. Add the wine and, using a wooden spoon, scrape the bottom of the pan to loosen any browned bits. Roast for another 5 minutes. Remove from the oven and transfer to a large saucepan.

3 Add the chicken stock and bring to a boil over medium-high heat. Lower the heat and simmer for 40 minutes. Remove from the heat and strain through a fine sieve into a clean saucepan, discarding the solids.

4 Add the cinnamon stick, orange zest, juniper berries, peppercorn and cloves and bring to a simmer over medium heat. Cook at a low simmer for about 20 minutes or until reduced by half and of a saucelike consistency. Strain through a fine sieve into a clean saucepan. Taste and, if necessary, season with salt and pepper. Reheat to serve hot. (Sauce may be made up to 2 days in advance of use and stored, covered and refrigerated. Reheat before serving.)

CHESTNUT-BRIOCHE CHARLOTTE

- 5 tablespoons unsalted butter ◆ 1 cup diced cooked chestnuts ◆ 1 cup diced porcini mushrooms ◆ 1 small onion, peeled and finely diced ◆ 1 rib celery, well washed, trimmed and finely diced ◆ 4 large eggs ◆ 2 cups heavy cream ◆ Coarse salt and freshly ground pepper ◆ 1 large brioche loaf, trimmed of crust and cut into pieces about ¼ inch thick and 3 inches long (or of a size to neatly fit the insides of a small charlotte mold) ◆ 2 teaspoons Fines Herbes (see page 235)

1 Preheat the oven to 300°F.

2 Heat 3 tablespoons of the butter in a medium sauté pan over medium-low heat and cook for about 4 minutes or until very aromatic and beginning to color. Add the chestnuts and sauté for about 3 minutes or until just beginning to take on some color. Stir in the mushrooms, celery and onion and sauté for about 5 minutes or until tender. Remove from the heat. Season with salt and pepper and set aside to cool.

3 Using the remaining 2 tablespoons of butter, lightly coat 6 small charlotte molds. Cut 6 circles of parchment paper to fit smoothly into the bottom of each mold. Fit one in the bottom of each mold and set aside.

4 Combine the eggs and cream in a bowl and whisk to blend. Working with one piece at a time, dip the brioche into the egg-cream mixture and then fit the brioche into the charlotte molds to completely line the inside of each mold. Ladle a small amount of the egg-cream mixture into each mold and let it soak in. Continue adding the egg-cream mixture to each mold until the liquid is floating on top and can no longer be absorbed into the filling.

5 Mix the Fines Herbes into the chestnut mixture. When well combined, fill the center of each mold with the chestnut mixture. Ladle a small amount of the egg-cream mixture to reach three-fourths of the way up the outside of the molds. Cover and place in the preheated oven and bake for about 20 minutes or until the custard has set. Remove from the oven and placing in a preheated 350°F oven for about 10 minutes or in a microwave for about 1 minute, until the point of a sharp knife inserted into the center comes out hot.) Do not unmold until ready to serve.

6 Place the filled molds in a roasting pan large enough to hold them with at least 1 inch between each mold. Add water to the roasting pan to reach three-fourths of the way up the outside of the molds. Cover and place in the preheated oven and bake for about 5 minutes before turning and reheated just before serving by covering and placing day and reheated just before serving. (The charlottes can be made early in the

7 When ready to serve, preheat the broiler. Place the warm, unmolded charlottes under the broiler and broil for about 2 minutes or until the tops are slightly crisp and golden. Watch carefully so that they do not begin to burn. Serve hot.

CRANBERRY-RED CURRANT COULIS

- 8 ounces fresh cranberries ◆ 1 cup fresh red currants ◆ 1 thin-skinned, seedless orange, well washed and quartered ◆ ¼ cup sugar ◆ Coarse salt ◆ Freshly ground pepper

1 Combine the cranberries and currants with the orange, sugar and pinch of salt in a medium nonstick saucepan over medium-high heat. Bring to a boil, then lower the heat and simmer for about 7 minutes or until the cranberries have popped and are tender. Remove from the heat and allow to cool.

2 Remove the orange from the cranberry mixture. Place the cranberry mixture in a food processor fitted with the metal blade and process until smooth.

3 Transfer to a small saucepan and season lightly with freshly ground pepper. Place over medium heat to warm just before serving. (May also be served at room temperature.)

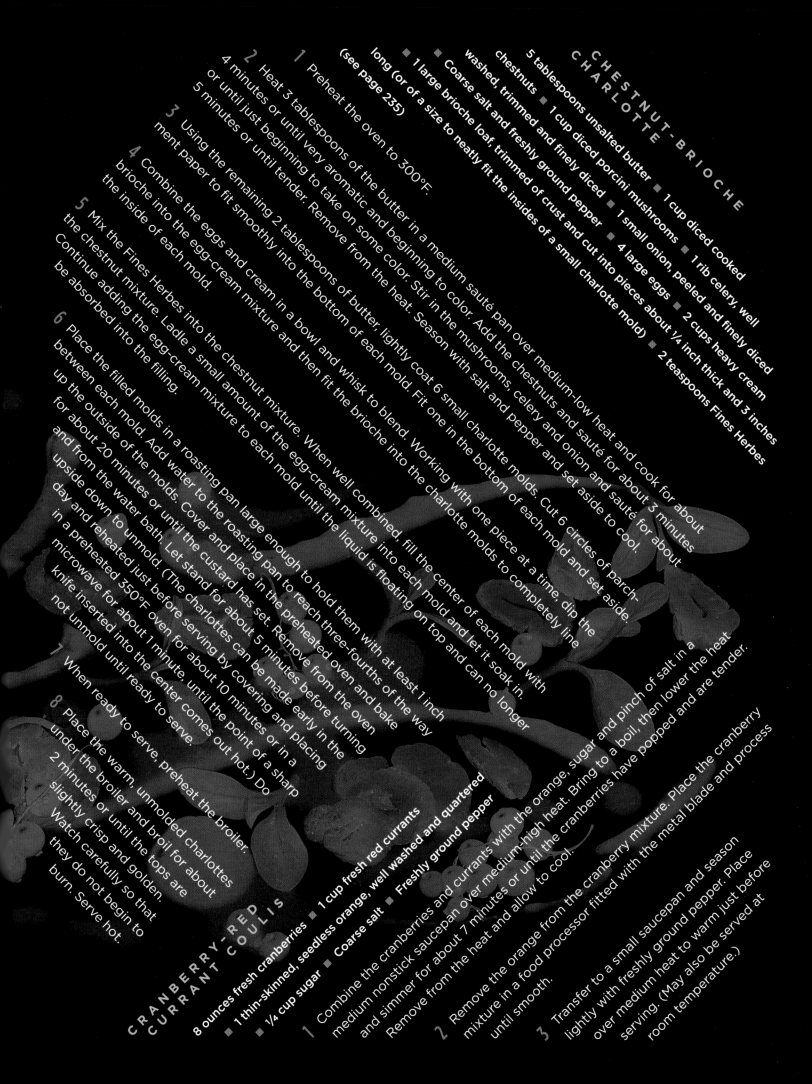

THE ART OF AUREOLE

FISH & SHELLFISH

Striped Bass
with Thyme-Roasted Tomatoes and Garlic-Scented Mussels

SERVES 6 **5 tablespoons olive oil** ■ **2 pounds striped bass fillet** ■ **1 lemon** ■ **2 cups olive oil** ■ **1 cup flat-leaf parsley chiffonade** ■ **1 cup chopped chervil leaves** ■ **½ cup roughly chopped tarragon leaves** ■ **¼ cup chopped chives** ■ **Fleur de sel** ■ **Thyme-Roasted Tomatoes** ■ **Garlic-Scented Mussels** ■ **Freshly cracked black pepper** ■ **1 cup micro-greens**

1 Chill 6 heatproof dinner plates.

2 Cut 6 pieces of parchment paper into large enough sheets to cover the chilled plates. Using a pastry brush and 1 tablespoon of the olive oil, lightly coat one side of the parchment paper with oil. Set aside.

3 Using a chef's knife, cut the bass, on a slight bias, into ⅛-inch-thick slices. Place an equal portion of the bass slices, slightly overlapping, in a circle about 1½ inches from the edge of each chilled plate.

4 Place a piece of the reserved parchment, oiled side down, over each plate to cover the fish. Refrigerate until ready to serve.

5 Make a small bowl of ice water. Set aside.

6 Using a vegetable peeler, zest the lemon, lengthwise, into long strips. Cut the strips into a fine julienne. Place the lemon julienne in a small saucepan with cold water to cover over high heat. Bring to a boil; then, drain and refresh in the ice-water bath. Remove from the ice-water bath, pat dry and set aside.

7 Juice the zested lemon into a small bowl and set the juice aside.

8 Combine the remaining ¼ cup of olive oil with the parsley, chervil, tarragon and chives as well as the reserved lemon zest in a medium mixing bowl. Season with fleur de sel and whisk to blend. Set aside.

9 Preheat the broiler.

10 Remove the fish plates from the refrigerator. Remove and discard the parchment paper. Using a clean pastry brush, lightly coat the fish with the reserved lemon juice.

11 Working with one plate at a time, place the plate under the broiler for about 1 minute or just long enough for the fish to become opaque and cook very slightly. Remove from the broiler and continue cooking the remaining fish.

12 Place an equal portion of the tomatoes over the fish on each plate. Place an equal portion of the mussels around the fish. Spoon the reserved herb oil over the fish and around the edge of each plate. Grind some pepper over the plate and season the fish with fleur de sel. Randomly sprinkle some micro-greens over each plate and serve immediately.

GARLIC-SCENTED MUSSELS

1 tablespoon olive oil ■ 1 clove garlic, peeled and
minced ■ 30 small mussels, beards removed and
scrubbed clean ■ 2 tablespoons white wine
■ 1/4 cup chicken stock ■ 1 tablespoon unsalted
butter ■ Coarse salt and freshly ground pepper

Heat the oil in a large shallow pan over medium
heat. Add the garlic and cook, stirring frequently, for about 4 minutes or until the garlic
is golden. Add the mussels and then the wine.
Raise the heat and boil for about 3 minutes or
until the wine has almost evaporated. Add the
chicken stock and butter and stir to blend.
Cook for a couple of minutes or until the sauce
has thickened slightly and the mussels have
opened. Remove from the heat and season
with salt and pepper. Serve hot.

THYME-ROASTED TOMATOES

30 small cherry tomatoes, blanched and peeled
■ 2 tablespoons thyme leaves ■ 1 tablespoon
olive oil ■ Coarse salt and freshly ground pepper

1 Preheat the oven to 200°F.

2 Combine the tomatoes with the thyme and
olive oil. Season lightly with salt and pepper.
Toss to evenly distribute the thyme and seasoning. Place the seasoned tomatoes in a
single layer in a nonstick baking pan and bake
for about 2 hours or until the tomatoes are
slightly dry but retain a bit of their moisture.
Remove from the oven and let stand at room
temperature until ready to serve.

Halibut Cheeks
with Beluga Lentils and Sorrel Purée

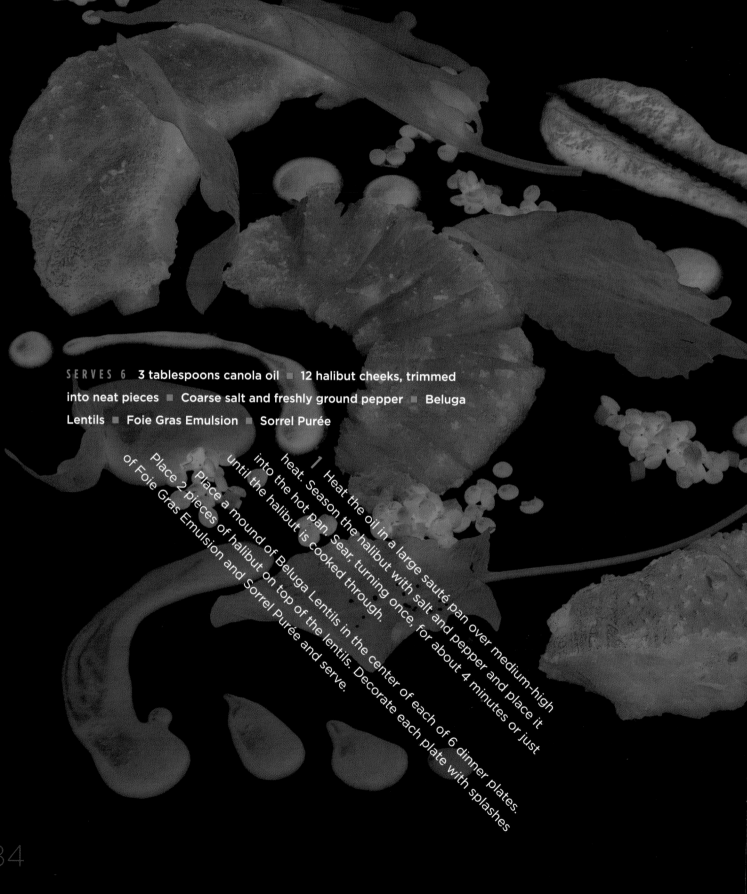

SERVES 6   **3 tablespoons canola oil** ■ **12 halibut cheeks, trimmed into neat pieces** ■ **Coarse salt and freshly ground pepper** ■ **Beluga Lentils** ■ **Foie Gras Emulsion** ■ **Sorrel Purée**

1 Heat the oil in a large sauté pan over medium-high heat. Season the halibut with salt and pepper and place it into the hot pan. Sear, turning once, for about 4 minutes or just until the halibut is cooked through. Place a mound of Beluga Lentils in the center of each of 6 dinner plates. Place 2 pieces of halibut on top of the lentils. Decorate each plate with splashes of Foie Gras Emulsion and Sorrel Purée and serve.

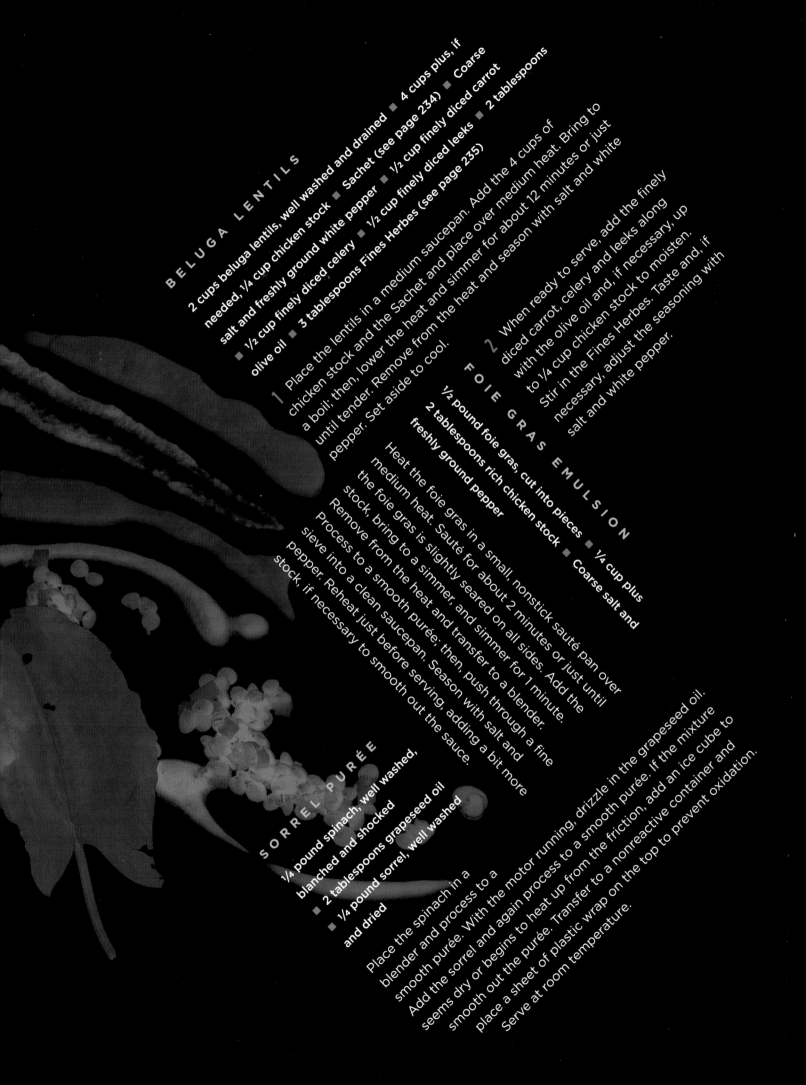

BELUGA LENTILS

2 cups beluga lentils, well washed and drained ■ 4 cups plus, if needed, ¼ cup chicken stock ■ Sachet (see page 234) ■ Coarse salt and freshly ground white pepper ■ ½ cup finely diced carrot ■ ½ cup finely diced celery ■ ½ cup finely diced leeks ■ 2 tablespoons olive oil ■ 3 tablespoons Fines Herbes (see page 235)

1 Place the lentils in a medium saucepan. Add the 4 cups of chicken stock and the Sachet and place over medium heat. Bring to a boil; then, lower the heat and simmer for about 12 minutes or just until tender. Remove from the heat and season with salt and white pepper. Set aside to cool.

2 When ready to serve, add the finely diced carrot, celery and leeks along with the olive oil and, if necessary, up to ¼ cup chicken stock to moisten. Stir in the Fines Herbes. Taste and, if necessary, adjust the seasoning with salt and white pepper.

FOIE GRAS EMULSION

½ pound foie gras, cut into pieces ■ ¼ cup plus 2 tablespoons rich chicken stock ■ Coarse salt and freshly ground pepper

Heat the foie gras in a small, nonstick sauté pan over medium heat. Sauté for about 2 minutes or just until the foie gras is slightly seared on all sides. Add the stock, bring to a simmer, and simmer for 1 minute. Remove from the heat and transfer to a blender. Process to a smooth purée; then, push through a fine sieve into a clean saucepan. Season with salt and pepper. Reheat just before serving, adding a bit more stock, if necessary to smooth out the sauce.

SORREL PURÉE

¼ pound spinach, well washed, blanched and shocked ■ 2 tablespoons grapeseed oil ■ ¼ pound sorrel, well washed and dried

Place the spinach in a blender and process to a smooth purée. With the motor running, drizzle in the grapeseed oil. Add the sorrel and again process to a smooth purée. If the mixture seems dry or begins to heat up from the friction, add an ice cube to smooth out the purée. Transfer to a nonreactive container and place a sheet of plastic wrap on the top to prevent oxidation. Serve at room temperature.

Sautéed Skate
with Crab-Stuffed
Zucchini Blossoms

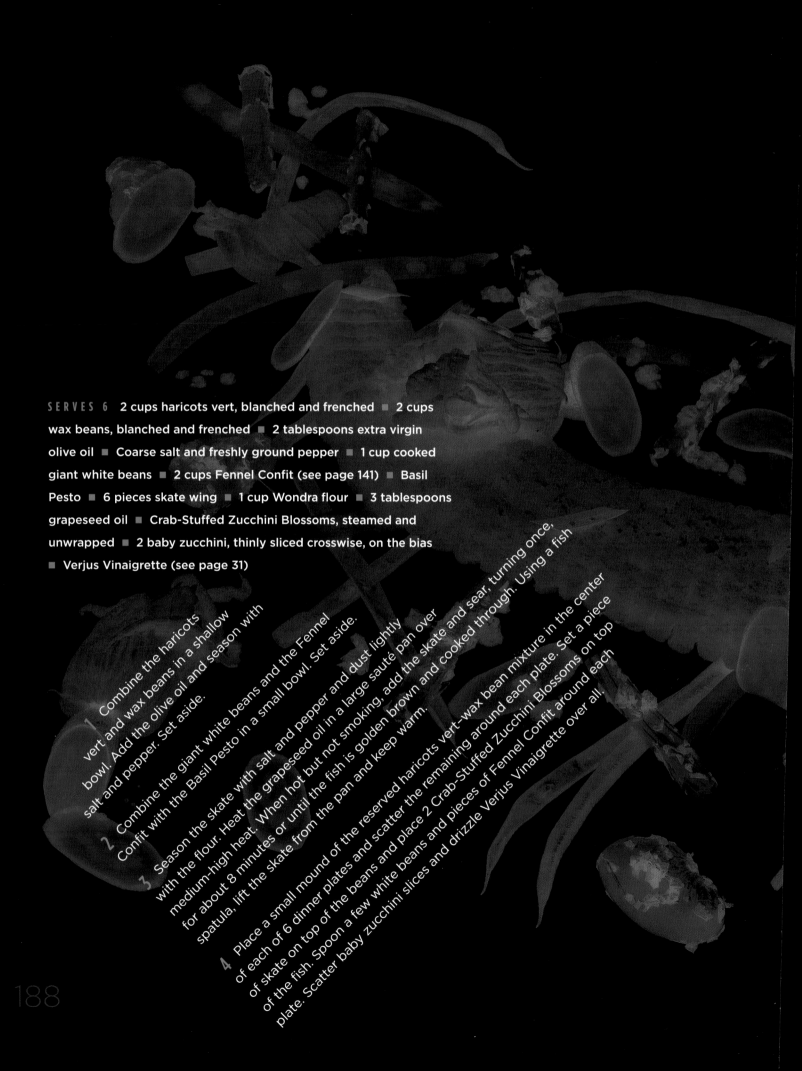

SERVES 6 2 cups haricots vert, blanched and frenched ■ 2 cups wax beans, blanched and frenched ■ 2 tablespoons extra virgin olive oil ■ Coarse salt and freshly ground pepper ■ 1 cup cooked giant white beans ■ 2 cups Fennel Confit (see page 141) ■ Basil Pesto ■ 6 pieces skate wing ■ 1 cup Wondra flour ■ 3 tablespoons grapeseed oil ■ Crab-Stuffed Zucchini Blossoms, steamed and unwrapped ■ 2 baby zucchini, thinly sliced crosswise, on the bias ■ Verjus Vinaigrette (see page 31)

1. Combine the haricots vert and wax beans in a shallow bowl. Add the olive oil and season with salt and pepper. Set aside.

2. Combine the giant white beans and the Fennel Confit with the Basil Pesto in a small bowl. Set aside.

3. Season the skate with salt and pepper and dust lightly with the flour. Heat the grapeseed oil in a large sauté pan over medium-high heat. When hot but not smoking, add the skate and sear, turning once, for about 8 minutes or until the fish is golden brown and cooked through. Using a fish spatula, lift the skate from the pan and keep warm.

4. Place a small mound of the reserved haricots vert-wax bean mixture in the center of each of 6 dinner plates and scatter the remaining around each plate. Set a piece of skate on top of the beans and place 2 Crab-Stuffed Zucchini Blossoms on top of the fish. Spoon a few white beans and pieces of Fennel Confit around each plate. Scatter baby zucchini slices and drizzle Verjus Vinaigrette over all.

CRAB-STUFFED ZUCCHINI BLOSSOMS

¾ pound peekytoe crabmeat, picked clean ■ **¼ cup olive oil plus more to coat plastic wrap** ■ **3 tablespoons minced chives** ■ **1 tablespoon minced shallots** ■ **1 teaspoon freshly grated lemon zest** ■ **Coarse salt and freshly ground pepper** ■ **12 zucchini blossoms with beginning squash forming**

1 Place the crab in a mixing bowl. Add the olive oil, chives, shallots and lemon zest and stir to combine. Taste and season with salt and pepper. Place in a pastry bag fitted with a medium tip.

2 Cut 6 pieces of plastic wrap about 8 square inches each. Using a pastry brush, lightly coat each piece of plastic wrap with olive oil.

3 Pipe the crab stuffing into each zucchini blossom. Place 2 stuffed blossoms on each piece of plastic wrap and loosely wrap the zucchini to completely enclose. Seal tightly but leave enough air in the packet to allow circulation around the blossoms so that they heat evenly.

4 When ready to serve, place the wrapped blossoms in a steamer basket over boiling water. Cover and steam for about 7 minutes or just until heated through. Remove from the steamer and keep warm until ready to plate.

BASIL PESTO

2½ packed cups basil leaves ■ **½ cup pine nuts or chopped walnuts** ■ **1 teaspoon minced garlic** ■ **½ cup freshly grated Parmesan cheese** ■ **1 teaspoon minced garlic** ■ **½ cup plus 2 tablespoons extra virgin olive oil** ■ **Coarse salt and freshly ground pepper**

Combine the basil, nuts, cheese and garlic in the bowl of a food processor fitted with the metal blade and process to a thick paste. With the motor running, slowly add ½ cup of the olive oil in a steady stream. If the sauce seems too thick, add the remaining olive oil, 1 tablespoon at a time. Season with salt and pepper. Scrape the pesto from the processor bowl into a clean container with a lid. Cover and refrigerate until ready to use. (Pesto may be stored, covered and refrigerated, for up to 1 week. However, the color may darken somewhat.)

Porcini-Dusted
Monkfish
Roasted on the Bone

SERVES 6 · 7 tablespoons unsalted butter (plus 3 more tablespoons if using 2 pans)

■ 12 medium porcini mushrooms, wiped clean, trimmed, and halved, lengthwise

■ 2 shallots, peeled and minced ■ 6 sprigs thyme (plus 3 additional if using 2 pans)

■ Coarse salt and freshly ground black pepper ■ 3 4-pound skinless monkfish tails

■ ¼ cup porcini powder ■ 6 tablespoons grapeseed oil ■ 3 bay leaves (plus

3 additional if using 2 pans) ■ 3 cloves garlic, peeled (plus 3 additional if using

2 pans) ■ 6 cups vegetable oil ■ 12 fingerling potatoes, well washed, dried, cut,

lengthwise, into 6 pieces each, and blanched ■ Sea salt and freshly ground white

pepper ■ Caramelized Fennel ■ 3 tablespoons porcini oil ■ Fleur de sel

1 Heat 4 tablespoons of the butter in a medium sauté pan over medium heat. Cook, stirring frequently, for about 4 minutes or until the butter is beginning to brown. Immediately add the mushrooms, cut side down, and lower the heat. Cook the mushrooms, shaking the pan occasionally to redistribute the fat, for about 6 minutes or until light brown and slightly crisp on the edges. Turn the mushrooms and cook, shaking the pan occasionally to redistribute the fat, for 4 minutes or until the mushrooms are almost cooked through. Add the shallots and 3 sprigs of the thyme and cook for an additional minute. Remove from the heat and season with salt and black pepper. Tent lightly with aluminum foil to keep warm.

2 Preheat the oven to 350°F.

3 Season the monkfish with salt and black pepper and dust the top with porcini powder. Set aside.

4 Heat equal portions of the grapeseed oil in two large, ovenproof sauté pans (unless you have one pan large enough to hold all of the fish) over medium-high heat. Add the seasoned monkfish and sear, turning occasionally, for 4 minutes or until the fish is well colored. Immediately transfer the pans to the preheated oven and roast the fish for 5 minutes. Remove the pans from the oven and return to medium-high heat. Turn the fish and add 3 tablespoons of butter to each pan. When the butter has melted, add 3 sprigs of the thyme, 3 bay leaves and 3 cloves of garlic to each pan. Lower the heat and baste the fish with the seasoned butter for about 4 minutes or until the fish is golden. Return the pans to the oven and roast the fish for 2 minutes. Remove from the oven and allow to rest for 5 minutes before serving.

192

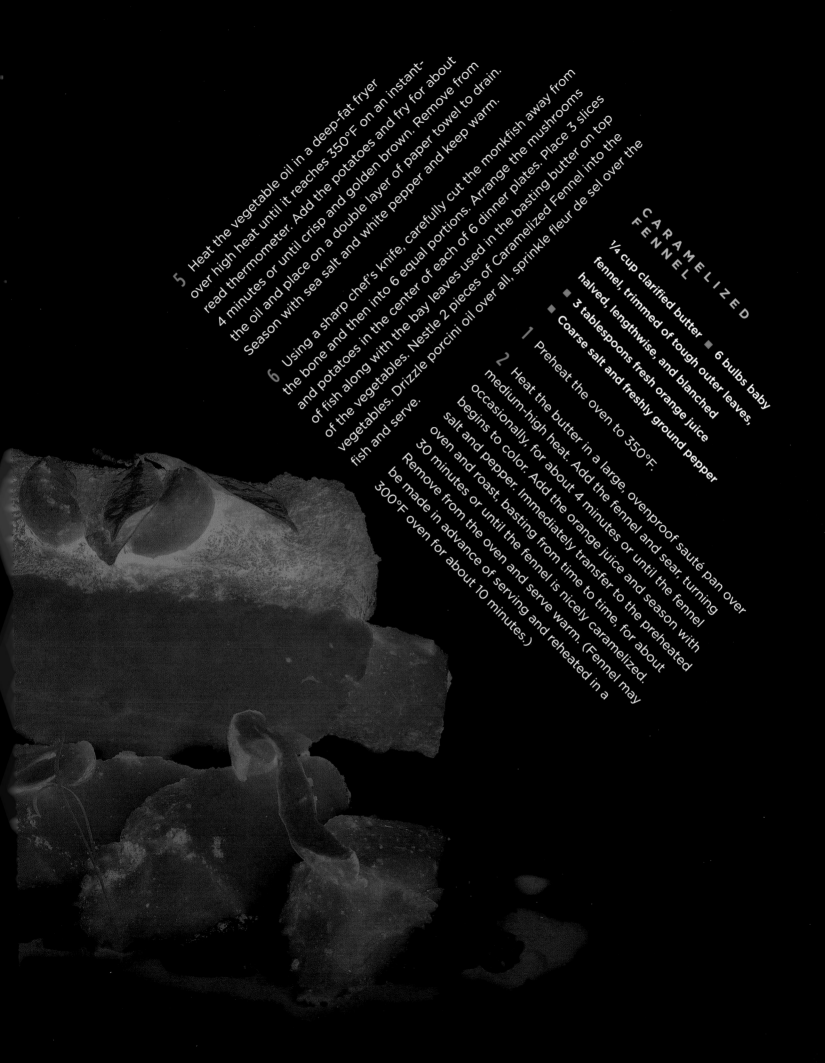

5 Heat the vegetable oil in a deep-fat fryer over high heat until it reaches 350°F on an instant-read thermometer. Add the potatoes and fry for about 4 minutes or until crisp and golden brown. Remove from the oil and place on a double layer of paper towel to drain. Season with sea salt and white pepper and keep warm.

6 Using a sharp chef's knife, carefully cut the monkfish away from the bone and then into 6 equal portions. Arrange the mushrooms and potatoes in the center of each of 6 dinner plates. Place 3 slices of fish along with the bay leaves used in the basting butter on top of the vegetables. Nestle 2 pieces of Caramelized Fennel into the vegetables. Drizzle porcini oil over all, sprinkle fleur de sel over the fish and serve.

CARAMELIZED FENNEL

- **¼ cup clarified butter**
- **6 bulbs baby fennel, trimmed of tough outer leaves, halved, lengthwise, and blanched**
- **3 tablespoons fresh orange juice**
- **Coarse salt and freshly ground pepper**

1 Preheat the oven to 350°F.

2 Heat the butter in a large, ovenproof sauté pan over medium-high heat. Add the fennel and sear, turning occasionally, for about 4 minutes or until the fennel begins to color. Add the orange juice and season with salt and pepper. Immediately transfer to the preheated oven and roast, basting from time to time, for about 30 minutes or until the fennel is nicely caramelized. Remove from the oven and serve warm. (Fennel may be made in advance of serving and reheated in a 300°F oven for about 10 minutes.)

Salmon Confit with Heirloom Potatoes

1 Place the duck fat in a sauté pan large enough to hold the salmon in a single layer. Place the pan over medium-low heat and bring to 170°F on an instant-read thermometer.

2 Generously season the salmon on both sides with the Five-Spice Powder. Carefully lay the seasoned salmon pieces in the duck fat. Return the heat to 170°F and cook, keeping the fat at a constant temperature, for about 7 minutes or until the salmon is medium-rare. Remove from the heat and allow the salmon to rest in the fat for about 5 minutes or until medium.

3 While the salmon is resting, heat the butter in a medium sauté pan over medium-high heat. Add the potatoes and stock and season with salt and white pepper. Cook, stirring occasionally, for about 5 minutes or until heated through. Remove from the heat and keep warm.

4 Using a slotted spoon, lift the salmon from the fat. Place a salmon piece in the center of each of 6 dinner plates. Spoon potatoes and Caramelized Cipollini Onions onto each plate. Garnish with Potato Chips and purslane sprigs and serve.

SERVES 6   Approximately 5 cups duck fat ■ Six 6-ounce pieces boneless, skinless salmon ■ 2 tablespoons Five-Spice Powder (see page 235) ■ 2 tablespoons unsalted butter ■ 2 pounds mixed tiny heirloom potatoes, peeled and cooked ■ 3 tablespoons chicken stock ■ Coarse salt and freshly ground white pepper ■ Caramelized Cipollini Onions ■ Potato Chips (see page 165) ■ 2 cups purslane sprigs, well washed and dried

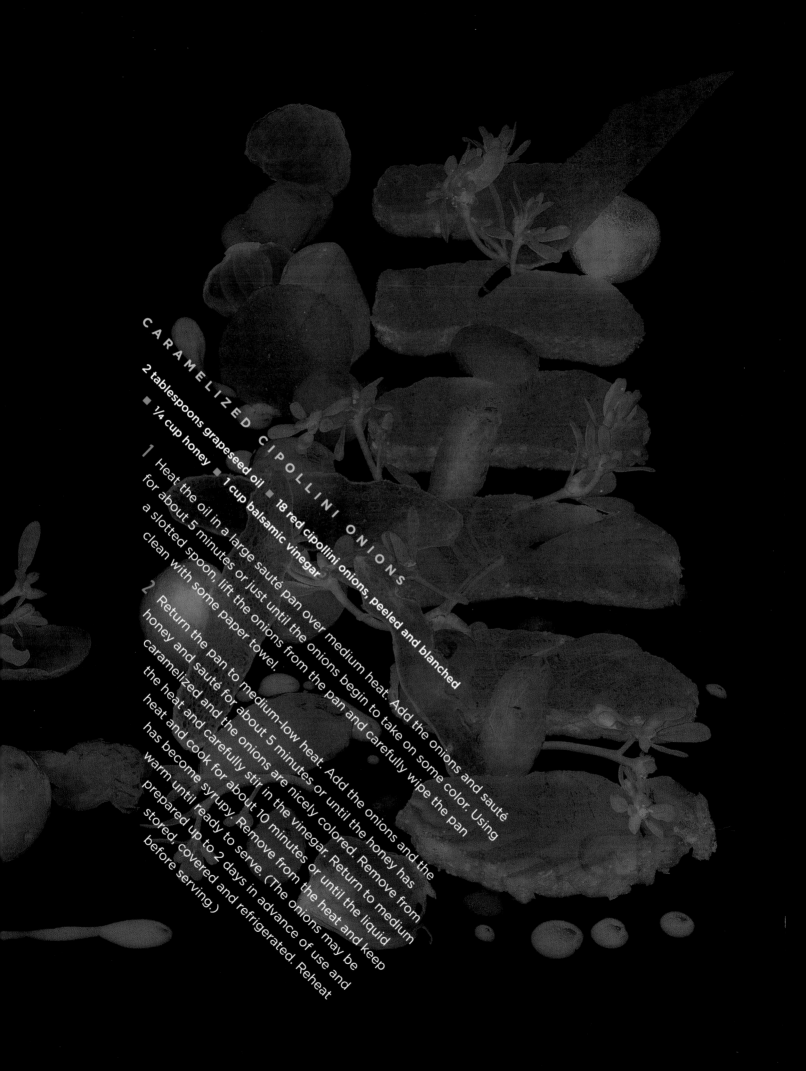

CARAMELIZED CIPOLLINI ONIONS

- 2 tablespoons grapeseed oil
- ¼ cup honey
- 1 cup balsamic vinegar
- 18 red cipollini onions, peeled and blanched

1 Heat the oil in a large sauté pan over medium heat. Add the onions and sauté for about 5 minutes or just until the onions begin to take on some color. Using a slotted spoon, lift the onions from the pan and carefully wipe the pan clean with some paper towel.

2 Return the pan to medium-low heat. Add the onions and the honey and sauté for about 5 minutes or until the honey has caramelized and the onions are nicely colored. Remove from the heat and carefully stir in the vinegar. Return to medium heat and cook for about 10 minutes or until the liquid has become syrupy. Remove from the heat and keep warm until ready to serve. (The onions may be prepared up to 2 days in advance of use and stored, covered and refrigerated. Reheat before serving.)

Rouget with
Arugula-Scented

Basmati Rice

SERVES 6 ¼ cup olive oil ■ 18 rouget ■ Coarse
salt and freshly ground pepper ■ Arugula-Scented
Basmati Rice ■ Squash Galettes ■ Grilled Eggplant
■ Tomato Vinaigrette ■ 2 cups amaranth greens

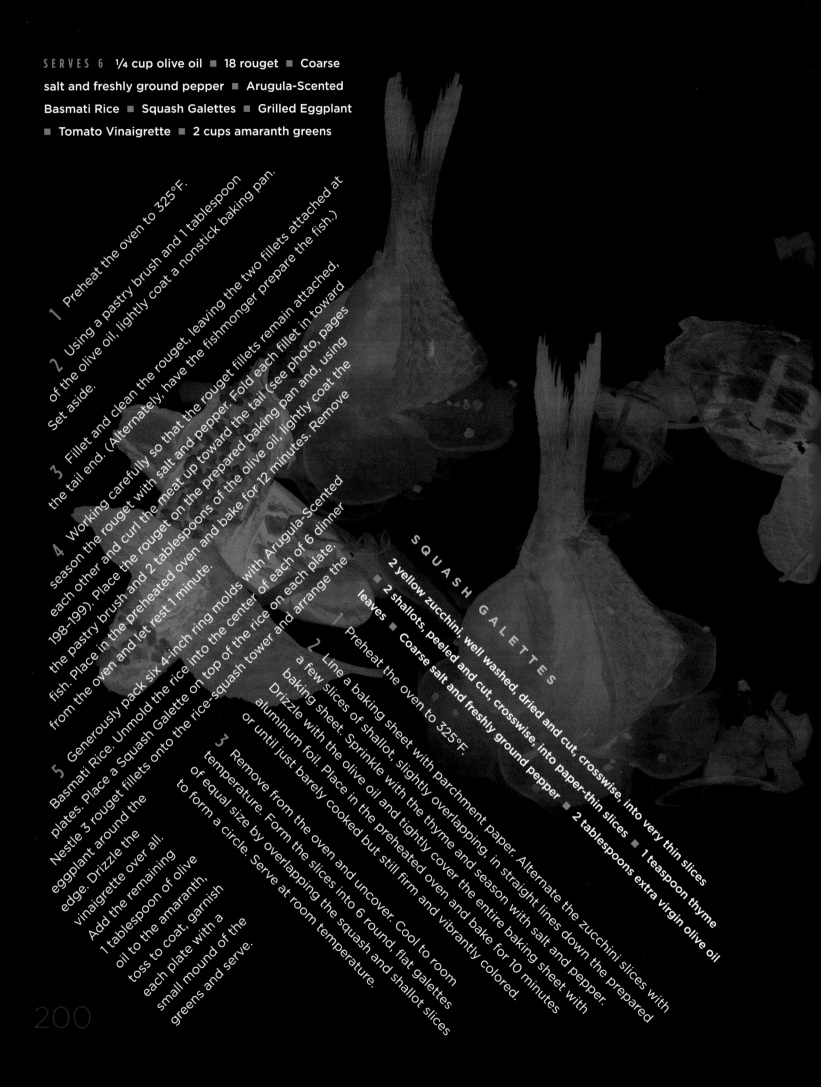

1 Preheat the oven to 325°F.

2 Using a pastry brush and 1 tablespoon of the olive oil, lightly coat a nonstick baking pan. Set aside.

3 Fillet and clean the rouget, leaving the two fillets attached at the tail end. (Alternately, have the fishmonger prepare the fish.)

4 Working carefully so that the rouget fillets remain attached, season the rouget with salt and pepper. Fold each fillet in toward each other and curl the meat up toward the tail (see photo, pages 198-199). Place the rouget on the prepared baking pan and, using the pastry brush and 2 tablespoons of the olive oil, lightly coat the fish. Place in the preheated oven and bake for 12 minutes. Remove from the oven and let rest 1 minute.

5 Generously pack six 4-inch ring molds with Arugula-Scented Basmati Rice. Unmold the rice into the center of each of 6 dinner plates. Place a Squash Galette on top of the rice on each plate. Nestle 3 rouget fillets onto the rice-squash tower and arrange the eggplant around the edge. Drizzle the vinaigrette over all. Add the remaining 1 tablespoon of olive oil to the amaranth, toss to coat, garnish each plate with a small mound of the greens and serve.

SQUASH GALETTES
■ 2 yellow zucchini, well washed, dried and cut, crosswise, into very thin slices ■ 2 shallots, peeled and cut, crosswise, into paper-thin slices ■ 1 teaspoon thyme leaves ■ Coarse salt and freshly ground pepper ■ 2 tablespoons extra virgin olive oil

1 Preheat the oven to 325°F.

2 Line a baking sheet with parchment paper. Alternate the zucchini slices with a few slices of shallot, slightly overlapping, in straight lines down the prepared baking sheet. Sprinkle with the thyme and season with salt and pepper. Drizzle with the olive oil and tightly cover the entire baking sheet with aluminum foil. Place in the preheated oven and bake for 10 minutes or until just barely cooked but still firm and vibrantly colored.

3 Remove from the oven and uncover. Cool to room temperature. Form the slices into 6 round, flat galettes of equal size by overlapping the squash and shallot slices to form a circle. Serve at room temperature.

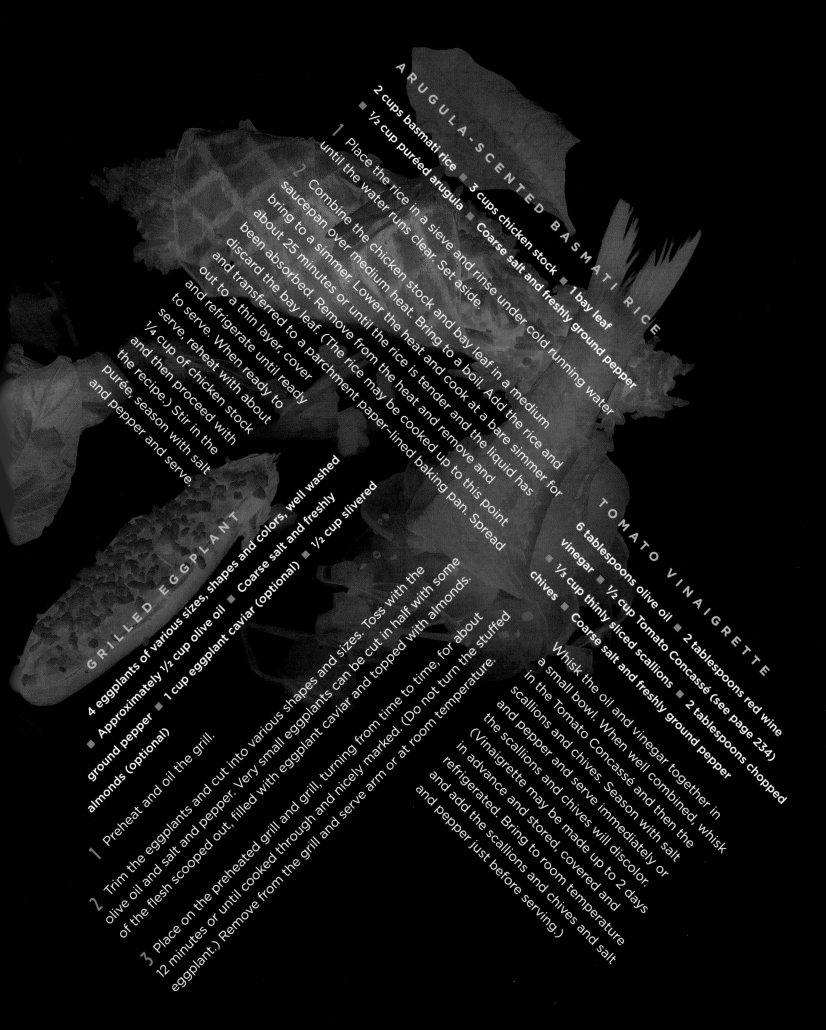

ARUGULA-SCENTED BASMATI RICE

■ **2 cups basmati rice** ■ **3 cups chicken stock** ■ **1 bay leaf**
■ **½ cup puréed arugula** ■ **Coarse salt and freshly ground pepper**

1 Place the rice in a sieve and rinse under cold running water until the water runs clear. Set aside.

2 Combine the chicken stock and bay leaf in a medium saucepan over medium heat. Bring to a boil. Add the rice and bring to a simmer. Lower the heat and cook at a bare simmer for about 25 minutes or until the rice is tender and the liquid has been absorbed. Remove from the heat and remove and discard the bay leaf. (The rice may be cooked up to this point and transferred to a parchment paper–lined baking pan. Spread out to a thin layer, cover and refrigerate until ready to serve. When ready to serve, reheat with about ¼ cup of chicken stock and then proceed with the recipe.) Stir in the purée, season with salt and pepper and serve.

TOMATO VINAIGRETTE

■ **6 tablespoons olive oil** ■ **2 tablespoons red wine vinegar** ■ **½ cup Tomato Concassé (see page 234)** ■ **⅓ cup thinly sliced scallions** ■ **2 tablespoons chopped chives** ■ **Coarse salt and freshly ground pepper**

Whisk the oil and vinegar together in a small bowl. When well combined, whisk in the Tomato Concassé and then the scallions and chives. Season with salt and pepper and serve immediately or the scallions and chives will discolor. (Vinaigrette may be made up to 2 days in advance and stored, covered and refrigerated. Bring to room temperature and add the scallions and chives and salt and pepper just before serving.)

GRILLED EGGPLANT

■ **4 eggplants of various sizes, shapes and colors, well washed** ■ **Approximately ½ cup olive oil** ■ **Coarse salt and freshly ground pepper** ■ **1 cup eggplant caviar (optional)** ■ **½ cup slivered almonds (optional)**

1 Preheat and oil the grill.

2 Trim the eggplants and cut into various shapes and sizes. Toss with the olive oil and salt and pepper. Very small eggplants can be cut in half with some of the flesh scooped out, filled with eggplant caviar and topped with almonds.

3 Place on the preheated grill and grill, turning from time to time, for about 12 minutes or until cooked through and nicely marked. (Do not turn the stuffed eggplant.) Remove from the grill and serve arm or at room temperature.

Legs,
and Sweet Pea Chantilly

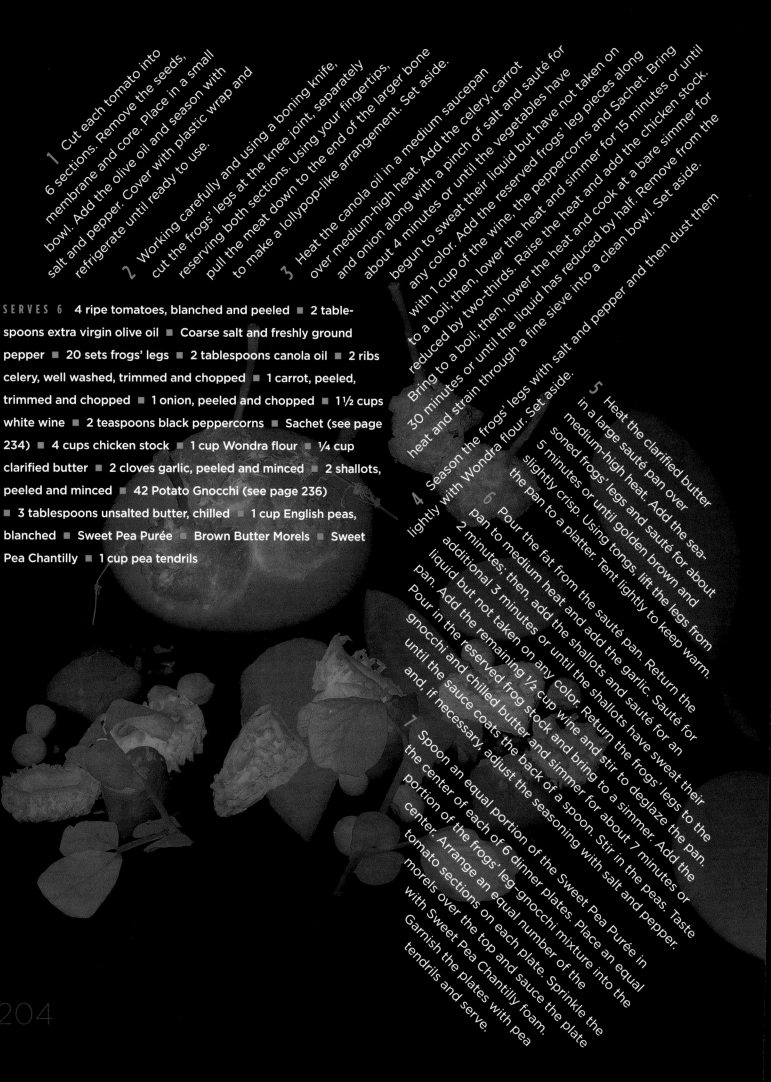

1 Cut each tomato into 6 sections. Remove the seeds, membrane and core. Place in a small bowl. Add the olive oil and season with salt and pepper. Cover with plastic wrap and refrigerate until ready to use.

2 Working carefully and using a boning knife, cut the frogs' legs at the knee joint, separately reserving both sections. Using your fingertips, pull the meat down to the end of the larger bone to make a lollypop-like arrangement. Set aside.

3 Heat the canola oil in a medium saucepan over medium-high heat. Add the celery, carrot and onion along with a pinch of salt and sauté for about 4 minutes or until the vegetables have begun to sweat their liquid but have not taken on any color. Add the reserved frogs' leg pieces along with 1 cup of the wine, the peppercorns and Sachet. Bring to a boil; then, lower the heat and simmer for 15 minutes or until reduced by two-thirds. Raise the heat and add the chicken stock. Bring to a boil; then, lower the heat and cook at a bare simmer for 30 minutes or until the liquid has reduced by half. Remove from the heat and strain through a fine sieve into a clean bowl. Set aside.

4 Season the frogs' legs with salt and pepper and then dust them lightly with Wondra flour. Set aside.

5 Heat the clarified butter in a large sauté pan over medium-high heat. Add the seasoned frogs' legs and sauté for about 5 minutes or until golden brown and slightly crisp. Using tongs, lift the legs from the pan to a platter. Tent lightly to keep warm.

6 Pour the fat from the sauté pan. Return the pan to medium heat and add the shallots and garlic. Sauté for 2 minutes; then, add the shallots and sauté for an additional 3 minutes or until the shallots have sweat their liquid but not taken on any color. Return the frogs' legs to the pan. Add the remaining ½ cup wine and stir to deglaze the pan. Pour in the reserved frog stock and bring to a simmer. Add the gnocchi and chilled butter and simmer for about 7 minutes or until the sauce coats the back of a spoon. Stir in the peas. Taste and, if necessary, adjust the seasoning with salt and pepper.

7 Spoon an equal portion of the Sweet Pea Purée in the center of each of 6 dinner plates. Place an equal portion of the frogs'-leg-gnocchi mixture into the center. Arrange an equal number of the tomato sections on each plate. Sprinkle the morels over the top and sauce the plate with Sweet Pea Chantilly foam. Garnish the plates with pea tendrils and serve.

SERVES 6   4 ripe tomatoes, blanched and peeled ■ 2 table-spoons extra virgin olive oil ■ Coarse salt and freshly ground pepper ■ 20 sets frogs' legs ■ 2 tablespoons canola oil ■ 2 ribs celery, well washed, trimmed and chopped ■ 1 carrot, peeled, trimmed and chopped ■ 1 onion, peeled and chopped ■ 1½ cups white wine ■ 2 teaspoons black peppercorns ■ Sachet (see page 234) ■ 4 cups chicken stock ■ 1 cup Wondra flour ■ ¼ cup clarified butter ■ 2 cloves garlic, peeled and minced ■ 2 shallots, peeled and minced ■ 42 Potato Gnocchi (see page 236) ■ 3 tablespoons unsalted butter, chilled ■ 1 cup English peas, blanched ■ Sweet Pea Purée ■ Brown Butter Morels ■ Sweet Pea Chantilly ■ 1 cup pea tendrils

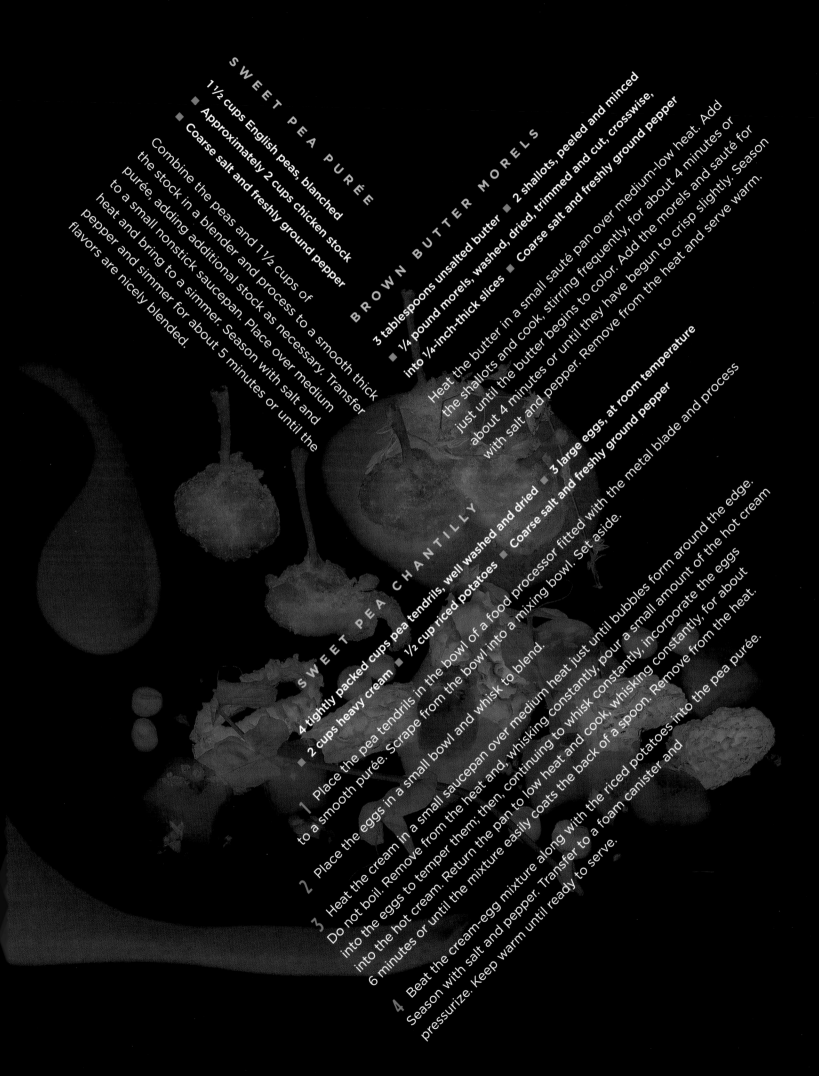

SWEET PEA PURÉE

- **1½ cups English peas, blanched**
- **Approximately 2 cups chicken stock**
- **Coarse salt and freshly ground pepper**

Combine the peas and 1½ cups of the stock in a blender and process to a smooth purée, adding additional stock as necessary. Transfer the purée to a small nonstick saucepan. Place over medium heat and bring to a simmer. Season with salt and pepper and simmer for about 5 minutes or until the flavors are nicely blended.

BROWN BUTTER MORELS

- **3 tablespoons unsalted butter**
- **2 shallots, peeled and minced**
- **¼ pound morels, washed, dried, trimmed and cut, crosswise, into ¼-inch-thick slices**
- **Coarse salt and freshly ground pepper**

Heat the butter in a small sauté pan over medium-low heat. Add the shallots and cook, stirring frequently, for about 4 minutes or just until the butter begins to color. Add the morels and sauté for about 4 minutes or until they have begun to crisp slightly. Season with salt and pepper. Remove from the heat and serve warm.

SWEET PEA CHANTILLY

- **4 tightly packed cups pea tendrils, well washed and dried**
- **½ cup riced potatoes**
- **3 large eggs, at room temperature**
- **2 cups heavy cream**
- **Coarse salt and freshly ground pepper**

1   Place the pea tendrils in the bowl of a food processor fitted with the metal blade and process to a smooth purée. Scrape from the bowl into a mixing bowl. Set aside.

2   Place the eggs in a small bowl and whisk to blend.

3   Heat the cream in a small saucepan over medium heat just until bubbles form around the edge. Do not boil. Remove from the heat and, whisking constantly, pour a small amount of the hot cream into the eggs to temper them; then, continuing to whisk constantly, incorporate the eggs into the hot cream. Return the pan to low heat and cook, whisking constantly, for about 6 minutes or until the mixture easily coats the back of a spoon. Remove from the heat.

4   Beat the cream-egg mixture along with the riced potatoes into the pea purée. Season with salt and pepper. Transfer to a foam canister and pressurize. Keep warm until ready to serve.

Soft-Shell
Crab with Apple-Fennel
Spicy Carrot Sauce

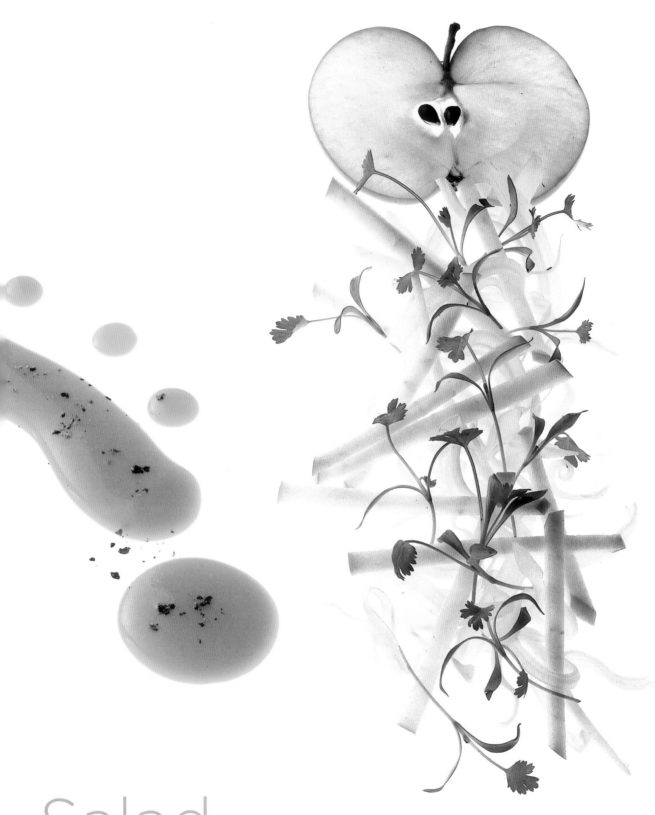

Salad,
and Simple Guacamole

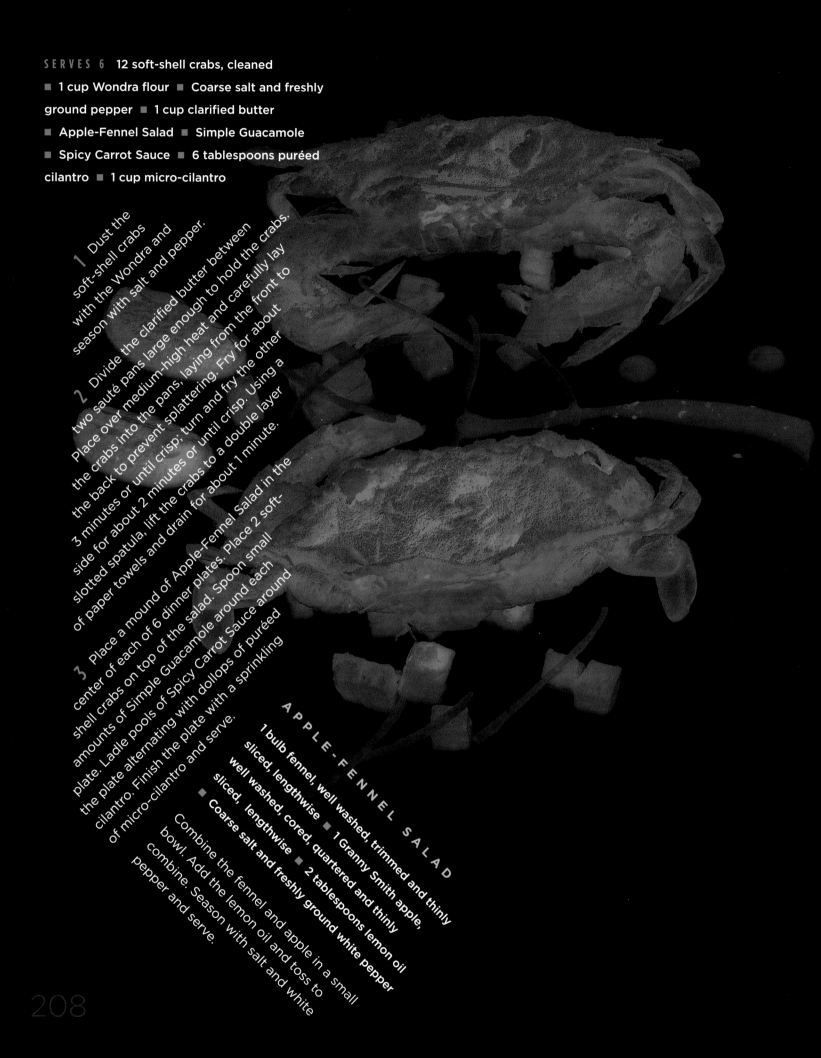

SERVES 6 ■ 12 soft-shell crabs, cleaned
■ 1 cup Wondra flour ■ Coarse salt and freshly
ground pepper ■ 1 cup clarified butter
■ Apple-Fennel Salad ■ Simple Guacamole
■ Spicy Carrot Sauce ■ 6 tablespoons puréed
cilantro ■ 1 cup micro-cilantro

1 Dust the soft-shell crabs with the Wondra and season with salt and pepper.

2 Divide the clarified butter between two sauté pans large enough to hold the crabs. Place over medium-high heat and carefully lay the crabs into the pans, laying from the front to the back to prevent splattering. Fry for about 3 minutes or until crisp; turn and fry the other side for about 2 minutes or until crisp. Using a slotted spatula, lift the crabs to a double layer of paper towels and drain for about 1 minute.

3 Place a mound of Apple-Fennel Salad in the center of each of 6 dinner plates. Place 2 soft-shell crabs on top of the salad. Spoon small amounts of Simple Guacamole around each plate. Ladle pools of Spicy Carrot Sauce around the plate alternating with dollops of puréed cilantro. Finish the plate with a sprinkling of micro-cilantro and serve.

APPLE-FENNEL SALAD

1 bulb fennel, well washed, trimmed and thinly sliced, lengthwise ■ 1 Granny Smith apple, well washed, cored, quartered and thinly sliced, lengthwise ■ 2 tablespoons lemon oil ■ Coarse salt and freshly ground white pepper

Combine the fennel and apple in a small bowl. Add the lemon oil and toss to combine. Season with salt and white pepper and serve.

208

SIMPLE GUACAMOLE

2 cups finely diced ripe avocado ■ 1 tablespoon
freshly grated lemon zest, blanched ■ 1 tablespoon
extra virgin olive oil ■ 2 teaspoons fresh lemon
juice ■ Coarse salt and freshly ground pepper

Place the avocado and zest in a small bowl. Add
the oil and lemon juice and season with salt and
pepper. Gently toss to just combine and serve.

SPICY CARROT SAUCE

2 tablespoons unsalted butter
■ 1 shallot, peeled and chopped ■ 2 carrots, peeled, trimmed
and diced ■ 1 cup fresh carrot juice ■ ½ teaspoon
Thai red curry paste ■ Coarse salt

1 Heat the butter in a medium saucepan over medium
heat. Add the carrots and sauté for about 4 minutes or just
until they have begun to sweat their liquid. Add the shallot
and sauté for an additional 3 minutes. Stir in the curry
paste and cook for another minute. Add the carrot juice
and bring to a simmer. Simmer for about 10 minutes or
until the carrots are tender.

2 Remove from the heat and transfer to a blender.
Process to a smooth purée; then, pour through a
fine sieve into a clean saucepan. Season with
salt and reheat when ready to serve.

Crab Ravioli in Tomato

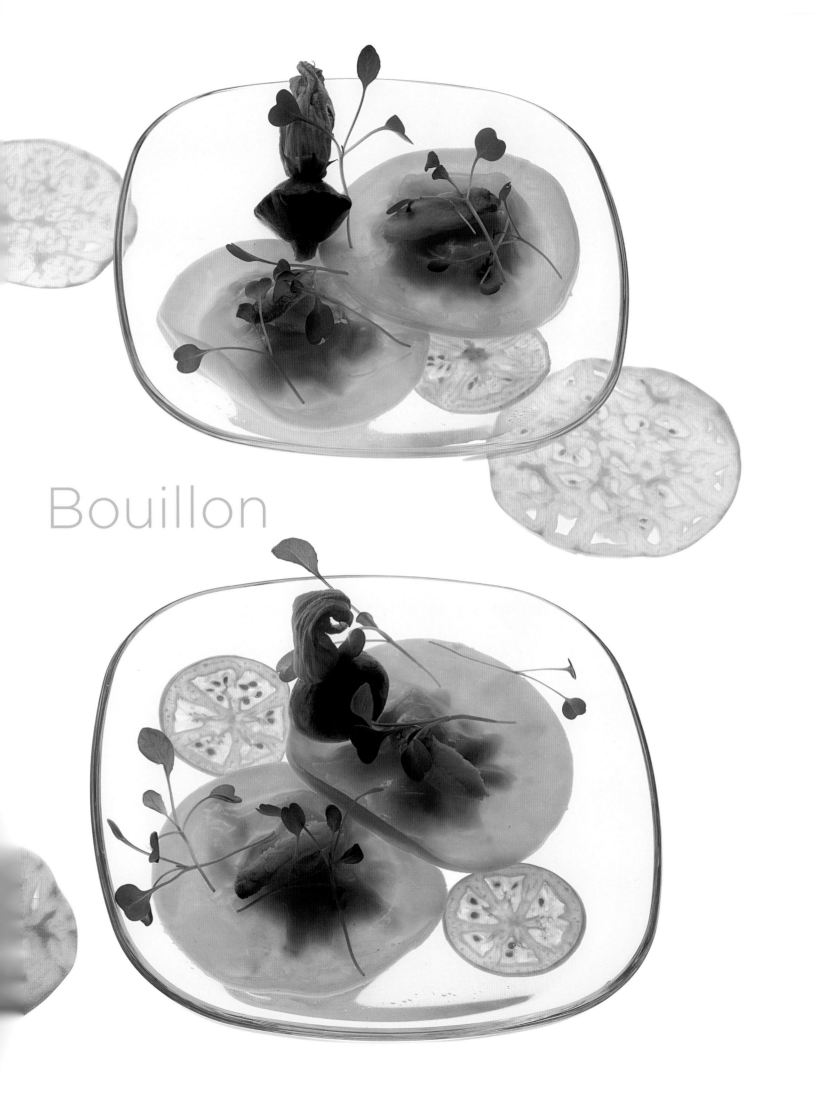

Bouillon

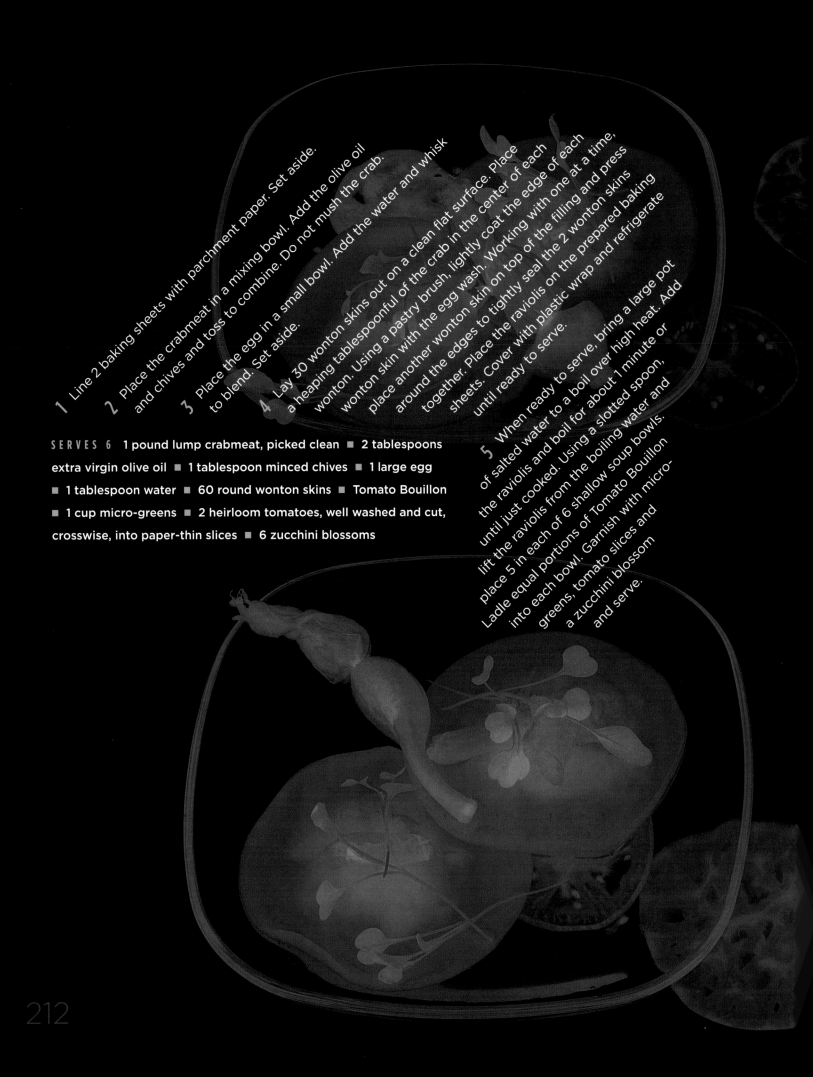

1 Line 2 baking sheets with parchment paper. Set aside.

2 Place the crabmeat in a mixing bowl. Add the olive oil and chives and toss to combine. Do not mush the crab.

3 Place the egg in a small bowl. Add the water and whisk to blend. Set aside.

4 Lay 30 wonton skins out on a clean flat surface. Place a heaping tablespoonful of the crab in the center of each wonton. Using a pastry brush, lightly coat the edge of each wonton skin with the egg wash. Working with one at a time, place another wonton skin on top of the filling and press around the edges to tightly seal the 2 wonton skins together. Place the raviolis on the prepared baking sheets. Cover with plastic wrap and refrigerate until ready to serve.

5 When ready to serve, bring a large pot of salted water to a boil over high heat. Add the raviolis and boil for about 1 minute or until just cooked. Using a slotted spoon, lift the raviolis from the boiling water and place 5 in each of 6 shallow soup bowls. Ladle equal portions of Tomato Bouillon into each bowl. Garnish with micro-greens, tomato slices and a zucchini blossom and serve.

SERVES 6   1 pound lump crabmeat, picked clean ■ 2 tablespoons extra virgin olive oil ■ 1 tablespoon minced chives ■ 1 large egg ■ 1 tablespoon water ■ 60 round wonton skins ■ Tomato Bouillon ■ 1 cup micro-greens ■ 2 heirloom tomatoes, well washed and cut, crosswise, into paper-thin slices ■ 6 zucchini blossoms

TOMATO BOUILLON

- 1 bay leaf
- 1 tablespoon chopped tarragon
- 1 tablespoon chopped thyme
- 2 teaspoons grapeseed oil
- 2 carrots, peeled, trimmed, diced and divided in half
- 2 ribs celery, well washed, trimmed, diced and divided in half
- 2 onions, peeled, diced and divided in half
- Coarse salt
- 1 cup white wine
- 1 tablespoon tomato paste
- Sachet (see page 234)
- 3 blue crabs, cleaned
- 1 teaspoon saffron threads
- 5 cups lobster stock or fish fumet
- 2 pounds ripe tomatoes, well washed, cored and quartered
- 1 cup shrimp shells
- 3 large egg whites
- Freshly ground white pepper

1 Place the bay leaf, tarragon and thyme in a cheesecloth bag tied with kitchen twine. Set aside.

2 Heat the oil in a large saucepan over medium heat. Add one-half of each of the carrots, celery and onions with a pinch of salt and sauté for about 5 minutes or just until the vegetables have sweat their liquid but have not taken on any color. Add the wine, tomato paste, saffron and Sachet and stir to combine. Stir in the crabs and the shrimp shells, smashing them up with a wooden spoon. Add the tomatoes and stock (or fumet). Raise the heat and bring to a simmer. Lower the heat and cook at a bare simmer for 30 minutes. Remove from the heat and strain through a fine sieve into a large saucepan, discarding the solids.

3 Combine the remaining carrot, celery and onion in a food processor fitted with the metal blade and process to slightly chop. Add the broth over medium heat. Cook for about 4 minutes or just until beginning to warm. Whisk in the chopped vegetable mixture and bring to a simmer, stirring and scraping the bottom of the pan from time to time. (Do not allow the egg to stick to the bottom of the pan or it will begin to burn.) Once the broth comes to a boil, do not stir. Simmer for about 30 minutes or until the egg foam begins to rise and cover the surface of the pan. As the foam begins to firm, using a gentle motion, poke a small hole in the center of the crust with the end of a wooden spoon. Lower the heat and cook at a bare simmer for another 30 minutes or until the egg mixture has formed a dense, solid crust on top of the broth.

5 Line a sieve with a double layer of damp cheesecloth. Remove the pan from the heat and very gently push an opening in the crust with a wooden spoon. Using a cup or a ladle, carefully pour the broth through the cheesecloth-lined sieve into a clean saucepan, discarding the solids. Season with salt and white pepper. (Bouillon may be made up to 2 days in advance and stored, covered and refrigerated.)

6 When ready to serve, reheat over medium heat.

Butter-Poached
Lobster with
Coconut Curry
Broth

SERVES 6 6 1¼ pound live lobsters ■ 6 baby bok choy, well washed and pulled into separate leaves ■ 1 cup reduced lobster stock ■ 3 cups plus 3 tablespoons unsalted butter ■ Coarse salt and freshly ground white pepper ■ 1 teaspoon finely minced garlic ■ 1 teaspoon finely minced fresh ginger ■ ¾ pound honshimeji mushrooms, brushed clean and trimmed ■ Freshly ground black pepper ■ Tempura Onion Rings ■ Coconut Curry Broth ■ Curry Oil (see page 235) ■ Lobster Roe Powder (see page 234)

1 Quarter the lobsters and clean the bodies. Set aside.

2 Make a large bowl of ice water.

3 Bring a large pot of salted water to boil over high heat. Remove the rubber bands from the lobster claws and place the claws and tails in the boiling water. Boil the tails for 3 minutes and the claws for 4 minutes. Immediately drain and shock in the bowl of ice water until cool. Remove from the ice-water bath.

4 Free the knuckle and claw meat from the shells, keeping the meat as intact as possible. Using a small, sharp knife, gently scrape away any white matter clinging to the meat. Set aside.

5 Split the tails in half, lengthwise, and remove the vein. Place all of the lobster meat on a platter. Cover with plastic wrap and refrigerate until ready to finish.

6 Blanch the bok choy leaves in boiling salted water for 30 seconds. Drain well and refresh under cold running water. Squeeze gently to remove any excess moisture. Set aside.

7 When ready to serve, place the lobster stock in a large shallow saucepan over low heat. When warm, whisk in 3 cups of the butter and season with salt and white pepper. Bring to 180°F on an instant-read thermometer. Do not let the temperature exceed 180°F.

8 While the lobster is poaching, heat the remaining 3 tablespoons of butter in a medium sauté pan over medium heat. Add the garlic and ginger and sauté for 3 minutes. Add the mushrooms and sauté for an additional 3 minutes. Add the reserved bok choy and stir to just heat through. Remove from the heat and season with salt and freshly ground black pepper.

9 Remove the lobster from the poaching liquid and remove the tail meat from the shell.

10 Mound an equal portion of the mushroom-bok choy mixture in the center of each of 6 shallow soup bowls. Arrange equal portions of the lobster on top of the mushroom mixture in each bowl. Place 2 Tempura Onion Rings on top of each serving. Spoon Coconut Curry Broth around the edge of the bowl. Drizzle Curry Oil around the broth. Sprinkle Lobster Roe Powder around the rim of the bowl and serve.

TEMPURA ONION RINGS

2 large white onions, peeled and ends trimmed ■ **1 cup Wondra flour** ■ **6 cups vegetable oil**

■ 1 cup all-purpose flour ■ **½ teaspoon baking powder** ■ **1½ cups ice-cold seltzer water**

1. Cut the onions, crosswise, into ⅛-inch-thick slices. Pull the slices apart to make individual rings. If using the rings only as a garnish, choose only the largest, most perfect rings for the tempura. Otherwise, tempura all of the rings.

2. Place the Wondra in a plastic bag. Working with a few rings at a time, place them in the Wondra and shake to coat very lightly. Continue until all rings are coated. Set aside.

3. Place the oil in a deep-fat fryer or medium saucepan over high heat. Bring to 365°F on an instant-read thermometer.

4. While the oil is heating, prepare the batter.

5. Combine the all-purpose flour and baking powder in a mixing bowl. Whisk in the seltzer until just blended—a few lumps are okay.

6. Working with one at a time, dip the floured onion rings into the batter. Drop into the hot oil and fry for about 1 minute or until golden brown and slightly puffed. Using a slotted spoon, lift the cooked rings from the oil and place on a double layer of paper towel to drain. Serve warm.

COCONUT CURRY BROTH

1 tablespoon grapeseed oil ■ **3 shallots, peeled and thinly sliced**

■ ¼ cup thinly sliced fennel ■ **1 stalk lemongrass, tender bottom only, thinly sliced on the bias** ■ **½ cup chopped cilantro leaves** ■ **1 tablespoon curry powder** ■ **1 clove garlic, peeled and thinly sliced**

1 tablespoon coarse salt and freshly ground pepper ■ **2 cups lobster stock** ■ **2 cups unsweetened coconut milk**

toasted coriander seed ■ **2 cups lobster stock** ■ **1 cup tapioca, soaked in water until soft** ■ **2 teaspoons ground ginger** ■ **2 kaffir lime leaves**

1. Heat the oil in a large saucepan over medium heat. Add the shallots, garlic, lemongrass, fennel and ginger and sauté for about 4 minutes or until they are very fragrant. Then, add the curry powder and coriander and sauté for 3 minutes and cilantro. Lower the heat and coconut milk and bring to a boil. Season with salt and pepper. Add the lobster stock and simmer for 15 minutes. Remove from the heat and pour into a blender. Process to a smooth purée. Pour through a fine sieve into a clean saucepan.

2. When ready to serve, add the tapioca and place over medium heat. Cook, stirring frequently, for about 5 minutes or until the tapioca is tender and the broth is very hot. Taste, and, if necessary, adjust the seasoning with salt and pepper.

Lobster, Lobster, Lobster

and Lobster Sauce

SERVES 6 6 1¼-pound live lobsters ■ 2 tablespoons canola oil ■ 2 ribs celery, well washed, dried and diced ■ 2 carrots, peeled, trimmed and diced ■ 1 large onion, peeled and diced ■ 5 tablespoons tomato paste ■ ¾ cup dry white wine ■ 12 cups lobster stock ■ ½ teaspoon black peppercorns ■ Sachet (see page 234) ■ ½ cup plus 2 tablespoons unsalted butter, at room temperature ■ Coarse salt and freshly ground pepper ■ 3 tablespoons clarified butter ■ 1 tablespoon minced ginger ■ 1 tablespoon minced garlic ■ 12 spring onions, well washed, trimmed, blanched and lightly grilled ■ Stuffed Artichoke Bottoms (see page 222) ■ Lobster Spring Rolls (see page 223) ■ 12 sprigs watercress, well washed and dried

1 Remove the claws and tail from the body of the lobster. Separately set all of the lobster pieces aside.

2 Make a large bowl of ice water. Set aside.

3 Bring a large pot of heavily salted water to a boil over high heat. Add the lobster claws and boil for 5 minutes. Using tongs, lift the claws from the boiling water and immediately immerse the claws in the ice-water bath.

4 When cool enough to handle, lift the claws from the ice-water bath and place on a double layer of paper towel to drain. Set aside. Do not turn off the heat; keep the water boiling.

5 Add additional ice to the ice-water bath and set aside.

6 Place the lobster tails in the boiling water and boil for 90 seconds. Drain and immediately place the tails in the ice-water bath.

7 When cool enough to handle, drain well and place on a double layer of paper towel to drain off any remaining water. Using a chef's knife, split the tails, lengthwise, and remove the vein, leaving the meat in the shell. Place the tails in a small bowl, cover with plastic wrap and refrigerate.

8 Carefully crack the claws and remove the claw and knuckle meat, keeping at least 6 claws intact. (If making the Stuffed Artichoke Bottoms, place the knuckle meat in a small bowl and set aside for use in the recipe.) Separately set the 6 whole claw pieces aside. (If making the Lobster Spring Rolls, roughly chop the remaining claw meat and set aside for use in the recipe.)

9 Pull the lobster bodies apart and scrape away all internal matter. Rinse the bodies under cold running water until the water runs clear. Using a chef's knife or cleaver, crush the bodies and set aside.

10 Heat the oil in a heavy-bottomed saucepan (such as a rondeau) over medium-high heat. Add the reserved lobster bodies and sauté for about 5 minutes or until the shells are bright red. Add the celery, carrots and onion and sauté for about 4 minutes or just until the vegetables are slightly tender but have not taken on any color. Stir in the tomato paste and cook, stirring constantly, for about 3 minutes or until the tomato flavor is well incorporated into the vegetables. Add the wine and stir to deglaze the pan. Cook, stirring occasionally, for about 10 minutes or until the liquid has reduced by two-thirds. Add 8 cups of the lobster stock along with the peppercorns and Sachet and bring to a simmer. Lower the heat and simmer for 30 minutes.

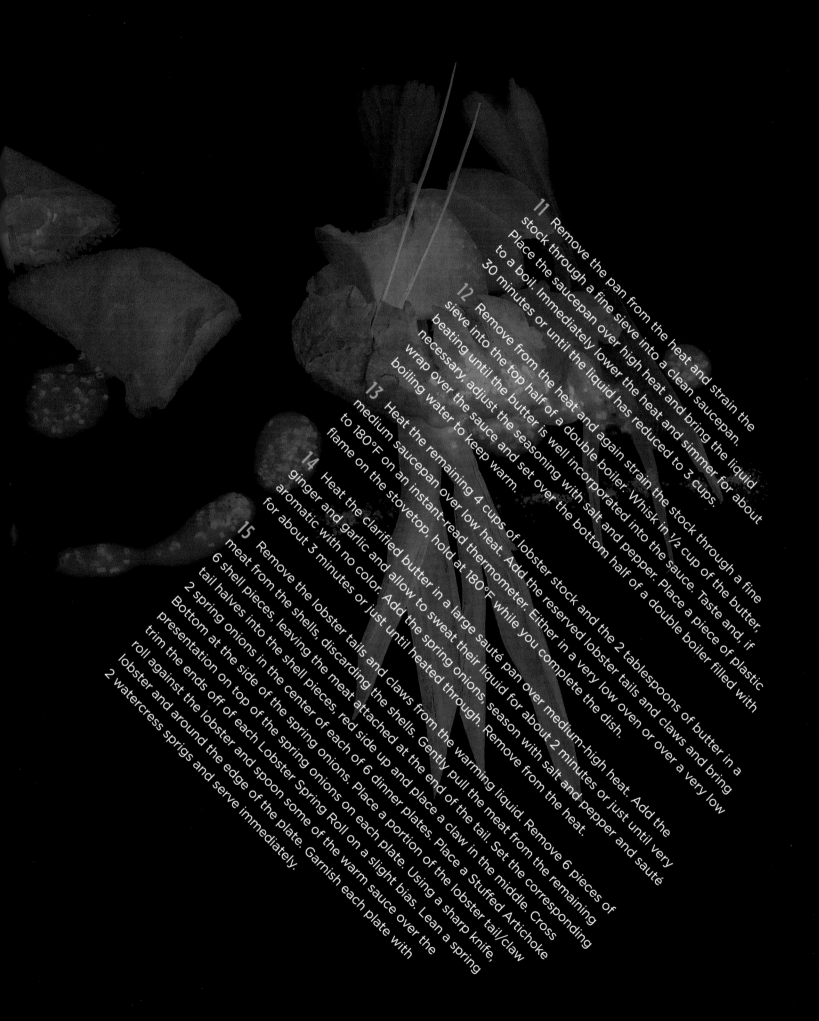

11   Remove the pan from the heat and strain the stock through a fine sieve into a clean saucepan. Place the saucepan over high heat and bring the liquid to a boil. Immediately lower the heat and simmer for about 30 minutes or until the liquid has reduced to 3 cups.

12   Remove from the heat and again strain the stock through a fine sieve into the top half of a double boiler. Whisk in ½ cup of the butter, beating until the butter is well incorporated into the sauce. Taste and, if necessary, adjust the seasoning with salt and pepper. Place a piece of plastic wrap over the sauce and set over the bottom half of a double boiler filled with boiling water to keep warm.

13   Heat the remaining 4 cups of lobster stock and the 2 tablespoons of butter in a medium saucepan over low heat. Add the reserved lobster tails and claws and bring to 180°F on an instant-read thermometer. Either in a very low oven or over a very low flame on the stovetop, hold at 180°F while you complete the dish.

14   Heat the clarified butter in a large sauté pan over medium-high heat. Add the ginger and garlic and allow to sweat their liquid for about 2 minutes or just until aromatic with no color. Add the spring onions. Season with salt and pepper and sauté for about 3 minutes or just until heated through. Remove from the heat.

15   Remove the lobster tails and claws from the warming liquid. Remove 6 pieces of meat from the shells, discarding the shells. Gently pull the meat from the tail. Set the corresponding 6 shell pieces, leaving the meat attached at the end of the tail. Set the corresponding tail halves into the shell pieces, red side up and place a claw in the middle. Cross 2 spring onions in the center of each of 6 dinner plates. Place a Stuffed Artichoke Bottom at the side of the spring onions. Place a portion of the lobster tail/claw presentation on top of each Lobster Spring Roll on a slight bias. Lean a spring trim the ends off of each Lobster Spring Roll on a slight bias. Using a sharp knife, roll against the lobster and spoon some of the warm sauce over the lobster and around the edge of the plate. Garnish each plate with 2 watercress sprigs and serve immediately.

STUFFED ARTICHOKE BOTTOMS

- ¼ pound pea tendrils, well washed and dried ■ ½ cup lobster
  knuckle meat (see page 220) ■ ¼ cup plus 2 tablespoons unsalted butter
- ⅓ cup minced shallot ■ ⅓ cup minced ginger ■ 2 tablespoons bias-cut
  scallion greens ■ Coarse salt and freshly ground pepper ■ 6 fresh artichoke bottoms,
  cooked ■ Approximately 2 cups lobster stock

1 Add the pea tendrils to the lobster knuckle meat and toss to combine. Set aside.

2 Heat ¼ cup of the butter in a small sauté pan over medium heat. Add the shallots and ginger and allow them to sweat their liquid for 3 minutes. Pour the shallot mixture over the pea-lobster mixture. Add the scallion greens and season with salt and pepper. Stir to lightly incorporate the butter.

3 Divide the mixture into 6 equal portions. Form each portion into a disk compact and large enough to fit firmly into the artichoke bottoms. Fit one disk into each artichoke bottom, using your fingertips to smooth the edges and make a neat fit. Place the filled artichoke bottoms on a plate, cover with plastic wrap and refrigerate until ready to serve.

4 When ready to serve, preheat the oven to 350°F.

5 Remove the Stuffed Artichoke Bottoms from the refrigerator. Uncover and place in a medium, ovenproof sauté pan. Add enough lobster stock to come up just under the rim of the artichoke bottoms and place over medium heat. Add the remaining 2 tablespoons of butter and season with salt and pepper. Bring to a simmer; then, immediately transfer to the preheated oven. Bake for about 15 minutes or until the filling is very hot and the tops are slightly crisp. Serve hot.

222

LOBSTER SPRING ROLLS

- 2 tablespoons clarified butter
- 1 tablespoon minced garlic
- 2 tablespoons minced ginger
- 1 cup carrot julienne
- 1 cup snap pea julienne
- 1 cup leek julienne, white part only
- ½ cup chopped chives
- 1 cup chopped lobster claw meat
- Coarse salt and freshly ground pepper
- Approximately ¼ cup Wondra flour
- 6 9-inch by 9-inch spring roll wrappers
- Approximately 8 cups vegetable oil
- ¼ cup

1   Heat the clarified butter in a large sauté pan over medium heat. Add the ginger and garlic and sauté for about 3 minutes or just until the aromatics have sweat their liquid but not taken on any color. Add the leek, carrot and snap pea juliennes and sauté for about 3 minutes or just until the vegetables are al dente. Season with salt and pepper, remove from the heat and set aside to cool.

2   When cool enough to handle, using your hands, squeeze out all excess moisture. Add the vegetable mixture to the lobster meat. Stir in the chives, taste and, if necessary, adjust the seasoning with salt and pepper.

3   Lightly flour a baking sheet with the Wondra. Set aside.

4   Lay the spring roll wrappers out on a flat surface. Place equal portions of the lobster filling into the center of each wrapper. Fold one end up and over the filling and then fold in each side to cover. Tightly roll up the wrapper to make a neat spring roll. Place the spring rolls on the prepared baking sheet, cover with plastic wrap and refrigerate until ready to use.

5   When ready to fry, line a baking sheet with a triple layer of paper towel and set aside. Remove the Lobster Spring Rolls from the refrigerator. Place the oil in a deep-fat fryer (or deep saucepan) over high heat and bring to 350°F on an instant-read thermometer. Carefully lower the spring rolls into the hot oil. Fry for about 4 minutes or until the rolls are golden brown and crisp. Using a slotted spoon, lift the rolls from the oil and place on the prepared baking sheet to drain. Lightly tent with aluminum foil to keep warm until ready to serve. (Rolls can be made a couple of hours in advance of use and stored, covered and refrigerated. Reheat in a preheated 350°F oven.)

Pan-Roasted Sea Scallops
and Truffle-Braised Pork Cheeks
with Watercress Coulis

2 tablespoons grapeseed oil ■ 12 large sea scallops, adductor muscle removed ■ Coarse salt and freshly ground pepper ■ 3 tablespoons unsalted butter ■ 2 teaspoons thyme leaves ■ Potato-Shallot Cakes ■ Truffle-Braised Pork Cheeks ■ Braised Baby Leeks ■ Watercress Coulis

1 Heat the oil in a large sauté pan over medium-high heat. Pat the scallops dry and season with salt and pepper. Place in the hot pan and sear, turning once, for about 3 minutes or until nicely colored. Lower the heat and add the butter and thyme. Cook, basting the scallops with the butter, for about 4 minutes or until the scallops are firm and cooked to medium (soft in the center with a slight rawness). Season with salt and pepper. Using a slotted spatula, transfer the scallops to a double layer of paper towel to drain.

2 Place 2 Potato-Shallot Cakes in the center of each of 6 dinner plates. Place a scallop on top of each cake. Spoon the pork cheeks with some of their sauce around the cakes. Garnish the plate with Braised Baby Leeks and Watercress Coulis and serve.

POTATO-SHALLOT CAKES ■ 4 large Idaho potatoes, well washed and dried ■ 1 large egg ■ ¼ cup minced shallots ■ 2 tablespoons mixed chives ■ Coarse salt and freshly ground white pepper ■ ¼ cup clarified butter

1 Preheat the oven to 350°F.

2 Prick the potatoes with a fork and place in the preheated oven. Bake for about 25 minutes or until just barely cooked. Remove from the oven and allow to cool.

3 When the potatoes are cool enough to handle, peel and grate them on a hand-held box grater. Place in a mixing bowl and add the egg, chives and shallots. Season with salt and white pepper and stir to blend well.

4 Line a baking sheet with parchment paper. Set aside.

5 Using a 3-inch ring mold, pack the potato mixture into the mold to make a firm cake. Continue making cakes until there are 12. Place the cakes on the prepared baking sheet, cover with plastic wrap and refrigerate for at least 4 hours or up to 24 hours.

6 When ready to serve, heat the clarified butter in a large sauté pan over medium-high heat. Remove the cakes from the refrigerator, unwrap and place them in the hot pan. Fry, turning occasionally, for about 12 minutes or until crisp and golden brown. Transfer to a double layer of paper towel to drain. Serve hot.

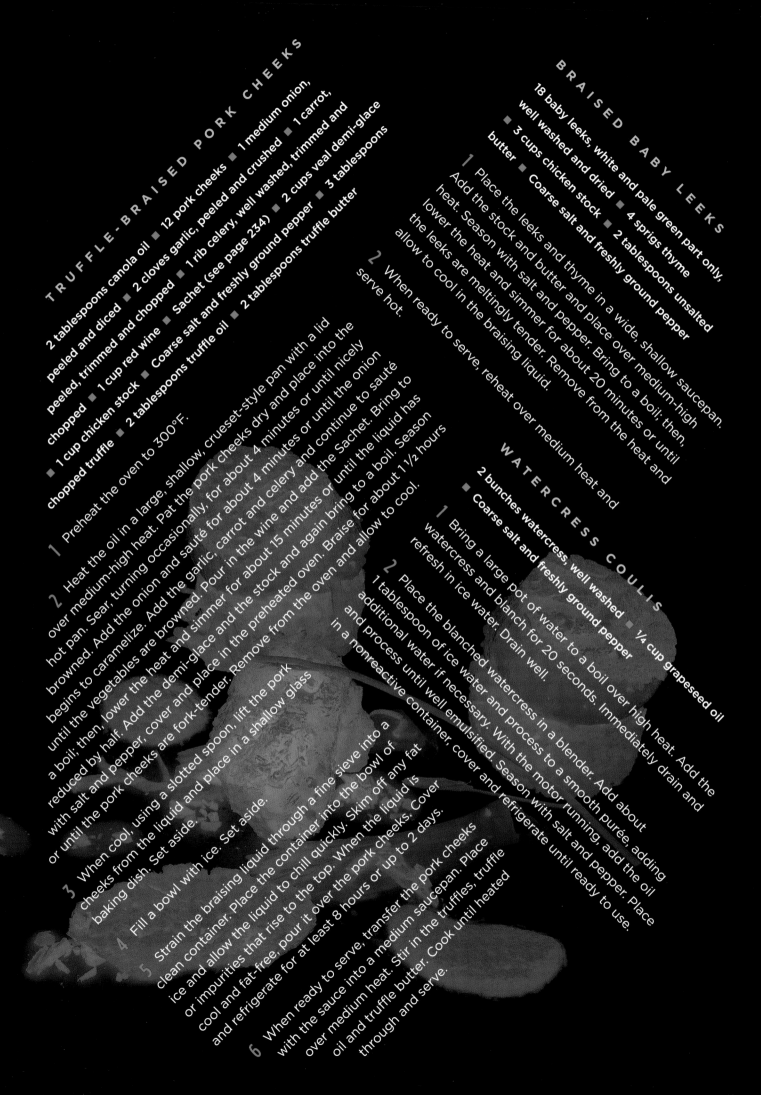

BRAISED BABY LEEKS

- 18 baby leeks, white and pale green part only, well washed and dried
- 3 cups chicken stock ■ 4 sprigs thyme
- 2 tablespoons unsalted butter ■ Coarse salt and freshly ground pepper

1 Place the leeks and thyme in a wide, shallow saucepan. Add the stock and butter and place over medium-high heat. Season with salt and pepper. Bring to a boil; then, lower the heat and simmer for about 20 minutes or until the leeks are meltingly tender. Remove from the heat and allow to cool in the braising liquid.

2 When ready to serve, reheat over medium heat and serve hot.

WATERCRESS COULIS

- 2 bunches watercress, well washed
- Coarse salt and freshly ground pepper ■ ¼ cup grapeseed oil

1 Bring a large pot of water to a boil over high heat. Add the watercress and blanch for 20 seconds. Immediately drain and refresh in ice water. Drain well.

2 Place the blanched watercress in a blender. Add about 1 tablespoon of ice water and process to a smooth purée, adding additional water if necessary. With the motor running, add the oil and process until well emulsified. Season with salt and pepper. Place in a nonreactive container, cover and refrigerate until ready to use.

TRUFFLE-BRAISED PORK CHEEKS

- 2 tablespoons canola oil ■ 12 pork cheeks ■ 1 medium onion, peeled and diced ■ 2 cloves garlic, peeled and crushed ■ 1 carrot, peeled, trimmed and chopped ■ 1 rib celery, well washed, trimmed and chopped ■ 1 cup red wine ■ Sachet (see page 234) ■ 2 cups veal demi-glace
- 1 cup chicken stock ■ Coarse salt and freshly ground pepper ■ 3 tablespoons chopped truffle ■ 2 tablespoons truffle oil ■ 2 tablespoons truffle butter

1 Preheat the oven to 300°F.

2 Heat the oil in a large, shallow, crueset-style pan with a lid over medium-high heat. Pat the pork cheeks dry and place into the hot pan. Sear, turning occasionally, for about 4 minutes or until nicely browned. Add the onion and sauté for about 4 minutes or until the onion begins to caramelize. Add the garlic, carrot and celery and continue to sauté until the vegetables are browned. Pour in the wine and add the Sachet. Bring to a boil; then, lower the heat and simmer for about 15 minutes or until the liquid has reduced by half. Add the demi-glace and the stock and again bring to a boil. Season with salt and pepper, cover and place in the preheated oven. Braise for about 1½ hours or until the pork cheeks are fork-tender. Remove from the oven and allow to cool.

3 When cool, using a slotted spoon, lift the pork cheeks from the liquid and place in a shallow glass baking dish. Set aside.

4 Fill a bowl with ice. Set aside. Strain the braising liquid through a fine sieve into a clean container. Place the container into the bowl of ice and allow the liquid to chill quickly. Skim off any fat or impurities that rise to the top. When the liquid is cool and fat-free, pour it over the pork cheeks. Cover and refrigerate for at least 8 hours or up to 2 days.

6 When ready to serve, transfer the pork cheeks with the sauce into a medium saucepan. Place over medium heat. Stir in the truffles, truffle oil and truffle butter. Cook until heated through and serve.

Five-Spice Langoustines with Roasted Watermelon

SERVES 6 1 teaspoon grapeseed oil ■ 12 2-inch square watermelon cubes

■ 30 langoustine tails, shelled ■ Coarse salt ■ Five-Spice Powder (see page 235)

■ 3 tablespoons unsalted butter ■ 1 cup Lobster Butter ■ Pickled Watermelon Rind

■ 1 cup micro-greens

1 Preheat the oven to 350°F.

2 Heat the grapeseed oil in a medium, ovenproof nonstick sauté pan over medium heat. Add the watermelon cubes and sear, turning frequently, for about 3 minutes or until almost black from the quick caramelization of the sugars. Transfer to the preheated oven and roast for about 2 minutes or just until heated through. Do not overcook or the watermelon will disintegrate. Remove from the oven and keep warm.

3 Season the langoustine tails with salt and dust with the Five-Spice Powder.

4 Heat the butter in a large sauté pan over medium-high heat and add the seasoned langoustines. Sauté for about 5 minutes or just until cooked through.

5 Place 2 pieces of watermelon on each of 6 dinner plates. Place 5 langoustine tails around the watermelon. Drizzle Lobster Butter over the langoustines and around the plate. Garnish with several pieces of Pickled Watermelon Rind and some micro-greens.

PICKLED WATERMELON RIND

- **1 teaspoon grapeseed oil** ■ **2 shallots, peeled and thinly sliced**
- ■ **1 clove garlic, peeled and thinly sliced** ■ **2 teaspoons Kanzuri**
- **(Japanese red chile paste)** ■ **2 sprigs mint** ■ **2¾ cups cold water**
- ■ **1 cup white wine vinegar** ■ **¼ cup fresh lemon juice** ■ **¼ cup yuzu**
- **juice** ■ **1 tablespoon sugar** ■ **1 tablespoon coarse salt** ■ **1 teaspoon**
- **black peppercorns** ■ **2 cups thinly shaved watermelon rind**

1   Heat the oil in a medium saucepan over
medium heat. Add the shallots and garlic and
sauté for about 3 minutes or until the aromatics
have begun to sweat their liquid. Add the
Kanzuri and cook, stirring occasionally, for an
additional minute. Add the mint, water, vinegar,
lemon juice, yuzu juice, sugar, salt and peppercorns and bring to a simmer. Remove from the
heat and allow to cool.

2   When cool, strain through a fine sieve,
discarding the solids.

3   Place the watermelon rind in a nonreactive container. Pour
the pickling liquid over the watermelon rind and store, covered
and refrigerated, for 24 hours or up to 3 days. Serve chilled or
at room temperature.

LOBSTER BUTTER

- ■ **3 tablespoons glace de homard**
- ■ **1 cup unsalted butter**

Heat the glace in a small
saucepan over medium heat.
When hot, whisk in the butter
until slightly thickened and
shiny. Remove from the heat
and serve.

THE ART OF AUREOLE

RECIPE COMPONENTS

Tomato Concassé

Tomato concassé is nothing more than peeled, cored and seeded very ripe tomatoes that have been finely diced or chopped.

Tomato Fondue

- **4 cups canned Italian plum tomatoes**
- **2 tablespoons olive oil**
- **1 teaspoon minced garlic**
- **1/4 cup minced shallots**
- **Coarse salt and freshly ground pepper**

1 Place the tomatoes in a sieve and push to extract all of the liquid. Working with one tomato at a time, cut the tomatoes open and remove the core and all seeds. When all of the tomatoes are cored and seeded, place the tomatoes in a food processor fitted with the metal blade and process just until coarsely chopped. Set aside.

2 Heat the olive oil in a large sauté pan over medium-high heat. Add the shallots and garlic and sauté for about 4 minutes or until beginning to soften. Add the reserved tomatoes and bring to a simmer. Lower the heat and most of the liquid has cooked out. Scrape into a nonreactive container with a lid and cool to room temperature. Cover and store, refrigerated, for up to 1 week.

Sachet

A sachet or *bouquet garni* is a group of herbs tied together or placed in a cheesecloth bag to be used to flavor sauces, soups or stews. The tying or bagging facilitates the herbs' easy removal from the pot. The traditional mix is parsley, thyme and a bay leaf. When Aureole recipes call for a sachet, it will require a bunch of parsley stems about the size of a little finger, 10 peppercorns, 1 teaspoon dried thyme and 2 bay leaves tied in a cheesecloth bag.

Crispy Leeks

- **2 leeks**
- **1/2 cup vegetable oil**
- **Coarse salt**

1 Trim the leeks of all green parts and cut in half, lengthwise. Holding each half together, wash all grit away under cold running water. Pat dry. Lay each half, cut side down, on a cutting board and slice, lengthwise, into fine julienne. Again, pat dry.

2 Heat the oil in a medium sauté pan over medium heat until just barely warm. Add the leek julienne and fry, turning over in a mass from time to time so that they color evenly, for about 3 minutes or until crisp and golden. Do not let the leeks get too brown as they hold the heat and will continue to color as they drain. Using a slotted spatula, transfer the leeks to a double layer of paper towels to drain. Season with salt. Serve warm or at room temperature. (The cooking oil may be strained and saved for use in vinaigrettes or marinades or as a dipping oil for bread.)

Natural Sauce

- **2 cups dark chicken or veal stock**
- **1 cup red wine**
- **1 teaspoon grapeseed oil**
- **2 tablespoons minced celery**
- **2 shallots, peeled and chopped**
- **2 tablespoons minced carrot**
- **2 tablespoons minced onion**
- **Coarse salt and freshly ground pepper**
- **1 tablespoon unsalted butter**

1 Place the chicken (or veal) stock in a small nonstick saucepan over medium heat. Bring to a boil, then lower the heat and simmer for about 20 minutes or until reduced by half. Remove from the heat and set aside. (Please note that a Natural Sauce can be made with almost any rich stock or a combination of stocks that will reduce to a glace.)

2 Place the red wine in a small nonstick saucepan over medium heat. Bring to a boil, then lower the heat and simmer for about 12 minutes or until reduced by half. Remove from the heat and set aside.

3 Heat the oil in a small sauté pan over medium heat. Add the shallots, carrot, celery and onion and sauté for about 4 minutes or until the vegetables are tender. Add the reserved reduced stock and wine. Raise the heat and bring to a boil. Lower the heat and simmer for about 15 minutes or until the liquid has reduced by half and is quite thick and smooth. Season with salt and pepper. Remove from the heat and strain through a fine sieve into a clean container.

4 When ready to serve, reheat the sauce in a small nonstick saucepan over medium heat. If desired, whisk in the butter to add sheen and body.

Lobster Roe Powder

- **1 cup lobster roe**

1 Preheat the oven to 200°F.

2 Place the lobster roe in a steamer basket over boiling water. Steam for about 5 minutes or until bright red and firm. Remove from the steamer and pat dry.

3 Break the roe apart and place in a small baking dish in the preheated oven and allow to dry for about 3 hours or until almost crumbly. Remove from the oven and place in a small electric spice grinder. Grind to a fine powder.

4 Place the powder in a fine sieve and shake it through to a clean container. Store, tightly covered, for up to 3 days.

Basil Oil

- **4 ounces basil, well washed**
- **1 cup grapeseed oil**
- **Coarse salt**

1. Bring a small saucepan of water to a boil over high heat. Add the basil and then immediately drain into a colander and rinse under cold running water until chilled. Pat dry.

2. Roughly chop the basil and place in a blender along with 1 tablespoon of cold water. Process until just puréed. Do not overprocess or the bright green color will fade and discolor. Scrape the purée into a small bowl and whisk in the oil. Season with salt. Pour into a nonreactive container, cover and refrigerate for at least 8 hours or up to 3 days. (If the basil is left in the oil for longer than 3 days, the color will muddy but the taste will not be affected.)

3. If you require a pure, green oil, slowly drain the basil oil through a fine sieve into a clean container. The oil can also be used in its rough-textured state for vinaigrettes, sauces or plate garnish.

Five-Spice Powder

- **2 tablespoons cumin seeds**
- **2 tablespoons coriander seeds**
- **2 tablespoons whole cloves**
- **2 tablespoons white peppercorns**
- **2 tablespoons ground cinnamon**

Combine the cumin, coriander, cloves and peppercorns in a spice grinder and process to a fine powder. Transfer to a clean glass container and add the cinnamon. Stir to blend. Cover and store in a cool, dark area for up to 1 month.

Fines Herbes

Fines Herbes is a mixture of equal parts finely minced chervil, flat-leaf parsley, tarragon and chives. It can be purchased dried but, under most circumstances, we prefer fresh herbs in all of our dishes.

Curry Oil

- **1½ cups grapeseed oil**
- **5 sprigs cilantro**
- **1 bay leaf**
- **2 tablespoons minced fresh ginger**
- **2 tablespoons chopped lemongrass**
- **1 tablespoon turmeric**
- **1 tablespoon curry powder**

1. Place the oil in a medium saucepan over very low heat. Add the cilantro, bay leaf, ginger, lemongrass, turmeric and curry powder, stirring to blend well. Bring to 180°F on an instant-read thermometer. Remove from the heat and allow to steep until cool.

2. When cool, strain through a fine sieve lined with a double layer of cheesecloth into a clean container. Cover and store at room temperature for up to 3 days.

Citrus Vinaigrette

- **1 cup plus 2 tablespoons olive oil**
- **Zest of 3 lemons**
- **3 shallots, peeled and chopped**
- **½ cup chopped white onion**
- **2 bay leaves**
- **½ cup chopped celery**
- **½ cup freshly ground pepper plus more**
- **½ cup fresh lemon juice**
- **¼ cup dark chicken stock**
- **½ teaspoon white wine vinegar**
- **Coarse salt**

1. Heat 2 tablespoons of the olive oil in a large sauté pan over medium heat. Add the shallots, lemon zest, bay leaves, onion and celery along with ½ teaspoon of the pepper. Lower the heat and sauté for 4 minutes or just until the vegetables are tender. Stir in ¼ cup of the lemon juice along with the chicken stock. Raise the heat to medium and simmer for about 5 minutes or until the liquid has reduced by half.

2. Remove from the heat and immediately strain through a fine sieve into a heatproof bowl, discarding the solids. Allow to cool.

3. Whisk in the vinegar and the remaining ¼ cup of lemon juice. When well combined, whisk in the remaining 1 cup of olive oil. Season with salt and pepper. Store, covered and refrigerated, until ready to use.

11 shallots, peeled ▪ **¾ cup olive oil** ▪ **¼ cup finely chopped onion** ▪ **¼ cup finely chopped carrot** ▪ **¼ cup finely chopped celery** ▪ **¼ cup red wine** ▪ **¼ cup red wine vinegar** ▪ **Coarse salt and freshly ground pepper** ▪ **2 tablespoons chopped flat-leaf parsley** ▪ **Sachet (see page 234)**

1. Finely mince 5 of the shallots. Heat ¼ cup of the olive oil in a small sauté pan over medium heat. Add the minced shallots and sauté for about 4 minutes or until translucent. Remove from the heat and set aside.

2. Chop the remaining 6 shallots and combine with the onion, carrot and celery. Heat 2 tablespoons of the olive oil in a medium sauté pan over medium heat. Add the chopped vegetable mixture and lower the heat. Sauté for 4 minutes or until the vegetables are tender. Add the red wine and raise the heat to medium. Bring to a simmer. Add the chicken stock and Sachet and again bring to a simmer. Simmer for about 5 minutes or until the liquid has reduced by half. Remove 4 minutes or until the pan is almost dry. Add the chicken stock from the heat and strain through a fine sieve into a clean bowl, discarding the solids. Allow to cool.

3. Whisk in the remaining 6 tablespoons of olive oil along with the red wine vinegar. Season with salt and pepper, then stir in the reserved minced shallots. Whisk in the parsley just before serving.

NOTE: Sherry-Shallot Vinaigrette may be prepared by replacing the red wine vinegar with sherry wine vinegar. Balsamic Vinaigrette may be prepared by replacing the red wine vinegar with balsamic vinegar.

Potato Gnocchi

2 pounds Idaho potatoes, well washed and dried ▪ **Approximately 2 tablespoons canola oil** ▪ **1 cup all-purpose flour** ▪ **3 large egg yolks** ▪ **2 tablespoons melted unsalted butter** ▪ **1 cup semolina flour** ▪ **1 tablespoon coarse salt** ▪ **1 teaspoon freshly ground white pepper**

1. Preheat the oven to 400°F.

2. Randomly prick the potatoes with the tines of a fork. Using your hands, lightly coat each potato with oil. Place the oiled potatoes on the center rack of the preheated oven and bake for about 1 hour or until easily pierced with the point of a small, sharp knife. Remove from the oven and immediately cut the potatoes in half, lengthwise.

3. Scoop the flesh from the jackets into a bowl, discarding the jackets. Transfer the flesh to a ricer and push it through into a clean bowl.

4. Using a wooden spoon, beat the egg yolks and melted butter into the potatoes.

5. Add the flours, salt and pepper and continue mixing until the potatoes and flours combine to make a heavy dough, adding additional flour, if necessary. Scrape the dough out onto a heavily floured surface and, using your hands, knead for about 5 minutes or until the dough is very smooth.

6. Roll a small amount of the dough into a log about ¾ inch thick. Cut the log, crosswise, into ¾-inch-long pieces to make small, even gnocchi.

7. Bring a small pot of salted water to a boil. Drop the sample gnocchi into the boiling water and boil for about 2 minutes or until they rise to the top. Using a slotted spoon, lift the gnocchi from the water. If, during this process, the gnocchi holds its shape and is a bit chewy after boiling, proceed in forming the remaining dough into four ¾-inch-thick logs. Cut the logs, crosswise, into ¾-inch-long pieces and cook, in batches, in boiling salted water as above.

8. When cooked, toss the gnocchi with olive oil and serve as directed in a master recipe or as a pasta course with freshly grated Parmesan cheese or any light-style pasta sauce.

9. If the gnocchi sample does not hold its shape in the trial boil, knead in additional flour, about 3 tablespoons at a time, and continue doing trial boils until the right consistency is reached.

(To prepare gnocchi in advance of use, do not cook. Place the raw gnocchi on a lightly floured baking sheet. For longer storage, freeze the gnocchi on the baking sheet until hard. Then transfer to plastic bags, seal, label and store in the freezer for up to 3 months. Do not thaw before boiling. Boil as directed above.)

KITCHEN COMPONENTS: THE CHEFS Just as every recipe has ingredients that come together to make the components of a noteworthy meal, the restaurant kitchen has skilled artists who come together to create the components of an inspired meal. When I became the chef-owner of Aureole, I carried with me years of training and manning the stove as well as inspiration from the history of my craft, the techniques of the classic French tradition, the bounty of America and the creativity of my mentors and peers. It was my desire to bring all of these components together to explore innovation and to define my own personal culinary style. As Aureole has matured and expanded, it has been upon the vision, craft and taste of the cooks who have developed their own personal culinary style in its kitchen. The Art of Aureole represents the perfect blending of the ingredients that exemplify its culinary esthetic with the artistry of the cooks who create it.

CHARLIE PALMER

TONY AIAZZI

DANTE BOCCUZZI

GERRY HAYDEN

BRYAN VOLTAGGIO

SCOTT ROMANO

ROB KERCHOFF

MARK PURDY

Index

Ten Speed Press
Box 7123
Berkeley, California 94707
www.tenspeed.com

Distributed in Australia by Simon & Schuster Australia, in Canada by Ten Speed Press Canada,
in New Zealand by Southern Publishers Group, in South Africa by Real Books,
and in the United Kingdom and Europe by Airlift Book Company.

Design assistant and production coordinator: Meghan Day Healey

Library of Congress Cataloging-in-Publication Data on file with publisher.
Printed in Italy by Mondadori Printing
First printing, 2003

1 2 3 4 5 6 7 8 9 10 — 08 07 06 05 04 03